EDUCATING FOR AN
ECOLOGICAL CIVILIZATION

INTERDISCIPLINARY, EXPERIENTIAL, AND RELATIONAL LEARNING

EDUCATING FOR AN ECOLOGICAL CIVILIZATION

INTERDISCIPLINARY, EXPERIENTIAL, AND RELATIONAL LEARNING

MARCUS FORD AND STEPHEN ROWE,
EDITORS

PROCESS
CENTURY
PRESS

ANOKA, MINNESOTA 2016

Educating for an Ecological Civilization: Interdisciplinary, Experiential, and Relational Learning

© 2017 Process Century Press

Process Century Press
RiverHouse LLC
802 River Lane
Anoka, MN 55303

Process Century Press books are published in association with the International Process Network.

Cover: Susanna Mennicke

An earlier, condensed version of Chapter 5, "Present Teaching: We Are Creating the Future Now and Reflections from a Project on Thinking What We Are Doing" appeared in *Change,* 11 August 2016 (vol. 48.3: 2016) titled, "In the Presence of Teaching: Reflections from a Project."

VOLUME XIII: TOWARD ECOLOGICAL CIVILIZATION SERIES
JEANYNE B. SLETTOM, GENERAL EDITOR

ISBN 978-1-940447-25-4
Printed in the United States of America

TABLE OF CONTENTS

INTRODUCTION: EDUCATION AS CIVILIZATION, *1*
  Marcus Ford and Stephen Rowe

1. THE ANTI-INTELLECTUALISM OF THE AMERICAN UNIVERSITY, *15*
   John B. Cobb., Jr.

2. THE LOSS OF AN INTELLECTUAL ORIENTATION AT
   COMMUNITY COLLEGE: A SEQUEL TO JOHN COBB'S "THE ANTI-
   INTELLECTUALISM OF THE AMERICAN UNIVERSITY," *31*
   France H. Conroy

3. WHY THE LIBERAL ARTS NEED A NEW WORLDVIEW, *51*
   Marcus Ford

4. FIELD-BUILDING, EQUITY, AND TRANSFORMATION
   IN EDUCATION: WHAT WE CAN DO, HOW TO
   DO IT, AND WHO WE NEED TO BE, *67*
   Sheryl Petty

5. THE OTHER CONVERSATION: DIALOGUE,
   MEDITATION, AND SERVICE, *93*
   Stephen Rowe

6. PRESENT TEACHING: WE ARE CREATING THE
   FUTURE NOW AND REFLECTIONS FROM A PROJECT
   ON THINKING WHAT WE ARE DOING, *105*
   Elizabeth Minnich, Brenda Sorkin, and Laura Gardner

7. THE PERILS OF EDUCATION: WHITEHEAD AND THE
   TURN TO AN ECOLOGICAL VALUE SYSTEM, *127*
   Howard Woodhouse

8. CULTIVATION OF HUMANITY THROUGH
   STRETCHING LIBERAL ARTS EDUCATION, *145*
   Jiahong Chen and Peimin Ni

9. "LIBERATING THE CURRICULUM" BY INTRODUCING TRANS-
   DISCIPLINARY AND HUMAN VALUES INTO UNDERGRADUATE
   EDUCATION AT THE UNIVERSITY OF TASMANIA, *167*
   Mark R. Dibben

10. LIBERAL EDUCATION AS COUNTER-HEGEMONIC MOVEMENT, *189*
    Vandana Pednekar-Magal

11. HUMANITIES ENTREPRENEURSHIP, *203*
    Abigail DeHart and Joseph Hogan

12. EDUCATION FOR CITIZENSHIP: ENVIRONMENTAL
    THOUGHT IN ACTION, *217*
    Mark Stemen

13. REDESIGNING EDUCATION IN A GRADUATE
    PROGRAM IN SUSTAINABILITY, *233*
    Sandra E. Lubarsky

14. ENCOUNTERING THE OTHER: A CASE FOR
    APPLIED LIBERAL EDUCATION, *247*
    Robert Neustadt

Contributors, 265

SERIES PREFACE: TOWARD ECOLOGICAL CIVILIZATION

We live in the ending of an age. But the ending of the modern period differs from the ending of previous periods, such as the classical or the medieval. The amazing achievements of modernity make it possible, even likely, that its end will also be the end of civilization, of many species, or even of the human species. At the same time, we are living in an age of new beginnings that give promise of an ecological civilization. Its emergence is marked by a growing sense of urgency and deepening awareness that the changes must go to the roots of what has led to the current threat of catastrophe.

In June 2015, the 10th Whitehead International Conference was held in Claremont, CA. Called "Seizing an Alternative: Toward an Ecological Civilization," it claimed an organic, relational, integrated, nondual, and processive conceptuality is needed, and that Alfred North Whitehead provides this in a remarkably comprehensive and rigorous way. We proposed that he could be "the philosopher of ecological civilization." With the help of those who have come to an ecological vision in other ways, the conference explored this Whiteheadian alternative, showing how it can provide the shared vision so urgently needed.

The judgment underlying this effort is that contemporary research and scholarship is still enthralled by the 17th century view of nature articulated by Descartes and reinforced by Kant. Without freeing our minds of this objectifying and reductive understanding of the world, we are not likely to direct our actions wisely in response to the crisis to which this tradition has led us. Given the ambitious goal of replacing now dominant patterns of thought with one that would redirect us toward ecological civilization, clearly more is needed than a single conference. Fortunately, a larger platform is developing that includes the conference and looks beyond it. It is named Pando Populus (pandopopulous.com) in honor of the world's largest and oldest organism, an aspen grove.

As a continuation of the conference, and in support of the larger initiative of Pando Populus, we are publishing this series, appropriately named "Toward Ecological Civilization."

~John B. Cobb, Jr.

OTHER BOOKS IN THIS SERIES

An Axiological Process Ethics, Rem B. Edwards
Panentheism and Scientific Naturalism, David Ray Griffin
Organic Marxism, Philip Clayton and Justin Heinzekehr
Theological Reminiscences, John B. Cobb, Jr.
Integrative Process, Margaret Stout and Jeannine M. Love
Replanting Ourselves in Beauty, Jay McDaniel & Patricia Adams Farmer, eds.
For Our Common Home, John B. Cobb, Jr., & Ignacio Castuera, eds.
Whitehead Word Book, John B. Cobb, Jr.
The Vindication of Radical Empiricism, Michel Weber
Intuition in Mathematics and Physics, Ronny Desmet, ed.
Reforming Higher Education in an Era of Ecological Crisis and Growing Digital Insecurity, Chet Bowers
Protecting Our Common, Sacred Home, David Ray Griffin

ACKNOWLEDGMENTS

There is one person we would like to thank first and foremost: John B. Cobb, Jr., who has dedicated his life to thinking clearly about the world that we live in and encouraging others to do the same. Both of the editors of this book have drawn inspiration and insight from John's voluminous writings on many topics, including higher education, and have long enjoyed his friendship. This volume of essays would simply not exist if John had not worked to organize the June 4–7, 2015 conference, "Seizing an Alternative: Toward an Ecological Civilization," which gave rise to most of the essays.

We would also like to publically acknowledge the excellent work of Ms. Elizabeth Stemen. She appeared just at the moment when we were really beginning to struggle with the complexities of format consistency in preparation of an anthology manuscript (when the analogy of "herding cats" became irresistible). And she went way beyond the call of formatting excellence, to become a valued participant in the process of both content and copy editing as well. We've wondered more than once whether this volume could have come into being without her calm, highly competent, and always encouraging presence.

Gratitude as well to the journal *Soundings* and the Society for Values in Higher Education for permission to reprint the John B. Cobb essay, "The Anti-Intellectualism of the American University" (Vol. 98, No. 2, 2015), and to the Center for Process Studies and Pomona College for organizing and hosting the conference

INTRODUCTION

EDUCATION AS CIVILIZATION

Marcus Ford and Stephen Rowe

MODERN LIBERATION REQUIRES POSTMODERN civilization; modern negation—beginning with Descartes' "methodological doubt," and later expressed as suspicion, reduction, deconstruction, and, finally, terror—requires postmodern affirmation. This is the proposition we wish to explore and advance.

As societies, and perhaps less obviously as individuals also, our attention has been lowered considerably in recent years, some to subsistence and below. In the developed world, we focus on material and economic conditions, employment, retirement, consumption, degradation of the environment, global instability—that is, when we are not jammed up in an ideological standoff that is remote from actually addressing any particular issue. Likewise in our approach to education, we come to regard liberal education, that cultivation of mature or civilized human beings which requires a modicum of security and leisure from the more basic necessities of life (the American form of which has been the envy of the world[1]), as a luxury we can no longer afford. And yet we have to wonder: Is not the absence of civility that accompanies our lowered attention, along with our urgent need for solutions to what some are calling "wicked" problems, precisely the reason we need liberal education more than ever before?

We are, then, taking the word "civilization" as *a verb rather than a noun*, a necessary undertaking rather than a settled state of affairs.[2] And we take the following to be among the most painful facts of life in our time: That in order to be able to address the overwhelming problems we face with any effectiveness, we need a kind of human development which has not yet occurred on this planet—at least not on a sufficient scale to make a real difference. This volume sees a little light in the very small space between impossibility and necessity, and seeks to open it up in the fashion indicated by John Dewey when he evoked what he called the "common faith" of humankind and the vocation of making that faith "more widely accessible and more generously shared."[3]

I

The subtitle of this volume might identify it as a project from the Progressive Era, when the approaches to education of William James, Dewey, and Maria Montessori were influential. Or it might have come from the burst of "alternative," "experimental," or "innovative" forms of education that surfaced in the 1960's and 1970's.

But instead this book arises from a very energetic and somewhat improbable conference that occurred at Pomona College in June of 2015: *Seizing an Alternative: Toward an Ecological Civilization.* Its thesis was that modern society is not simply unsustainable—it is actively suicidal. It is not enough to attend to the vast array of problems caused by modern modes of thought; we must seize an alternative to modernity itself and build alternative institutions, alternative civilizations, and an alternative world order. And we must be aware that an alternative is available.

The conference featured big-name speakers—Bill McKibbin, Vandana Shiva, Wes Jackson, Sheri Liao, Herman Daley, and John Cobb (who was the principal organizer of this conference)—and over fifty "tracks," as theme or issue-oriented working groups which met continuously throughout the four days of the conference. (See Pando Populus at <pandopopulus.com> for information and papers from the broader conference and various projects which have grown out of it.) As a somewhat unorthodox academic conference, the aim of the organizers was to build a popular movement, a cultural shift towards a more enlightened postmodern world.

Our track was on Higher Education and dealt with the present and future of liberal education, primarily in North America: education that aims for something more ambitious than training for careers, that is concerned foremost with a student's maturation and transformation into the kind of adult we so urgently need. We did not begin with the assumption that there is one form of liberal education, or that the kind of education needed at this time in our history will closely resemble what currently exists or what existed at some previous time. We also did not begin with the assumption that what is needed here is what is needed elsewhere, say in China or in Ivory Coast, or even that formal schooling is necessarily a universal human need.

The authors in this volume share the belief of the conference organizers that the present state of affairs is ruinous, and that a pervasive culture shift is not only necessary, but possible. Hence the papers gathered here can be read as ventures into the shape and texture of what the new paradigm will look like and how liberal education — or that which grows out of it — could help to bring about this cultural shift. They could be useful for reformers, as well as those who think we need the founding of new institutions and communities of education. They are presented in the spirit of our mutual commitment to the embodiment of a very particular and yet not fully articulated alternative, one many of us have experienced in our better moments of teaching, community engagement, or curriculum design. It might be called "civilizing education," to indicate a broader and more commonly shared function of cultivating adulthood than is comprehended by the older Western term "liberal education."[4]

"Civilizing education" is a term that has entered our ongoing inquiry rather recently. At the conference, and in development of the education track for almost a year before the June 2015 meetings, participants took as the focus of our concern the challenges to and possibilities for liberal education, specifically as articulated in the appended description of the track (included at the end of this introduction.) As the inquiry continued after the conference was over, the term "civilizing education"—again, a term inclusive of but not exclusive to the Western, Greek idea—entered our conversations and began to take center stage. We understand the new ideal to be relational, ecological, pluralistic, dialogical—indeed, reflective of a new worldview and a real alternative that is struggling to emerge in our time. In fact, awareness of this essential quality, and the conversation partners with whom we pursued it, led us to invite a few essays in this volume from colleagues who, for one reason or another, did not actually attend the conference but who we think bring important insight to the ongoing and broader inquiry about liberal/civilizing education in the global age.

II

To understand the origins of our concerns and the alternative world view we seek to explore, some background is necessary. The worldview that is now dominant, what may be called the "modern scientific world view," the "modern mindset," or more generally "the way things are" is in fact a historical artifact rooted in 17th and 18th century Western philosophy and 17th century physics. This worldview has become widespread, exported around the world by European conquest and colonization and, more recently, by education, commerce, and popular culture. But its roots go back to a very particular moment in European history, almost as specifically as that moment when René Descartes sat down and began his project of seeking certainty through doubt.

Certainly the modern worldview has been enormously successful for some purposes, especially in the natural sciences, industry, and technology, and it has supported the development of social institutions and habits of mind that have been truly liberating. To dismiss this way of thinking as completely false or as doing only damage is an overreaction and a dangerously simple-minded reading of our situation. And yet, the modern worldview has also been enormously destructive. It has stripped the world of moral and aesthetic values and promoted endless economic expansion as the only measure of cultural progress or well-being; encouraged people to think of nature as a resource that can and must be managed by humans for economic gain; devalued non-Western civilizations and indigenous cultures; reinforced the idea that "might makes right"; and promoted a kind of atomistic individualism that undermines social life and human meaning. The harm now being done in the name of modernization vastly outweighs the good. Once a blessing and a liberation, modernity has now become exceedingly problematic.

One possible alternative to the modern world might be to revert to some kind of pre-modern worldview and the various types of pre-modern civilizations supported by these worldviews. Whether or not this is really a viable option is debatable. So much has changed in the intervening centuries that returning to "the way things were" at some time in the past is likely not possible, and, if it were, it is easy to romanticize pre-modern civilization and forget that it was built on assumptions concerning race, class, and gender that we now find abhorrent.

The organizers of this conference at the Center for Process Studies advocated another alternative—moving forward into a postmodern world. More specifically, they called for a profound reorganization of modern civilization based on the postmodern philosophy first laid out in some detail by the British-American physicist, mathematician, and philosopher, Alfred North Whitehead (1861–1947).

The term "postmodern" is fraught with difficulties, chief among which is that this term has been associated with one particular type of postmodernism—the deconstructive, entirely negative and critical postmodernism. David Griffin, a co-founder of the Center for Process Studies and one of the leading proponents of Whiteheadian thought, has argued that Whitehead's philosophy constitutes another type of postmodernism, what Griffin calls "constructive postmodernism." Both types of postmodernism reject all or most aspects of modernism. Where they part company is on the issue of whether it is even meaningful to speak of reality—a set of events that exists independently of human awareness. Deconstructive postmodernism rejects not just the modernist conception of reality, but any and all conceptions of reality, and therefore the idea that it is possible to make any true statements about reality at all, leaving us in a quagmire of nihilism as the breeding ground of terror and terrorizing. Constructive postmodernism, on the other hand, rejects only the modernist conception of reality, not reality itself; constructive postmodernists reject the truth claims of modernists, but not the concept of truth itself. The deconstructionists, then, have a kind of anti-worldview worldview, whereas the constructive postmodernists offer up an alternative worldview, one that is developmentally more ambitious.

The world that exists independently of human thought—and the world that includes human thought, according to Whitehead—is made up of events, not bits of matter. Everything actual, including a moment of human experience, has the same basic characteristics: The actual has some intrinsic value—value for itself—; is related to everything else; has some agency; and is temporal. Whitehead called his worldview a "philosophy of organism," highlighting the fact that everything actual had some type of experience (however dim), agency (however minimal), and was shaped by its environment. Others have called it "process philosophy" or "process-relational philosophy," drawing attention to the fact that, according to Whitehead, all things are events and all events are related. Whatever language is used, Whitehead articulated a way of describing the actual world that is wholly unlike the descriptions offered up by modern philosophy, which took for granted that most or all of reality was made up of lifeless bits of matter, devoid of experience, agency, and relationality. The modernists, Whitehead maintained, most importantly Descartes, Locke, and Kant, were not wrong in believing that there is a real world outside of and including human experience, and they were not wrong in thinking it is possible to say true things about this reality. They were profoundly mistaken, however, in how they described that world—as one of lifeless matter manipulated by abstracted ideas.

So what? On one level, the distinction between modern and postmodern thought and the various types of postmodernism is, quite literally, "merely academic"—a phrase that has come to mean, in our modern world, "of no real importance." What difference does it make if the world is made of events or of bits of matter? Why does philosophy matter? Philosophy matters because how we think about reality, at the deepest level, determines how we structure our lives and our societies. The social institutions we create—the governments and business, the religious institutions and the military forces, the labor unions and the schools — are grounded in how we understand reality. To paraphrase the great English poet Shelley, our worldviews are "the unacknowledged legislators of the world."

A worldview, such as Whitehead's, that emphasizes intrinsic value, relationality, agency, and temporality supports a very different type of civilization or civilizations than a worldview that implicitly or explicitly denies intrinsic value, relationality, agency, and temporality. The alternative worldview to which we point places human beings in nature, not outside of it or above it; it attributes value to all human beings — female and male, old and young, educated and uneducated, rich or poor; it values all living things regardless of their usefulness for humans; it encourages peaceful resolutions of differences; and it elevates intellectual and spiritual development rather than economic growth. In his introduction to the SUNY Series in Constructive Postmodern Thought (launched in 1989), Griffin writes about the contrast between the kind of postmodern civilization, built on a postmodern worldview such as Whitehead's, that intrigues us and contemporary society with its modernist foundation. "Going beyond the modern world will," he writes, "involve transcending . . . individualism, anthropocentrism, patriarchy, mechanization, economism, consumerism, nationalism, and militarism. Constructive postmodern thought provides support for the ecology, peace, feminist, and other emancipatory movements of our time, while stressing that the inclusive emancipation must be from modernity itself." "A postmodern world," he contends, "will involve postmodern persons, with a postmodern spirituality on the one hand, and a postmodern society, ultimately a postmodern global order, on the other."[5]

Because higher education has, for the last hundred years or more, been committed to a modern worldview, it has been, on the whole, an unwitting promoter of individualism, anthropocentrism, economism, consumerism, militarism, nationalism, mechanization, and patriarchy. In short, it has been a supporter of the kind of modern civilization that we currently have in the West and are seeking to globalize — the kind of civilization that is destroying the planet, undermining human communities, and robbing human life of deep meaning.

There are exceptions to this generalization. There are individual institutions and programs within institutions, and individuals within programs, who are working against some or all of these aspects of modern civilization. Some of the essays in this volume detail how it is possible, even within an institution that is, on the whole, advocating such concepts as extreme individualism and economism, to foster a sense of human community and moral responsibility. Universities, and even relatively small colleges, are complex institutions. Exceptions to the rule, however, do not disprove the rule.

The essays in this volume push beyond traditional liberal education to begin envisioning a constructive postmodern form of civilizing education, one that will help to usher in a postmodern global civilization.

III

Also by way of background, Whitehead's view of history is informative. According to Whitehead, both "persuasive" and "senseless" agencies have been present over time. Whitehead speaks of the persuasive in broad historical terms as democracy, "the greatness of the human soul,"[6] and "the tender elements of the world, which slowly and in quietness operate by love."[7] In our time he would likely see the alternative we perceive as a form of that same persuasive possibility, which has appeared in previous times of reform and advance—flickering in and out of availability, "nerving the race in its slow ascent."[8]

But neither Whitehead nor the Center for Process Studies are particularists; they appreciate the fact that the constructive postmodern worldview that is emerging in our midst has many embodiments and articulations, and that—just as God is greater than religion—the reality of the possibility we pursue could not be contained in any single formulation. The many articulations and embodiments of this worldview exhibit the post-traditional hermeneutical sophistication to affirm dialogue, substantive democracy, and deep pluralism as necessary ongoing sources of growth, correction, and insight for both thought and action. These qualities they share with other articulations, including those of some pragmatists, feminists, Confucians, environmentalists, advocates of dialogue, and reformers in education. Together they present a world-view and a way of being that is life-affirming, pluralistic, ecologically responsible, relational, and oriented to transformation in the direction of thriving.

The contemporary Whiteheadians who convened the 2015 Claremont conference shared with the others present the agreement that our time is unprecedented. Ours must be a Second Axial Age.[9] For modernity has melted traditional cultures, with all of their ambiguities, and brought us to a barbaric place. The center of the new age must be the achievement of maturity, full humanity, or what has been known in the West as the liberally educated person. But people like Amartya Sen remind us that, in the same way democracy is not an exclusive product of the West,[10] so also there are non-Western traditions and resources for transformative education in many parts of the world. We need a global network of these approaches so we can wake each other up, share resources, and collaborate on the global problems we face. For if we don't, it is quite unlikely that we will have the wisdom to invent the policies that will save us from death by our own technologies, let alone from the soul death of meaninglessness, loneliness, and consumption. Perhaps Tu Weiming is right that the movement from modern liberation to postmodern civilization will require the adoption of education as a civil religion.[11]

IV

A note on the essays: We considered writing in this introduction about each of the essays separately, but finally decided, since the titles are clear and each essay begins with an abstract, that this is sufficient by way of overview. What we do want to say here about the essays that follow is that, taken together, they exemplify the values they discuss, namely those of inclusion, engagement, diversity, the comparative approach and ecological/global perspective. They point toward the cultivation of our commonly shared yet endlessly diverse humanity for a form of adulthood and being in the world that is more advanced than those which have been generated before. We are talking about the emergence of a new humanity out of the crumbling of the historic traditions in the 20th century and its replacement with a homogenizing modernity of a least common denominator that is finally expressed in revulsion and terror. We are talking about a form of humanity that is capable of an appreciative pluralism; a form of humanity that could allow us to live together as neighbors without reducing us all to the sameness of consumer society and help us develop wise policy for the deployment and development of the technologies on which our lives depend.

ADDENDUM: ORIGINAL CONFERENCE DOCUMENT
SEIZING ALTERNATIVE HIGHER EDUCATION: TOWARD AN
ECOLOGICAL CIVILIZATION

www.ctr4process.org/whitehead2015
June 4th-7th, 2015
Pomona College
Claremont, California

The Higher Education Track of Section VIII, Reimagining and Reinventing Education

The atmosphere of higher education, and more specifically liberal education, today is often gloomy, with diminishing support, mechanistic and merely numerical forms of accountability and planning, and widespread questioning about the value of education beyond short term economic considerations.

Meanwhile, the problems of the world are very real. On the one hand, there are the problems of climate change, species extinction, loss of democratic institutions, and the great disparity of income and opportunity; on the other hand, there is a crisis of meaning, hope, and well-being, especially in affluent, highly industrialized countries such as the United States. Higher education, in its present form, is doing a remarkably poor job of addressing either of these two sets of issues, which we believe to be intertwined.

And yet, there are some encouraging developments. There are discoveries and claims that point to a new era and a new paradigm for education that are extremely hopeful. With focus on capacities-based purposes in education, and the support of sophisticated, science-based evidence as to the dimensions of healthy human development and thriving, we can speak of transformative and integrative education, and demonstrate the concrete values of service learning, civic engagement, and inclusion. Organizations such as the Association for the Contemplative Mind in Higher Education (ACMHE) and YES+ are working within with universities to provide programs aimed at helping students better understand themselves and their potential, using age-old techniques of breathing and meditation and drawing on the latest discoveries of neuroscience.

There are also some encouraging developments on the environmental and social justice front. Increasingly, students are becoming aware of the problems that the modern world has created for itself and are taking action. For example, 350.org and other student-based groups are working to mobilize citizens in the U. S, and around the world for effective political action to combat climate change, including a campaign for colleges and universities to divest their endowments of fossil fuel stocks.

For the most part, these two efforts—toward personal development and social justice—have been separate from each other and, although loosely tied to higher education, "extracurricular." The standard academic curriculum remains more or less unchanged and rooted in a way of thinking about the world that does not support either personal meaning or social justice. Environmental problems are thought to be largely scientific issues, difficult to understand, and amenable to technical solutions. Issues of meaning and value are thought to be entirely private and "non-academic."

So here is the *problematique*: We'd like to take the few sessions of the *Seizing an Alternative* conference that are allotted to our track to talk about what we can do as educators who remain committed to liberal education as a deep and ineffable ideal associated with the developed capacity to live an "examined life." For us, this includes a clear understanding of the world we live in, its problems, and a willingness to act. More specifically, the question becomes one of how we can be effective for and with our students in the world of today—at a time of creative challenges and great opportunities — and how we can transform our institutions of higher education so as to make them relevant to the deeper needs of both persons and society.

It seems fitting to have this conversation under the umbrella of Whitehead as a worldview alternative, since his is indeed one of the most powerful articulations of the relational worldview and its implications for education (see especially *The Aims of Education*). Whitehead encourages us to sharpen our question one step further: Given the hope we hold in and for the *relational* vision, how can we organize and present liberal education as a most persuasive path for students today?

We have eight sessions stretching across three days, so we can have a real workshop in which we weave some pre-selected presentations into a genuine inquiry (speaking of liberal education!). So if you have a paper or presentation abstract you'd like to submit, we will happily consider these. And if we can help with institutional support, we will write you a letter of invitation with specific mention of acceptance of your proposal.

Next June at the conference, we'll basically begin a face-to-face inquiry with the statement above, with other such statements that emerge electronically through the next academic year, and presentation proposals received. We'll converse, hear some presentations, converse some more, and see how far we can go.

Marcus Peter Ford and Stephen Rowe, Co-chairs
August 12th, 2014

NOTES

1   Fareed Zakariah, *The Post-American World* (New York: Norton, 2008), 190.

2   For a book on education which takes something like this approach in relation to the core curriculum at Columbia University and in Asia, see William Theodore de Bary, *The Great Civilized Conversation: Education for a World Community* (New York: Columbia University Press, 2013).

3   John Dewey, *A Common Faith* (New Haven: Yale University Press, 1934), 87.

4   On this possibility, Martha Nussbaum's study of Indian education is suggestive, in *Not for Profit: Liberal Education and Democratic Citizenship* (Princeton: Princeton University Press, 2012).

5   David Ray Griffin, *God and Religion in the Postmodern World: Essays in Postmodern Theology* (Albany: SUNY Press, 1989), xi.

6   Alfred North Whitehead, *Adventures of Ideas*, 1933 (New York: Free Press, 1967), 19.

7   Whitehead, *Process and Reality* (New York: Free Press, 1969), 404.

8   Whitehead, *Adventures of Ideas,* 18.

9   See Karl Jaspers, *The Origin and Goal of History* ((New Haven: Yale University Press, 1953) and Armstrong, *The Great Transformation: The Beginning of our Religious Traditions* (New York: Alfred A. Knopf, 2006).

10 See Amartya Sen's famous article on the global origins of democracy, "Democracy and Its Global Roots," *The New Republic* (Oct. 6, 2003): 28–35.

11 Weiming Tu, "Implications of the Rise of 'Confucian' East Asian," *Daedalus* 129, no. 1 (Winter 2000): 203.

I. THE ANTI-INTELLECTUALISM OF
THE AMERICAN UNIVERSITY

John B. Cobb, Jr.

ABSTRACT: *The dominant ideal of the American university is to excel in research. To this end it has organized itself in terms of academic disciplines. These discourage critical thought. Their goal of good research could be realized in the context of intellectual inquiry. But the most prestigious universities today are those that have most fully rejected this alternative. The liberal arts colleges that hire their graduates have great difficulty maintaining the tradition of liberal arts. Concern for the holistic development of students is in the tension with studies that aim to be "value free." Value-free research is done for the highest bidder. There is no place in the university for discussing its assumptions. If the academic disciplines operate on mutually inconsistent assumptions, the university does not consider this worthy of study. The experts produced by the anti-intellectual university contribute more to the global crisis than to a positive response.[1]*

IT MIGHT BE BETTER IF, instead of writing about the American university, I specified "the research university" as my topic. I could state my objection to allowing the model of the research university to dominate all higher education. There has been criticism of this tendency all along, but it has had little effect in deflecting the movement in this direction, so far as I know.

However, I know so little about the situation in other countries that I will consider only how this has happened in this country. I recognize and celebrate the fact that there are universities in the United States that differ from what I describe, but I believe that what I call "the American university" is very widespread in this country. So I choose the title "The Anti-Intellectualism of the American University."

To those who consider all rational thinking, scholarly research, and diligent study "intellectual," my title is, of course, ridiculous. There is lots of careful thought, refined scholarship, and hard work going on in American universities, and an enormous amount of information is produced every year. But according to my understanding, scholarly research is not, as such, an intellectual activity.

Before proceeding, let me acknowledge that there is little that is really new in my critique. The American research university is the epitome of the modern, and long ago, in *Science and the Modern World*, Whitehead identified modernity as an "historical revolt," and wrote: "It is a great mistake to conceive this historical revolt as an appeal to reason. On the contrary, it was through and through an anti-intellectualist movement."[2] The modern research university is a collection of academic disciplines, what the Germans called "Wissenschaften." Heidegger wrote an essay whose title asserts that these do not think. I want to try my hand at spelling out this anti-intellectual character of the research universities in this country.

I

Colleges and universities are very conservative institutions. Long after the beginnings of modernity, universities continued their medieval traditions and remained centers of intellectual activity. As recently as a hundred years ago, the general image of post high school education in the United States was the liberal arts college. Speaking very generally, these aimed at the cultural development of students with the expectation that this would enable them to be better leaders in society. Although these colleges were not primarily oriented to the intellectual life, they did not discourage it. They were not anti-intellectual.

In addition to liberal arts colleges there were by then a good many universities. Most of these were liberal arts colleges with associated professional schools and some graduate programs. These graduate programs could not compete in quality of research with those in Europe. Americans looked especially to German research universities to lead in the advance of scholarship. Ambitious Americans went to Germany for graduate work. A few American institutions were modeling themselves on European ones. However, post high school education was assumed to be in what could properly be called a liberal arts college. Research was not their primary goal.

American universities did not have an articulated alternative to the German research universities for their PhD programs. Hence they modeled themselves on systems that were successful in producing researchers. After one was educated in a liberal arts program, one could choose a specialty, structured as an academic discipline, and get a PhD. This supposedly qualified one to become a professor in a liberal arts college.

There is a rather obvious misfit here. The professor in a liberal arts college had qualified to teach, not by becoming excellent in the liberal arts, but by developing skills in research in an academic discipline. The task of teaching liberal arts was quite different from research in an academic discipline. Many made the adjustment well, being themselves graduates of liberal arts colleges. But teaching liberal arts was not conducive to advancing research in the disciplines in which they had specialized.

Measured in terms of research, American scholars lagged behind their German colleagues for two other reasons. First, Germans completed their gymnasium and started their training for specialized research two years earlier than Americans completed liberal arts colleges. Second, there was an added step in Germany for the really serious researchers. They continued their studies and wrote a second dissertation in close association with an established scholar. They were then habilitated, qualified not only to teach in gymnasia but also in universities. American universities produced by chance a few scholars who could be considered in this elite category, but overall, even during the Nazi era in Germany, Americans looked to Germany for leadership in most academic disciplines.

Meanwhile, in the United States, academics increasingly prized research, and the prestige of academic disciplines as the loci of research grew. People forgot that the purpose of organizing around such disciplines was quite different from that of liberal arts colleges. Indeed, there was little reflection about liberal arts and almost no effort in graduate schools to prepare students to teach them. The closest the universities could come to liberal arts was in interdisciplinary or multidisciplinary courses.

As a result, college teachers more and more taught introductions to their disciplines rather than liberal arts. Those who majored in a discipline were well prepared by the time of their college graduation to pursue a PhD. At the cost of abandoning liberal arts education, Americans caught up with Germans in research.

Today the research university makes no pretense of helping students to mature, developing cultural understanding, or preparing students for leadership in their communities. It prepares students to become skilled specialists in some branch of research. In terms of its self-definition as a research university, its organization in terms of academic disciplines instead of liberal arts has been a great success. Just why this has ever been regarded as the normative form of higher education is not so clear.

Of course, training for research is not all that goes on in universities. They also prepare people for jobs. They teach the specialized knowledge needed in different forms of employment. In part this is a matter of particular academic disciplines, but in part it is skills of various sorts. The older idea of professional schools has faded as the distinction between professionals and employees has largely disappeared.

II

Organizing a university as a collection of departments each committed to promoting an academic discipline worked well in promoting research. I have stated that scholarly research as such is not an intellectual activity. Before proceeding to describe the anti-intellectual character of the American university, I want to make clear my own judgment that research can be done in an intellectual context.

I am quite sure of this because I had the good fortune to study in an intellectual university. Perhaps the best way for me to clarify what I miss in the American university today is to describe my own educational experience. I attended the University of Chicago at the peak of the influence of Robert Maynard Hutchins. He was struggling against the reduction of academia to preparation for research in segregated disciplines. At the time I did not realize how unusual my experience of higher education was. It seemed to be what education should be.

I went to Chicago with my childhood faith largely intact. There had been nothing intellectual about my studies in junior college in Georgia, but in the Army I had Jewish and Catholic friends from New York, who introduced me to the life of the mind. I became aware that the progressive culture of the time considered the culture in which I had been raised naïve and backward. This did not shake my desire to serve professionally in the church, but it did make me eager to test my faith by full exposure to the contemporary world of thought.

I enrolled in the Humanities Division and chose a non-departmental program on "The Analysis of Ideas and the Study of Method." To work in that program one was required to state one's topic of special interest. I chose the reasons that modern culture had rejected belief in God.

I did not complete that program. Within a year I had learned what I needed to know. The problem with belief in God was not that arguments against belief had proved stronger than arguments for it. Rather, modern thought was largely founded on the assumption that everything about nature and history could be explained in terms of nature and history. No one supposed that this project was complete. But science and history were both pursued in the faith that this was the right project. Failure to accept this project was to exclude oneself from participation in modern culture and, of course, in the university. Can you imagine hiring someone to teach in a history department who declares her project to be to identify the acts of God in history?

Since modernity excluded God from acting in nature or history, the only act that could be attributed to God was as originator of the whole. This fell outside the bounds of any academic study. When evolution brought the creation of the world we know into the bounds of the nature we study, the role of initiation lost interest. There was no longer any reason to posit a beginning. God disappeared from the realm of efficient causes. Meanwhile modernity as a whole grew up out of the rejection of final causes, and formal causes were purely abstract. This left only material causes, and belief in God continued here and there as the ultimate in the line of material causes. That is, everything is ultimately an instantiation of Being Itself. This could be said without threatening the modern faith, but the connection of Being Itself with the God portrayed in the Bible is obscure.

This means that there is a deep conflict between biblical faith and modern faith. For modern faith, the sphere of finite entities is self-contained and self-explained. For biblical faith it is not. But this sort of formulation of the issue is not part of the modern discussion.

Although this formulation of my conclusions expresses my current thinking rather than the way I would have formulated things then, I do not think it distorts my thinking of that time. I ceased to be interested in arguments for or against God. My interest shifted to basic worldviews. During the year in the Humanities Division, I became aware that there were criticisms of the modern worldview and that other worldviews were proposed. My limited contacts with Divinity School faculty made me aware that they were concerned with worldviews. I transferred to the Divinity School.

I hope you will understand my use of the term "intellectual" with respect to the year I have described. I was asking an intellectual question and found an intellectual answer. But my point here is not that my personal quest was intellectual. It is that the university supported me in this quest. It invited me into a program that I could shape to enable me to pursue my quest. It created a climate among students that encouraged interchange of ideas of this sort.

What I have said about the support of intellectual activity in the university as a whole was true in spades of the Divinity School under the deanship of Bernard Loomer. For him faculty and students were engaged in a joint quest for truth about reality and meaning. We were required to pass exams in various fields, but these were subsidiary to coming to our own convictions about matters of ultimate orientation.

The climate of discussion emphasized the need to think facts and values together, although anyone who was convinced that they should be kept separate would receive an open hearing. In this respect it was postmodern, even though the term was not used. The faculty was keenly interested in scientific developments that showed the limitations of the mechanistic worldview that excluded value from the world studied by science. The climate of the school urged faithfulness to experience. In this sense it emphasized empiricism, but the empiricism it favored was "radical" over against the exclusive emphasis on sense data. This meant that aesthetic, moral, and religious experience should be taken seriously. The boundaries of modernity were being stretched. Indeed, I think the new naturalism, which many of my professors affirmed, broke with modernity.

Some of them, however, retained the notion of the world of finite things being self-contained. They thought that, by vastly enriching the world of nature, its self-contained character became plausible. One did not have to deny the existence of purpose, for example, in order to explain everything mechanically, because one no longer needed to limit explanations to efficient causes. Henry Nelson Wieman showed both the possibility and the limits of thinking in richly naturalistic terms when one broke with the rigidities of modern thought.

Others believed that systematization of the new naturalism, grounded in new developments in science and in the methods of radical empiricism, required re-introducing God into the explanations of what is and what happens. Charles Hartshorne, in the Philosophy Department, belonged to this group. He had been an assistant to Whitehead at Harvard. My empirically minded professors in the Divinity School also talked much of Whitehead. He was the thinker who pursued the discussion furthest and most rigorously.

I hope you will also understand why I say that the Divinity School was an "intellectual hothouse." Issues of fundamental importance were discussed in a context in which all opinions were heard and criticized. Nothing was more strongly supported than students coming to their own convictions, as long as they were prepared to defend them in open discussion. Since this is just what I needed and wanted, I flourished there.

The Chicago of Robert Maynard Hutchins and the Divinity School of Bernard Loomer ended. In this sense the experiment with the focus on intellectual freedom and activity failed. Soon after I left, the trustees fired Hutchins and within the next few years the Divinity School faculty under which I studied scattered. The replacements changed the nature of the school.

III

Because of my personal experience I know that a university can be supportive of intellectual reflection and that scholarly research can be guided by intellectual concerns. I think I have been able to support such reflection in my own teaching, and I am sure that this is true of many others. Intellectual reflection goes on to some extent in many universities without reduced interest in scholarly research. When I describe universities as anti-intellectual I do not want to belittle this.

Nevertheless, I hold to the thesis that American universities are organized in a way that discourages intellectual activity. As a result of this discouragement the amount of intellectual activity there has declined. I will illustrate first by changes in philosophy departments.

At Chicago when I was there we took for granted that those who taught us philosophy were persons who had worked out their own philosophical ideas. We expected these to provide answers to existential questions and to cosmological ones as well or to explain why they did not do so. Even when I was in the Divinity School I took half my courses with philosophers.

Even then, there were those who taught the history of philosophy without betraying their own judgments. Their gift was to help us confront the thinking of persons other than our own teachers. Expanding the range of those we encountered was thought to contribute to our coming to our own convictions. Although I think Chicago was particularly strong in thinking of philosophy in this way, on many campuses it was the major locus of intellectual activity.

However, philosophy departments today are much more like other departments in the university. They understand that philosophy should be one academic discipline alongside others. For this, it requires a subject matter that can be distinguished from others and a suitable methodology for dealing with it. What I described as intellectual activity is seen as speculation, and this is discouraged. The goal in any academic discipline is the increase of knowledge, and this can be attained only by limiting ourselves to rigorous methods of analysis and testing.

Professors are selected for their expertise in these specialized activities. Since philosophy as a discipline wants to claim its heritage from earlier forms there is also historical teaching about the past. The current focus, of course, influences the approach, but history provides its own norms of objectivity. It, too, tends to focus on more technical issues in past philosophies rather than their comprehensive worldview or responses to existential questions. My generalization is that a student with an interest in broad or deep issues would find little help today in most university philosophy departments.

Two other departments in many universities continued to seek holistic answers to broad questions. Geography expanded from simply learning about the landscape and the location of human habitat to a deeper reflection on how human beings related to their natural contexts and how this affected these contexts. Anthropology sought to understand the world inclusively from the perspective of the people it studied. These approaches cut against the general trends of university culture and departments of geography and anthropology began to disappear.

In the sixties there were protests by students that important topics were ignored by universities. As a result many universities introduced new "programs" such as Black studies, women's studies, peace studies, ecological studies. These often encouraged intellectual reflection. However, they were considered temporary concessions rather than models of how universities should reorganize. Professors in these programs were encouraged to engage in the sort of teaching and scholarship that is done in academic disciplines. Mary Daly described what happened in women's studies programs as "methodicide." Universities worked toward absorbing these programs into established disciplines or developing new disciplines out of them.

I will approach this description of directions taken in universities in one other way. There has been a considerable literature about economic issues recently that is of great interest to the general public, but very little of this comes from academic departments of economics. Some of it is dealing with what is happening in the real world, and no department of the university deals much with current events.

Nevertheless, we might expect a department whose teaching has so much influence among decision-makers to be somewhat interested in what happens, at least in a general way. In the past fifty years financial institutions have become far more important than industrial ones. But the books describing this shift are rarely written by academicians in departments of economics, and the change in the nature of the economy has had very little influence on what is taught.

One glaring example is with respect to money. One might expect this to be a major topic among economists. It is not. As banks and their creation of money have become more formative of the whole of society, the literature on this topic has grown. But most of this has come from outside of academia.

Economic theory deals chiefly with how to increase market activity. Occasionally, an economist raises the question as to whether such increase is always desirable. This question arises from intellectual interests. If colleagues in the department had intellectual interests, they would engage such questioners. Such discussions might lead to reaffirmation of the central importance of increasing market activity. But they might not. They could lead to significant changes. However, because there is such a lack of intellectual interest, the response is simply to view such questioners as nuisances and to silence them.

It is my judgment that intellectuals teaching in departments of economics would be interested in actual economies and attempt to throw light upon them. That there is so little of this interest points to the discouragement of intellectual activity in these departments. Scholars can do their work without attending to such things.

IV

One cause of the anti-intellectual character of universities is their self-designation as "value free." They boast of this. Scholarship, they think, can be trusted only if it is pursued for its own sake rather than in an effort to support an established belief or commitment or preference. There is, of course, a significant point being made here. Scholars should freely examine the data and do so as objectively as possible.

One place where values might intrude is in the selection of research topics. One might make a selection based on the judgment that certain information is important in order to pursue some reform. But this would imply that the researcher was committed to that reform, and this is not acceptable. Or it would lead to discussion of whether that reform was desirable. The academic disciplines of the university aim not to be drawn into such intellectual discussions.

The only importance recognized by the discipline is importance for the discipline. If past research has led in a certain direction but is being impeded by ignorance of some matter, then it is important to gain additional information. Research is properly guided by such considerations. The narrowness of the parameters for decision prevents such discussions from engaging the sort of issues that involve one in intellectual discussion.

That the university and its disciplines seek to advance knowledge disinterestedly is an ideal of some merit. However, universities actually compromise the ideal on a large scale. Research takes time. Sometimes it takes expensive equipment. Often one must pay people for their contributions. All this is expensive. Universities have limited budgets. Accordingly, in practice, the greater part of research is done at the behest of funders, or is, at least, dependent on finding funders. Indeed, the budgets of universities often depend on a portion of the research grants that meet the concerns of outsiders. These outsiders are certainly not free of values. Money is available for medical research, and the value of healing diseases and extending life lies behind these grants, as well as profits of particular businesses. But the values of most of the corporations served by universities are more problematic. And much research is paid for by the Department of Defense. Just because universities are value free they serve various interests uncritically. A value-free university sells its services to the highest bidder.

One value prized by the value-free university is accuracy and honesty in scholarly work. Hence the university intends that its scholars provide those who pay them for research with accurate and honest conclusions. Sadly the lack of emphasis on moral norms weakens this implicit value. This weakening is advanced by the decline of the view of truth as correspondence. Although the defenders of other views of truth do not intend this result, a de-emphasis on the need for results to correspond with the way the world is opens the door to adjusting results to the needs of the situation—generally defined by what the one who pays for the results wants to hear.

Much the same can be said of the job-training dimensions of the university. Since the institution is value free, it does not ask about the value of the jobs for which it prepares people. It certainly does not ask about the health of a society that employs people for some lines of work and not for others. To be value free is to be free from critical thought.

Many individual professors have strong values and commitments. These tend to influence their teaching. They want students to share their concerns. As the prospects for the human future become more dire, more professors feel the need to influence students to attend to the questions this danger raises. They want to make a positive difference. Recognizing this tendency, a leading educator, Stanley Fish, wrote a book, addressed to professors. One might have hoped that he would agree that as the global situation becomes more critical universities should think about how their work could become relevant to the world's needs. But this is not his message. His title says it all: *Save the World on Your Own Time*.[3]

The university hires people to advance their disciplines by research and by preparing students to take up this task. Saving the world is not its job. If professors want to use their free time in that way, OK, that is none of the university's business. But don't mix that into one's life as a teacher.

V

Another dimension of the university's anti-intellectual character is its lack of interest in assumptions. Academic disciplines do not encourage efforts to articulate their assumptions. They socialize students into the existing pattern of assumptions and procedures. They rarely state their assumptions, presumably assuming that they are not problematic. In some cases there is study of the history of the discipline. In such a history, it may become clear that assumptions do change over time. Even if this is presented simply as progress so that adopting the current assumptions is encouraged, this does raise the possibility of critical discussion — an intellectual activity. However, this is rarely encouraged.

If we move from the individual disciplines to the university as a whole, the situation is similar. Courses in the history of higher education are rare. Still rarer is any attempt to use historical knowledge to raise questions about the value of the modern value-free university. Almost any self-study in a university is limited to questions of efficiency of the use of resources within the existing context of assumptions.

In my view, the modern research university is deeply Cartesian. I may, or may not be right about this. In either case, in an institution with intellectual interests, such a thesis would be considered worthy of discussion. But the university provides no locus for it. Obviously individuals can raise all sorts of questions, but these have no foothold in the disciplines and are not the sort of thing that could be brought up at a meeting of faculty, administrators, or trustees.

A particular problem in the university is that the assumptions underlying research in various fields are not coherent with one another. A particularly glaring example is that the assumptions of contemporary relativity theory cannot be reconciled with the assumptions of contemporary quantum theory. For anyone with intellectual interests this raises challenging questions. But the organization of the university discourages such questions. It is bad manners for practitioners of one discipline to criticize what takes place in another. As long as a discipline advances in its own research, matters of this sort are ignored.

VI

Actually, the situation is worse than I have described thus far. The lack of attention to assumptions has left unexamined some metaphysical assumptions that force scholars to neglect evidence and to defend positions that are obviously false. This is the real situation, while the university continues to present itself to the world as the source of unbiased knowledge. It places its prestige in support of a particular worldview, one that is demonstrably false. It socializes the elite to accept this unhealthy mental climate.

How this came about can be explained quite briefly. Thoughtful persons concerned to advance knowledge of the physical world called for a break with the dominant, Aristotelian, science of the Middle Ages. That science had allowed investigators to rest too easily with explanations in terms of final causes. One "understood" an organ in the human body when one identified its function. Satisfaction with this understanding blocked investigation of just how it actually worked. The thinkers who noted this problem called for a focus on efficient causes. They thought that these could be observed, and that science could best advance by seeking observable causal relations in the natural world. They bracketed questions of what things were in themselves or for themselves. The world of the objectively given, or the world of objects, was taken to be the nature that was investigated, and it was to be explained without reference to anything external to it.

This move toward objectivity served the natural sciences very well for a long time. The wonderful achievements of this science supported treating its view of nature as ultimate truth. A nature that functions entirely by efficient causes and exists only objectively is, of course, totally determined and explicable in reductionist ways.

Until the middle of the nineteenth century human beings were understood as fundamentally different from this mechanistic nature. However, the study of organisms led inexorably to the understanding of evolution and the relocation of human beings within nature. This was, from my perspective, a great gain and a great opportunity for new thinking. If human beings were part of nature, then nature was much richer than had previously been recognized. Nature included subjective experience, and the final causes that had been banished must be allowed a place. There was a burst of intellectual activity along these lines.

Sadly, the university chose a different path. The inclusion of human beings within nature meant that human beings also were to be understood ultimately reductionistically as matter in motion. Scholars is some academic disciplines were allowed to continue talking about reasons for historical events that included human purposes, but this was within a context that assumed that at a deeper level purposes were to be explained in terms of efficient causality.

This choice was partly a matter of inertia. The physical scientists were certainly not interested in rethinking their whole approach. It was also partly the victory of the greatest thinker of the eighteenth century, Immanuel Kant. He overcame the extremely problematic metaphysical dualism of nature and humanity by shifting to a duality of theoretical and practical reason. Theoretical reason he identified with the study of efficient causation and the Cartesian view of nature. However, he assumed that for practical purposes it was necessary for human beings to think in a quite different way. This was simplified by later Kantians into the distinction of fact and value. From this perspective evolution just showed that from the perspective of fact, the mechanistic understanding applies to everything.

The Kantians who resolved the crisis in this way had no intention to belittle value. But this result is inevitable. If values have no basis in reality, they lose status for thought as well. Universities declared themselves value free.

At one level this may seem to be wonderfully consistent. However, consistency of this kind is not possible. The person who proclaims that he or she is a machine does not really understand saying this as expressing simply the way the machine happens to be programmed. If those who hear it understood it in this way there would be no reason to consider the idea, much less to organize a university on this assumption. Anyone who really understood herself or himself as a machine would have to be institutionalized.

Nevertheless, the commitment to the metaphysics is so strong that the evidence against it must be denied, ignored, or at least bracketed. The most dramatic evidence against it is found in parapsychology. This evidence is not only anecdotal. It is based on thousands of carefully controlled experiments. Efforts to undermine this evidence have been unsuccessful. But universities have not responded by adjusting their assumptions. On the contrary, they have ended this research and created a climate in which anyone who takes it seriously loses status. They do this while continuing to ridicule the Aristotelian scientists of the papal court for refusing to look through Galileo's telescope.

The evidence for the causal role of subjects shows up in many places. Often it is acknowledged and then ignored. There is plenty of evidence from neuroscience that brain and mind interact. The most difficult evidence for the university to deal with is the growing body of physics, especially at the quantum level, that does not fit the metaphysics into which physicists have been socialized. This gives some hope for change. But thus far, these "anomalous" facts have simply been bracketed.

VII

I'm sure that many of you will feel that my criticisms are exaggerated. If I were describing the personal beliefs and attitudes of the people who make up the university community, what I have said would be highly misleading. I have tried to make it clear that this is not my topic. I am speaking of the value-free research institution and the academic disciplines that carry out the research. The people who are hired to do anti-intellectual work are much more than simply employees. As individual human beings they are concerned with values and ideas.

Nevertheless, I will conclude with a negative statement. The structure and assumptions of the university have had a great effect on those who study and work there. The university understands itself to be entrusted with the task of producing experts, and the experts it produces generally see the world in the way the university has socialized them to see it. Overall they contribute more to leading the world into catastrophes than to steering us away.

NOTES

1   Reprinted with permission from *Soundings,* vol 98.2 (2015), 218–32.

2   Alfred North Whitehead, *Science and the Modern World,* 1925 (New York: The Free Press, 1967), 8.

3   Stanley Fish, *Save the World on Your Own Time* (Oxford: Oxford University Press, 2008).

2. THE LOSS OF AN INTELLECTUAL ORIENTATION AT COMMUNITY COLLEGE:

A SEQUEL TO COBB'S "THE ANTI-INTELLECTUALISM OF THE AMERICAN UNIVERSITY"

France H. Conroy

I. PRELUDE

IMAGINE HAVING THE "GOOD FORTUNE TO STUDY in an intellectual university," as John B. Cobb Jr. describes: an "intellectual hothouse" where "nothing was more strongly supported than students coming to their own convictions, as long as they were prepared to defend them in open discussion"—and then teaching at a community college.[1]

Why would one do that? Nobody would do that, one might argue.

Besides, it's inappropriate. Community colleges are ground zero for "workforce readiness." Everyone these days agrees on this, from Obama to the conservatives, whatever one's view of the mission of universities. The debate is whether or not taxpayers should take on the cost of making these two years free; if so, they would certainly demand efficiency, which means quantitatively measured skills for today's global corporate economy: nothing less.

And yet—have we lost our memories?

Wasn't it not long ago that there was another era? In my case, for example, when I was hired in 1979 at Burlington County College (NJ), we *were* a little bit of an intellectual hothouse. East Campus, a collection of Quonset huts and a small brick building, was home to Social Science, Humanities and "College Skills" divisions, each alive with a talented, well-credentialed, and free-thinking faculty. These professors and their students would have understood Cobb's praise for how at the University of Chicago "we were required to pass exams in various fields but this was subsidiary to coming to our own convictions about matters of ultimate orientation." Not everyone had an educational philosophy like that, but it was definitely part of the mix. Because professors were respected as independent intellectuals, differences were expected. The homogenizing regime of outcomes, compliance, and "accountability" hadn't set in yet. Students were not yet "customers." Most of the men and women in that faculty cohort retired early. I was younger and had to stay later, finishing my career somewhat like a professor from another planet.

I can identify with Prof. Cobb's re-introduction of the word "intellectual" into public discussion. In this article, I want to take further his use of the word. I am afraid that his analysis, tucked in the back of an issue of the Society for Values in Higher Education's journal *Soundings*, will be of little interest to ordinary people. It sounds like an effete issue: whether great research universities should be called "intellectual" or not owing to their separation into departments and the loss of older conceptions of the university. I taught 10,000 students, and only a few would find this issue compelling. Therefore, I will try to write an article that rescues Cobb's issue from its elitist shell. Why is it important that even community colleges, not only universities and liberal arts colleges, be organized in a way that encourages, not discourages, intellectual activity—in the sense Cobb describes? Why might this be important even in orienting K-12? This is the task I have set out for myself.

I will be briefly autobiographical, for the same reasons as Cobb. Before proceeding to his direct analysis of universities' anti-intellectual character, he notes, "Perhaps the best way to clarify what I miss in the American university today is to describe my own educational experience." My experience, likewise, should help clarify my subsequent analysis of how community colleges have lost something important from the 1970s to today.

There was a seminal statement that I encountered in 1971 that forever changed my educational trajectory. Cobb's concluding statement that the experts trained in today's universities overall "contribute more to leading the world into catastrophe than to steering it away" reminds me of this statement. I had been a discontented first-year graduate student at Yale University in philosophy when I encountered a 26-page photocopied catalogue of another graduate program, without departments, without walls, integrating theory and practice, built around "arduous intellectual endeavor and hypothesis testing." Most important, the catalogue began with this statement: "The Union Graduate School has developed in response to the fact that for many competent students existing graduate programs are too limited, too prescribed and inflexible, and *poorly adapted to the needs of a society in crisis*" (my italics).[2] This statement reminds me of Cobb's. Both discern that the world is in crisis. In 1971, no other institution I was aware of put that front and center, but it was obvious.[3] In 2015, I contend that it is again obvious; see Pope Francis's recent Encyclical on the environment if you need details.[4]

Furthermore, I agree with Cobb that research universities, separated into departments that keep producing narrow forms of "knowledge," are unable to respond appropriately to such a crisis. Nor at a more populist level are community colleges, partly because they are derivative from these universities and partly from their own workforce-ready imperatives derived directly from the dominant neoliberal regime. I will argue that Cobb's conception of "intellectual" implies that all persons, elite and ordinary, are called as a matter of "ultimate orientation" to respond in a life-defining way to avert impending catastrophe. Education must be sufficiently broad, deep, free, and providing of critical distance from current power structures to enable them to do that.

Returning to my biography, my transfer from Yale to a shoestring, experimental free school was a defining moment, but my introduction to intellectual life began much earlier. Cobb remarks that "there had been nothing intellectual about (his) studies in junior college in Georgia," but for me there was something intellectual already about my senior year of high school in Hawai'i. I mention this in part because later I want to include in my argument the years leading up to college. For me at age 17, coming out of a good, even very good, but conformist suburban East Coast public school, the senior year 1965–66 at Punahou School in Honolulu was suddenly and distinctly "organized in a way that *encourages* intellectual activity."[5] My senior English course introduced me to a jazz reading of Plato's *Republic*; had me meet Victor Frankl, in two lectures at the University of Hawai'i; exposed me to the films *Les main sales* and *No Exit* by Jean-Paul Sartre; and had me work with my French teacher, a translator himself at the Nuremberg trials, to write a senior thesis on Albert Camus about killing. Furthermore, the school exposed me to a range of assembly speakers from the head of the student body during the Free Speech Movement at Berkeley to Gen. William Westmoreland of the U. S. Army, Vietnam, and on and on.

Coming to Haverford College in 1966, I found not only the philosophy department, but also the college overall organized in such a way as to be an "intellectual hotbed." It seemed to be in the air—perhaps it was the Quaker heritage—that we were encouraged to concern ourselves with "ultimate orientations"; and periodically the campus community, due to the crises of the Vietnam War, assassinations, etc., came together to make overall judgments.

The philosophy department was a central part of this whole. It attracted the most majors from my class of 1970, 17 out of about 150 graduates. The department had been completely rebuilt in the early 1960s as the older Quaker leadership of Douglas Steere and others gave way to a new mix. Cobb says, "We took for granted that those who taught us philosophy were persons who had worked out their own philosophical ideas," both "existential" and "cosmological." This was certainly true here. Paul Desjardins, chosen by Steere to build the department, reinforced for me a *Republic* that would stay for a lifetime, and Confucius as well; he in turn chose Richard J. Bernstein, who taught a young Marx that stirred in me a sense of justice and discernment for the hidden workings of class. This was not, as Cobb notes concerning the modern research university, "one academic discipline among others," requiring "a subject matter that can distinguish itself from others and a suitable method for dealing with it," aimed at "an increase in knowledge."[6] It was the opposite, broad and non-sectarian. In a way that Aquinas, Aristotle, and Confucius would understand, it helped pull all the other departments of the college into a coherent whole. This was what would stay with me as I moved on, confused, into the philosophy department at a research university, Yale.

Paul Desjardins, for whom I returned to Haverford to do an internship in 1972–73, would write in his 1975 recommendation for me that I was "weighty and well-versed," demanded "a good deal of us morally and intellectually," was "a good philosopher and a good person" (adding, "one would like to find this statement redundant!") — then, "being egalitarian to a flaw, he has things to say about feminism, the third world, and the working class."[7] There in a sentence you have the transition from my identity as bearer of the intellectual mantle of hey-day University of Chicago or Haverford to introducer of the more questionable corollary: that truly intellectual learning has relevance to ordinary people. Thus we can quickly complete the transition from autobiography to analysis and get to the main focus of this article: the particulars of what has happened to community colleges. Suffice it to say that my studies at the Union Graduate School, freed of the pretensions and privileges of Yale, led me to be able to do what Yale philosopher George Schrader called "one of the most interesting graduate projects with which I have ever been associated in something like twenty-five years of graduate teaching," and led me to be from then on suspicious of the scent of the intelligentsia. In my 1971–75 participant-observer research, I became excited by the very idea of the "working class intellectual." I was able to live at the peak of those "greening of America" times combining an Odyssean mode of contemporary journeying with an analysis of the leading theories of social change, anti-imperialist, democratic socialist, communist, existentialist, third world, and feminist. I wrote it all up like a symphony. The product, *Becoming Revolutionary Persons,* presents a window into the early 1970s that I haven't seen portrayed in the media: neither hippies nor Weathermen, *both* counter-culture *and* classical culture — just human beings who sometimes, dreaming of a different future from the one that we have now, became young-Marx communists. Eighteen months after achieving a doctorate of everything, I went to work in a factory; four years later, a community college.

What I need to do then is, starting from Cobb, expand on characteristics of an intellectual orientation in college; explain how it was possible to incorporate such an orientation in community colleges through the early 1990s; then delineate how community colleges changed to make it impossible; and finally, address why the issue is important and what I propose going forward.

Let me note that I will be proposing that community colleges were (and can be again) *semi*-intellectual spaces, not *fully* (like Cobb's Chicago). By *semi* I don't mean diluted or compromised; I mean hybrids that include fully intellectual areas alongside others.

II. "INTELLECTUAL"

From my teaching experience as well as my training, then, I suggest there may be at least four characteristics of an intellectual orientation: (1) it risks being considered useless; (2) it depends on a fragile mix concerning motivation for learning; (3) it puts front and center the notion of "coming to our own convictions about matters of ultimate orientation"; and (4) it remains ever-open to questioning assumptions, while still honoring the need for foundations. I follow with a second list. These are five structural features specific to the community college when I arrived (c. 1975-1990) that I found hospitable to the above: (a) pluralist educational philosophy; (b) adequate public funding; (c) empowered faculty, especially liberal arts and science; (d) organic, not corporate managerial, administrative leadership; and (e) part of a larger society not yet distorted by severe inequality.

1. THE RISK OF SUPPOSED "USELESSNESS"

This recalls Plato's *Republic*. Socrates uses this word to describe young men and women who seek truth and raise critical questions, agreeing with his students that they do not have a specific usefulness, such as winning battles in war or making profits in business, so some societies might tend to ignore them. Socrates proposes that it may be the fault of the societies, not the young men and women.[8] Flashing forward 2400 years, I often wonder what the students who over the years were most attuned with me think as they reflect now on what I emphasized. In view of the direction society has changed, I wonder if they say to themselves, "What Conroy taught turned out to be useless after all!" During my last fall, I started my Introduction to Philosophy classes by confiding to my 100 students in three sections that what they were about to learn would be useless. I later had them write term-essays on revolution. I decided to do this because I had increasingly come to the conviction that the real motivation behind "outcomes assessment" was to make all courses rationalize themselves in terms of workforce readiness for the neoliberal economy and compliance with neoliberal culture. Since my course would emphasize tools to critique the severe inequalities in the neoliberal model and the erosion of liberty in its culture, my course would provide no measurable quantities for "succeeding" within that system: hence useless.

2. THE "FRAGILE MIX" OF INTELLECTUAL ORIENTATION

What's that? Let me approach my point at first through analogy. I recently heard a remark by economist Joseph Stiglitz that he hadn't realized as he was growing up how the functionality of capitalism, so taken for granted in the 1950s–60s, was really based on a fragile mix of regulation and freedom.[9] He didn't notice it until it went away, resulting in the dysfunctional capitalism of today. Analogously, I was not aware how fragile was the wondrous educational arrangement I found growing up. Things were set up so that if one plunged into humane learning in the arts and sciences, one would eventually be invited into the leadership of society. This was because the adults in influential positions in government, business, healthcare, security, et al., were in part, to use Plato's term, like guardians. They had been promoted for *their* humane learning, at least as much as for technical skills, and they were looking for younger replacements who would carry this on. I experienced a steady stream of examples growing up, such as how Harvard Medical School would rather have aspiring undergraduates major in history or

philosophy than chemistry or biology. The community college I joined
in 1979 still seemed to be in the universe of this fragile mix. Within it,
intellectual activity could thrive.

3. "COMING TO OUR OWN CONVICTIONS ON MATTERS OF ULTIMATE ORIENTATION"

Cobb has already developed this: What can I add? A broad swath of my
students animated this principle, particularly when I team-taught holistic programs. For example, from my first five years in "College Skills,"
I think of a returning adult who eventually became a security guard
at the college who was touched holistically by the text I used, Howard
Zinn's *A People's History of the United States.* From my second decade in
a liberal arts core program, I think of a young man so transformed by
the insights of *Habits of the Heart* that when author Robert Bellah visited
upstate to address the New Jersey Council on the Humanities, he made
the trip and afterwards was first to engage Bellah in conversation. From
my third decade, when pluralism was disappearing, I could still attempt,
less satisfactorily, to address students holistically within isolated philosophy courses. I think especially of a young woman who wrote in her 101
journal, amidst thousands of words, that she was "a child of Camus."

I should say before leaving "conviction" that this word is in danger
of becoming a cliché. Commercial media today regularly gushes
self-serving praise on "convictions," usually about fame and profit seeking, hardly ever ultimate orientation, and rarely collective dreams. Even
C-SPAN. Consider this example from the commencement speech of one
Jason Kilar at the University of North Carolina May 10, 2015. Leaving
no doubt that he considered himself a success, this young billionaire's
main message to graduates was that they, like him, should "have a passion"; "believe in" themselves; approach their work "with a mission";
"take risks." If you have a conviction, no amount of adversity can stop
you, he testified, comparing himself to Churchill. But what was the
content? First, Kilar dared to join, early on, Amazon; then later risked
leaving to launch Hulu. His mission: to "transform the way television
is delivered." "If you think the world is broken in a certain way," Kilar
pronounced, "and you have a way to fix it, don't hold back from pursuing your dream."[10]

But is this really about fixing the world? Consider these words of Pope Francis:

> Do we realize that something is wrong in a world where there are so many farmworkers without land, so many families without a home, so many laborers without rights, so many persons whose dignity is not respected? Do we realize that something is wrong where so many senseless wars are being fought and acts of fratricidal violence are taking place on our very doorstep? Do we realize something is wrong when the soil, water, air and living creatures of our world are under constant threat?[11]

4. QUESTIONING ASSUMPTIONS

We could transition to this from just where we left off above, by bringing up how to handle "left" versus "conservative" (and other) assumptions. For example, I am aware that sentiments such as Kilar's can be part of a worldview that might be "defended in open discussion." Conservative Charles Krauthammer recently published a book called *Things that Matter*. It concerns his 2012 prediction that President Obama, if re-elected, would set the U.S. on a path to becoming a European-style social democracy, not a dynamic cradle-of-innovation.[12] The very title raises this to a level near ultimate concern. My point is not to exclude such arguments from the "intellectual hotbed." Rather, I think they must be tested in argument, not just accepted as assumptions, while going outside them is dismissed as foolishly idealistic. Is a conviction to launch Hulu on a par with a conviction about—well, important things? Here is where we get to foundations, such as what Aquinas suggested when he argued that material goods, honor, glory, etc. could not possibly be the highest good. The search for such foundations provides a horizon, even if the foundations are never locked down. Perhaps even when young people "have a passion" to sing, play tennis, or run a large enterprise, they need to be encouraged to relate it to the world's central needs, such as Camus describes in his essay "The Artist and his Time."

Turning to the second list, these were features I found at the community college in the late 1970s when I joined.

The first (a) was a pluralist educational philosophy. While some professors already believed in pedagogy built around the predecessors of outcomes, others found this ill-suited for what they taught. All were united in a loose and tolerant coalition around an arts and sciences core. At our college, the main major was just liberal arts and sciences, with a concentration in various departments, such as sociology, English, and biology. Therefore the separation into departments didn't seem particularly absolute, and the overall ethos of getting a college education was emphasized.

The second (b) was public funding. Community colleges in 1979 were still close to the intended three-thirds split among state, county, and student. I think there is actually a tie-in between a community college's having an intellectual orientation and justifying taxpayer expense. It involves the relationship between the hothouse and civic vibrancy. Coming to one's own convictions about matters of *ultimate* orientation may be the top goal, but matters of ultimate *societal* orientation are a close second. The hothouse is where citizens learn to think. As the community college became privatized there has been less interest in the hothouse, more in job-preparation. This argument has conservative as well as left roots. As Fox News' Juan Williams argued recently against Ann Coulter on a *Hannity* panel, studying texts (like Plato's *Republic*) deserves public funding because it trains people to do what "we are doing here," Williams said: debating which way society should go.[13]

The third (c) was an empowered faculty, especially in the arts and sciences. When I arrived in 1979, the faculty ran the college. They determined curriculum. They chose the books. They figured out who taught what. Faculty set the tone not only in the classroom but also in the halls and extra-curricular assemblies. They did not pay excessive attention to student "evaluations," or to administrative review. I would say, they had the upper hand, and well they might: like doctors in medicine, they had the education and self-confidence to be authors of their own work. Some would say they had too much power. In my state, they were organized in the NJEA (New Jersey Education Association), Governor Chris Christie's avowed enemy. I should note that I think Christie's attacks on K-12 destroy preparation for respecting what is intellectual and discourage good teachers. However, I admit that one of the reasons in New Jersey's higher education that we got to where we are today might have been a backlash against the sometimes too indiscriminate use of power by the union to protect faculty. I would have been more comfortable with the American Association of University Professors. On the other hand, although unionization in the college setting was unfamiliar to me, faculty running a college was not. If you want to have intellectual colleges, you have to set free a faculty that can think. Certain people give forth great energy when set free, but close down when they are watched over by corporate supervisors. As Confucius predicted, they'll do what they're told—until you stop watching them.

The fourth (d) was organic leadership. In 1979, the chairpersons of divisions largely came up through the ranks. They were professors who wanted to try administration. Higher administrators—deans, provosts, and vice presidents—were comparable. Liberal arts-and-science humanism was a common theme, even among New Jersey community college presidents. My president in 1979 was a gentleman scholar who shuffled between county funders, the state house, the Princeton Mid-Career Fellowship program, and our own faculty. The administration and faculty all went to the same parties and celebrations. I remember showing a film once to my college skills students called "Puerto Rico: Paradise Invaded" in which an employee finds herself with a promotion and this advice (paraphrased): "Now that you are a manager, it is important *not* to fraternize any more with the people who used to be your friends." That certainly did not describe the community college when I arrived; it would years later.

The fifth (e) was "part of a larger society not distorted by severe inequality." I am not talking about inequalities of opportunity for female, African-American, Latino, or LGTB persons, which were worse in earlier decades. I am talking about the vibrancy of the middle class and the extent of the gap between rich and poor, as documented in the work of Robert Reich, for example. Conditions were much more functional before Reaganomics set in. This affected the atmosphere at the community college. I will say more when I consider the flip side, the distorted society, in part III.

III. "ANTI-INTELLECTUAL"

How did the second list, the structural features, change since the late 1990s to make characteristics on the first list—the distinctions of intellectual orientation—no longer possible?

First and foremost (a), the pluralism of educational philosophies at the community college is gone, destroyed by structural re-adjustment akin to that of economies like Greece and Argentina. At the community college, there became only one acceptable way: a philosophy of education based on "outcomes." To consolidate its hegemony, the outcomes architects used the term "culture of outcomes" to describe what was to penetrate into every hall of the college, and hopefully every crevice of student and faculty minds. Once pluralism was gone and the "one" enshrined, all five characteristics of an intellectual orientation became difficult; only through contortions could one fit our beloved useless, fragile mix into quantitative behavioral outcomes assessment, as monitored by corporate-style management.

This transition was first sold to community college faculty as a non-substantial change that would only systematize better what professors were already doing. I can remember the day the transition was introduced; it is not a hyperbole to call it a coup. Faculty such as described above—diverse, talented, well-credentialed, freethinking, energetic—were sat down in a computer room and told to cram everything they wanted students to do into short sentences with performance-oriented verbs like "List the causes." The need for us to do this, we were told, had to do with a new accreditation emergency coming up from the South, which was now apparently the vanguard region. Many liberal arts and science faculty found the experience infantilizing. We were assured that it wouldn't change anything; it changed everything.

For example, the change has been destructive in two areas highlighted by Cobb: questioning assumptions and being value-free. Cobb notes that in today's anti-intellectual university there is a "lack of interest in assumptions" on two levels, departmental (no encouragement to articulate assumptions; instead socialization into the existing pattern) and university-wide ("Almost any self-study...is limited to questions of efficiency within the existing context of assumptions").[14] These are echoed at the community college, especially the second: Self-studies for regional accrediting agencies have become a major vehicle for imposing neoliberal restructuring, not the opportunity to consider a variety of orientations. Moreover, from institutional down to course levels, outcomes policing has encouraged a kind of historical amnesia. Longitudinal studies are discouraged. For example, I once suggested, in a document that the regional accrediting agency would see, that a longitudinal study of student writing in comparative religion from 1999 to 2013 might uncover a decline in standards; this was redacted with no explanation. With regard to "value-free," community colleges in the neoliberal period, like research universities, have turned increasingly to value-free claims to guard the prevailing order and protect it from alternatives. Yet echoing Cobb, these claims "compromise the ideal on a large scale." Funding constitutes one compromise, e.g., the world's leading weapons manufacturer Lockheed-Martin funds science research at our community college. Further, as Cobb points out, does "value-free" training for jobs mean we cannot "ask about the value of the jobs"?[15] But training for those often less-than-meaningful jobs imposes its own value.

How was such a transformation consolidated? There were many prongs to the attack, but in retrospect overwhelmingly two: the imposition of a new "accountability" from the top and heightened emphasis on "student evaluations" from the bottom. Accountability, innocuous sounding at first, didn't turn out to be just any accountability but a neoliberal version. The default accountability was re-set to the emerging global corporate society, with its accelerating transfer of wealth from bottom to top and privatizing the commons. The market as God is how theologian Harvey Cox described it in 1999; we would now be accountable to the new God.[16] The accompanying emphasis on student evaluations, in turn, did not turn out to be just any student evaluations, but opinion surveys in the vogue of the new "customer satisfaction" craze. A professor now must try to please "customers" as figured by calculations of marketing "success."

In the midst of these changes, the fragile mix all but disappeared. Neither faculty nor students could pretend anymore that, in this society, learning to be human (Confucian phrase) turns out also to attract a respected paid position. Students' very attitude toward education changed. True, just as in the 1970s, those up from uneducated backgrounds would still say things in 2014 like "I finally got the light" and "now I can see the importance of education"; but when further questioned to specify *what* is important, the recent ones usually say "keeping up my GPA" and "getting my degree"—not awakening intellectually. It is about compliance and getting ahead, not improving the republic or "ultimate orientation."

Increasingly there seemed to grow a disingenuousness about the very words "education" and "college." In the early 2000s worldwide, education would be lauded and demanded as every person's right, by the Pakistani young woman Malala Yousafzai, for example. Would Malala suggest risking life for corporate job training? For an SAT prep course? Most students today major in business or a trade to make themselves workforce-ready. If they do go against the current and major in one of the liberal arts, then of late they are tempted to become single-minded about this, too, taking the narrow track to beat out all others in that separated discipline, again as a way to employment; the stakes in an extremely unequal society are too frightening to do otherwise. And if students go into teaching, then they face submitting to the same rules of compliance—measurable test-driven outcomes, "accountable" lesson plans—and the whole process comes full circle.

We can address the other three changed structural features of the community college more briefly because they flow directly from the above. "Public funding" (b) has eroded. Today students and faculty alike are exposed to the bare truth of unregulated capitalism, that there are no strong collective entities like counties or states that fund much of anything. Tuition plus corporate charity have had to step in, and faculty help by accepting to teach for stunningly low salaries considering they are highly educated persons.

Accordingly, "empowered faculty" (c) is a thing of the past. One of the prongs of the attack has been the laying off and encouraged early retirement of faculty who experienced the freer regime, and their replacement by millennials who never have. The changeover also would not have been possible without the outsourcing to adjuncts of most positions.

"Organic administration" (d) is also gone. A corporate managerial administrative structure has been superimposed over leadership that emerges up from the faculty. Individual administrators within this system might be good people, but the structure itself is too confining for them to do much.

Finally, the "larger society" (e) has changed dramatically. William Greider writes in a 2011 *Nation* article, "severe inequality is not just a question of morality; it is the source of disorder that leads to crisis." The ancients knew this, Greider points out. He cites Hebrews and Babylonians and might have added Confucius and Plato.[17] Reich, as well as Stiglitz, has detailed this rising inequality spanning the last 35 years, 1980–2015.[18] Radical educator Henry A. Giroux has written about the same period in education, with the rise of the neoliberal and fall of the civic.[19] Bad societies lead to bad schools. In the U.S. case the extremism that has led to dysfunction is market extremism, the opposite kind that led to the dysfunction of late Soviet society. But in either, dysfunctional economies affect intellectual aspirations in schools. Beset by society-imposed blinders, learners cannot entertain the full spectrum of thought. With alternatives eliminated, the only practical education is one in which one learns how to get ahead within the system. Approaches to higher and broader things, Cobb's "ultimate orientations," seem strange and pointless.

IV. "COLLEGE"

Cobb's argument for universities becoming intellectual again may generate great-university discussion and even some action, but my argument for more intellectual community colleges is in danger of falling flat. Current national proposals are moving rapidly in the opposite direction; local officials in charge are likely to do nothing lofty or impractical; liberal arts, increasingly compliant, has found a small niche after a record retreat (but who cares?); and the word "intellectual" isn't all that popular. This is why I am going to suggest, in conclusion, not so much emphasis on the words "intellectual" and "anti-intellectual" and more on the word "college."

I propose that what we now call a community college be re-named a Global Corporate Training Center in the Community. Within that there could be a smaller entity called "the College." It would be an intellectual space, even a hotbed.

But before we go on, let me address a possible general objection. Why listen any further to me? I finished my 35 years at a community college with dubious status. So what is this? A last-ditch effort to salvage some respectability? Sour grapes? Why don't I just walk away? "Leave community college alone!" I think about this a lot. My life takes most of its meaning from my family anyway; just write off my foolish attempt to bring what I learned at Haverford, etc. to the public as a wasted career that at least supported my kids.

Yet for some reason I have a pestering urge to account for myself. By habit since age 18 (Punahou, Haverford), I can't help interpreting my life trajectory in Plato's Socrates' terms: as one of a guardian trainee. In the *Republic,* Socrates has the students who participate in dialogues on *everything* in their early thirties then spend 15 years in "practical posts." Well, I spent 35; it went by quickly. So now what? In Plato's story, next comes the re-convening of the guardian cohort, when each person gives an account of what he or she learned. Then all proceed with the highest studies of all, the dialectic and beyond, until some of them achieve enlightenment and take their turns at governing the state. Moving back to 2015, it is time to re-convene. But with whom?

Cohorts: I have been reflecting on them lately. One's cohorts can have an immense power. The alumni magazines from Punahou, Haverford, Yale, and Princeton (where I was a post-doc) pour into my house. There I read of the people with whom, by socialization, I am encouraged to share lifelong camaraderie, accountability, and giving back. Elite school PR departments play upon our desires to feel important, and highlight those whose "success" can bring treasure. They oppose what some have called socioeconomic "class treason," and tenaciously reproduce the class structure. To me it feels that my schools, after teaching me the opposite for 1-4 years, have left me with a rest-of-life supply of seductive but ultimately self-serving (dis)information, as my society and planet lurch toward catastrophe.

But what do I want them to do? Close down? Isn't everyone self-serving, they and I? So we cancel? Favored classmates report back their success in business, thinking this gives their lives meaning: how self-serving! I write an article to question their meaning and salvage mine: how self-serving! Only a few seem to escape this conundrum: Thomas Aquinas, I am told, went virtually silent his last six months, distancing himself from everything he had written. Clamoring ego disturbed it all, as Simone Weil might have said:

> May I disappear, in order that those things that I see may become perfect in their beauty from the very fact that they are no longer things that I see. I do not in the least wish that this created world should fade from my view, but that it should no longer be to me personally that it shows itself. ...If I go, then the creator and the creature will exchange their secrets.[20]

After such cleansing, can we begin somewhere?

I would like to reconvene as grandparents who care deeply about leaving behind a world worth living in for their grandchildren. Ultimate orientation does not mean we have to decide as to markets or socialism, God or Tao. I have a grandson who is half-South American, half-North American. Can I insist at least that he and every life be treated with dignity? Whether he goes to a research university, community college, or something in-between, I would like him to be able to experience a hotbed and to confront the whole picture. Furthermore, I would like his K-12 education to build toward this orientation with as much wonder-building as skill-crunching.

Returning to my argument, a small part of a Global Corporate Training Center in the Community would be "the College." That part would be run in a strikingly different way. It would be more concerned with inputs than outcomes. Its faculty would be hired and set free using the best of renewed older practices. Trusted as "good philosophers and good persons" (geographers, biologists, etc.), they would experience their creativity unleashed. We can learn much from the Confucian model in this regard.

The College would be frugal. We would need tenure, but no merit pay, nor steep raises. Socrates' wording might guide us here: maintain lovers of wisdom at the state's expense (like infrastructure or trees). The society in certain periods might become more entrepreneurial or more communal, but this inner group would be protected. No one would work for these low wages? I suspect there is actually a backlog of people who would like to work in this kind of arrangement: secure but not rich. Such persons currently feel hopeless amidst the preoccupation with beating out others and climbing to the top. It could be part of a global shift toward collectives or co-ops, bringing a little closer together the once polarized models of, say, Cuba and the United States. "The College" could be run as a sort of collective.

The College might be a new dawn for the liberal arts, or more accurately liberal arts *and sciences*. After all, this is not a power struggle against STEM (Science, Technology, Engineering and Math). It would help science, too. "STEM" without "liberal"—I concur with Cobb on this—gives us mostly the situated and biased science of defense contractors and pharmaceutical giants. As an example, the College might become a hothouse for innovative integral medicine, escaping the assumptions of conventional modern medicine, or for brainstorming in a new ecological paradigm about climate change.

Although avoiding the chopping block of outcomes assessment, the College should aim to be transparent as to what kind of long-range good it can contribute. In terms of viability, for example: Faced with a choice between "global corporate training" and college, will some students choose college? Will some who want to train for medicine or business nonetheless choose *part* of their coursework in "the College"? By changing the words—what Confucian tradition calls rectification of names—we may exert a gentle coercion toward eventually returning to the fragile balance. The society could keep unobtrusive track of how the "College way" is doing compared to the "Global Corporate Training way" when the latter is stripped of its unfair usurpation of the name "college."

The modern research universities Cobb discusses might also be renamed, perhaps "Global Corporate Research Centers in the Cities." Within each of these, as well, there could be an intellectual hothouse called the College. It could be accessible to students at any level: undergraduate, graduate, and professional.

All this might seem too rhetorical and unlikely, but my hope is that it helps advance the discussion. Reversing Cobb's closing sentence, a freer school with a more urgent and ultimate focus, right within each of our existing institutions, may contribute "to steering the world away from catastrophes more than leading it into them."

NOTES

1   John Cobb, "The Anti-Intellectualism of the American University," *Soundings* 98, no 2 (2015): 219; Alfred North Whitehead, *Science and the Modern World* (Cambridge: Cambridge University Press, 1925).

2   Union of Experimenting Colleges and Universities. "The Union Graduate School," 1971.

3   See Martin Luther King's analysis in *The Radical King* (Boston: Beacon, 2015) with introduction by Cornel West, if you need details.

4   Pope Francis. "Laudato Si: Encyclical Letter of the Holy Father Francis on Care for our Common Home," widely available online.

5   Cobb, "The Anti-Intellectualism of the American University."

6   Ibid.

7   1975 letter on file with author.

8   Plato, *The Republic of Plato,* Francis MacDonald, trans. and ed. (London: Oxford University Press, 1945).

9   Joseph Stiglitz, *The Great Divide: Unequal Societies and What We Can Do About Them* (New York: W. W. Norton, 2015).

10   Jason Kilar, University of North Carolina Commencement Speech, May 10, 2015.

11   Pope Francis, "Speech at the World Meeting of Popular Movements," July 9, 2015.

12   Charles Krauthammer, *Things that Matter: Three Decades of Passions, Pastimes and Politics* (New York: Crown Forum, 2013).

13   Juan Williams on *Hannity,* Fox News, broadcasted May 30, 2015.

14   Cobb, "The Anti-Intellectualism of the American University."

15   Ibid.

16   Harvey Cox, "The Market as God," *The Atlantic,* March, 1999.

17   William Greider, "Debt Jubilee, American Style," *The Nation* (Nov. 14,

2011): 11-17.

18   Robert Reich, *Inequality for All,* directed by Jacob Kornbluth (2013; Los Angeles, CA: Radius TWC), DVD.

19   Henry A. Giroux, *Neoliberalism's War on Higher Education* (Chicago: Haymarket Press, 2014).

20   Simone Weil, "Reality, from Gravity and Grace," in *Reality,* Carl Levenson and Jonathan Westphal, eds (Indianapolis, Indiana: Hackett, 1994), 180–81.

3. WHY THE LIBERAL ARTS NEED
A NEW WORLDVIEW

Marcus Ford

ABSTRACT: *A civilization that does not encourage the intellectual, moral, and aesthetic development of its young people is a danger to itself and the planet, and that the modern scientific worldview—the dominant worldview of higher education—undermines this type of education. So long as the modern scientific worldview goes unchallenged, we cannot reestablish the tradition of a liberal arts education. Whitehead's constructive postmodernism offers a viable alternative to both Cartesian dualism and scientific materialism and provides the basis for a new, non-anthropocentric, form of liberal arts education.*

FOR MORE THAN TWO THOUSAND YEARS, liberal arts education has been judged to be critically important both for human development and democracy. Lately, we have convinced ourselves that it is unnecessary; that so long as we have technical knowledge we will flourish. But judged by the measures of environmental health and social justice, we are not thriving. Indeed, we are in immense peril. I suggest that we need to reevaluate the cultural importance of a liberal arts education.

The consequences associated with not getting education right are enormous. In 1929, Whitehead wrote,

> When one considers in its length and in its breadth the importance of this question of the education of a nation's young, the

broken lives, the defeated hopes, the national failures, which result from the frivolous inertia with which it is treated, it is difficult to restrain within oneself a savage rage. In the conditions of modern life the rule is absolute, the race which does not value trained intelligence is doomed. Not all your heroism, not all your social charm, not all your wit, not all your victories on land or at sea, can move back the finger of fate. To-day we maintain ourselves. To-morrow science will have moved forward yet one more step, and there will be no appeal from the judgment which will then be pronounced on the uneducated.[1]

By "trained intelligence," Whitehead did not mean individuals educated narrowly. The proper goal of education, he believed, is producing individuals "who possess both culture and expert knowledge."[2] Today, we have delinked the two, devaluing the importance of the kind of education designed to promote culture and giving enormous importance to expert knowledge.

The danger associated with producing individuals who have specialized knowledge without culture, specialized knowledge in a vacuum, should be obvious: without some understanding of how everything fits together and what it all means, we lack the capacity to evaluate how best to use our specialized knowledge and the virtue needed to transcend our narrow self-interest. We have become a danger to ourselves and to the planet.

The argument that will be outlined in the following pages is that we are failing as a civilization because we have adopted a way of thinking about reality that does not make sense and a form of higher education that reinforces this worldview. There are no viable, long-term, solutions to our current situation short of rethinking our most basic assumptions regarding the nature of reality. We need a different metaphysics and a different form of education so that we can fundamentally remake our civilization.

****

Liberal arts education was invented in Athens twenty-five hundred years ago for two related purposes: to transform self-interested individuals into citizens and to refine the human spirit. A life of civic engagement, which for the Greeks included military service, and a life of contemplation and aesthetic enjoyment pull one in different directions, but for the Greeks, there was the sense that these two ideals were not fundamentally in opposition. A fully realized individual was someone devoted to truth, goodness, and beauty, but also fully committed to the collective life of the community.

When this form of higher education was absorbed into Christian culture, the understanding of these objectives — of personal refinement and service to others — was reconstructed in light of Christian theology, but their fundamental expression and practice remained quite similar. The goal of citizenship was reinterpreted to mean service to God and God's creation, but in practical terms, service to God and God's creation was interpreted to mean service to one's fellow human beings. Likewise, for both Greeks and Christians, material wealth was viewed as an impediment to the virtuous life. According to Plato, wealth, like poverty, corrupts the soul. The Christian position was even more severe: the love of wealth is a form of idolatry.

The primary form of higher education in the United States, prior to 1950, was a liberal arts education rooted in the Christian faith. Here is how one liberal arts college in Arkansas, described its mission in 1910:

> Since Hendrix College is under Church auspices, and because education without religion is a mockery and a failure, the Christian religion is made to underlie and permeate all our instructions… [T]he morals of those entrusted to our care will be faithfully cultivated… While we recognize the necessity for practical education, we do not pander to the depraved money-born cry, "Nothing but the practical!" The education which, ignoring culture, burdens the student's mind with tables and technical terms, simply because these may be of use to him in his business or profession, is… injurious in the extreme. The student who has learned to think, not merely memorize, who has secured permanent culture and wisdom, who has absorbed and assimilated… is the one who will be felt, wherever he may go… To make such men, cultured in mind and heart, to give to our country and to our God strong, manly Christian men, shall be our object and our ambition.[3]

In its understanding of the goals of higher education, Hendrix College was no different than any other liberal arts college. Education was about culturing the "mind and heart;" teaching people to think for themselves; and contributing to the common good. It was *not* about getting rich.

Robert Maynard Hutchins, the president of the University of Chicago from 1929–1945, makes this last point explicitly, recalling a meeting with a former Oberlin College classmate who had made a good deal of money and was obviously embarrassed by this fact. Rather than bragging about his wealth, Hutchins reports, this Oberlin graduate insisted upon telling his fellow alumni privately that he devoted his extracurricular life to civic betterment. As Hutchins recounted, it was "an Oberlin assumption that a man might be rich or honorable, but hardly both."[4]

We have since radically reassessed our views on wealth, individual success, and the purpose of a liberal arts education. In 1997, John Mearsheimer, a distinguished member of the faculty at the University of Chicago, in the annual "The Aims of Education" address (named in honor of Whitehead's essay by the same title) said this to the incoming students:

> [T]he fact that a degree from here [the University of Chicago] increases the prospects that you will make a lot of money, and maybe even become very rich, is also great news. I don't say that because I expect that you will use that money to lead a life of debauchery. On the contrary, I believe that you will soon become adults with significant responsibilities, and to meet those responsibilities, you will need lots of money. For example, most of you will marry, have children, and buy a house. Putting a roof over your head and sending Billy and Suzy to the University of Chicago will certainly cost you a lot of money when your time comes. So be prepared, which is another way of saying, make sure you have a lot of money in the bank, and the more of it you have, the better.[5]

Mearsheimer's contention that the primary value of a liberal arts education from a top-ranked school is economic, is exceptional only in terms of its candor. Most people use language that is more subtle. A liberal arts education, they say, will "open up new opportunities" and "prepare one for success." In most cases what that means is precisely what Mearsheimer said: a liberal arts education will increase the prospects of making a lot of money.

How did a liberal arts education, once devoted to the twin goals of citizenship and wisdom, and then to service to God and God's creation, become transformed into an education for upward mobility and financial success? How did a twenty-five hundred year old tradition of believing that money corrupts the soul and is a form of idolatry give way to the idea that money is a good thing and "the more you have of it the better"?

The short answer to these questions is the secularization of higher education. When the liberal arts tradition cut its ties with the Christian faith, it severed its connections with a set of moral principles. The moral values of the Christian tradition have been replaced by the economic values of modern secular society.

The longer answer to this question is that the liberal arts have embraced the modern scientific worldview — a worldview that is not only atheistic but also rules out the ideas of intrinsic value, moral and aesthetic norms, and personal agency. In the absence of aesthetic and moral norms, the door is open to valuing personal wealth and power.

***

In its original form, the modern scientific worldview was not atheistic, deterministic, or value-free. Descartes, the "father of modern philosophy," did not doubt that he existed or that he had free will; indeed, this was the one thing that he said he could not consistently doubt. And he did not seem to seriously doubt that God existed or that there were moral and aesthetic norms. From the fact that he had the idea of God, he quickly concluded that God must exist. It was only later, in order to make this new worldview more coherent, that others rejected the idea of divinity, experience, agency, and moral and aesthetic norms.

Having convinced himself that he, and others like him, existed, and that God existed, Descartes went on to postulate another kind of reality — extended substances. Only God, he thought, was truly self-sufficient, but mental substances (minds) and extended substances (atoms) were nearly self-sufficient in that they required only God in order to exist. Mental substances, Descartes speculated, did not need extended substances or other mental substances in order to exist, and extended substances did not require mental substances or other extended substances in order to exist.

The most shocking aspect of Descartes' new worldview was his proposal that, with the exception of the human mind or soul, the universe was comprised of dead matter. The world of nature is not obviously lifeless. Many things move and some things, most notably animals, seem to have feelings. To hypothesize, as he did, that animals are in fact only very complex machines — incapable of feeling, cognition, and agency — was an act of bold philosophical speculation in the 17th century.

Descartes' proposal that the universe was a giant machine, governed by laws of efficient causation, proved to be a very useful way of thinking about certain phenomena. In the astronomy and physics of the 17th and 18th centuries, and then in the chemistry of the 19th century, nothing of any importance seemed to have been lost by assuming that the entities under consideration were lifeless and, indeed, a great deal of precise knowledge was gained in terms of how such entities moved.

The primary problem for Descartes, and for those who came after him, was accounting for the interaction between the human psyche and the body. The mental decisions we make *seem* to result in bodily action and, conversely, what happens to the body *seems* to influence our experience. When our body is injured we feel pain. When we make up our mind to go for a walk, our body usually obliges. Descartes' speculation that the mind was a metaphysically different type of substance than the substances that make up the body made any natural explanation of mind-body or body-mind interaction metaphysically impossible. The inability to provide any explanation for something as basic as the relationship between the human mind and the human body counts heavily against the plausibility of metaphysical dualism.

One "solution" to this philosophical conundrum was to deny the existence of mental substances. If there is only one type of substance — extended substances — then the problem of how two metaphysically distinct types of substances can interact never arises. This is the "solution" favored by most scientists today. Human experience, it is postulated, does not technically exist. What we call "experience" is nothing more than the interaction of entities—cells, molecules, electrons, and so on—all devoid of experience. Human beings are very sophisticated robots.

Bertrand Russell summed up the modern scientific worldview in his 1902 essay *A Free Man's Worship*:

> That Man is the product of causes which had no prevision of the end they were achieving; that his origin, his growth, his hopes and fears, his loves and his beliefs, are but the outcome of accidental collocations of atoms; that no fire, no heroism, no intensity of thought and feeling, can preserve an individual life beyond the grave; that all the labors of the ages, all the devotion, all the inspiration, all the noonday brightness of human genius, are destined to extinction in the vast death of the solar system, and that the whole temple of Man's achievement must inevitably be buried beneath the debris of a universe in ruins—all these things, if not quite beyond dispute, are yet so nearly certain, that no philosophy which rejects them can hope to stand...Only within the scaffolding of these truths, only on the firm foundation of unyielding despair, can the soul's habitation henceforth be safely built.[6]

The universe is devoid of moral and aesthetic norms, purpose, and human agency. Human beings are the product of material forces, signifying nothing.

A more recent, and less literary, summary of the modern scientific worldview comes from William Provine, a historian of science:

> Modern science directly implies that the world is organized strictly in accordance with deterministic principles or chance...There are no purposive principles whatsoever in nature. There are no gods and no designing forces that are rationally detectable...Second, modern science directly implies that there are no inherent moral or ethical laws...Third, human beings are marvelously complex machines. The individual human becomes an ethical person by means of only two mechanisms: deterministic heredity interacting with deterministic

environmental influences. That is all there is... Fourth, we must conclude that when we die, we die and that is the end of us... There is no hope of life everlasting... [F]ree will, as traditionally conceived, the freedom to make uncoerced and unpredictable choices among alternative possible courses of action, simply does not exist... [T]he evolutionary process cannot produce a being that is truly free to make choices... The universe cares nothing for us... Humans are as nothing even in the evolutionary process on earth. There is no ultimate meaning for humans.[7]

Reality is nothing but matter blindly and mechanistically following the laws of the universe—laws that arose for no reason and provide no reason. This is the metaphysical context for the modern university. In this setting, the traditional goals of a liberal arts education—to transcend one's own interest, refine one's character, serve God and God's creation—are pointless, even foolish.

***

In the early part of the 20th century, Whitehead developed an alternative to both Cartesian dualism and scientific materialism. Given the inadequacy of these two forms of modernism, it is an alternative worthy of consideration.

Whitehead formulated his postmodern worldview as a response to the internal contradictions and inadequacies of the modern scientific worldview. A worldview that compels intelligent people to conclude that they are machines—lacking purpose, intrinsic value, and freedom—is a worldview deserving of reevaluation. A fully adequate worldview must be able to make sense of the person who holds this worldview, including how they talk and act when they are not doing philosophy, and it must make sense of the world as revealed by the best science of the time. For a hundred years, it has been clear that the world is not comprised of bits of matter but rather of units of energy. Neither Cartesian dualism nor scientific materialism adequately reflects this.

Whitehead called his metaphysics "a philosophy of organism," more commonly known as "process philosophy" or "process-relational philosophy." David Griffin, one of the chief expositors of Whitehead's metaphysics and a philosopher in his own right, has called Whitehead's position "panexperientialism with organizational dualism." Although less mellifluous, Griffin's nomenclature has the advantage of being more precise.

Reality, Whitehead speculated, is best explained in terms of experiential units. He called them "actual occasions." Everything actual—a quantum of energy, a moment of human consciousness, a moment of divine experience (if there are such experiences)—is an actual occasion. To be anything is to be something for oneself (an experience), to have an environment (made up of other events), to have some agency, to be temporal, and to become part of the environment of all future actual occasions. These are universal characteristics. All actual occasions, by hypothesis, share these in common.

Griffin's term "organizational dualism" alludes to Whitehead's hypothesis that actual occasions organize themselves in two fundamentally different ways. What Descartes thought of as an extended substance or a collection of extended substances, Whitehead thought of as an aggregate society of actual occasions. A rock, for example, is a myriad of actual occasions, each with some agency and subjectivity, but the rock itself is simply an aggregate of these entities and as such has neither agency nor subjectivity. Descartes' error, according to Whitehead, was in attributing metaphysical status to these aggregates of actual occasions. If there is only one way to be actual, the central problem of metaphysical dualism—how can metaphysically unique entities interact?—never arises. In this respect, Whitehead's philosophy is like scientific materialism: it posits only one way of being actual. Where it differs from scientific materialism is in terms of the characteristics of this one type of actuality. All actual occasions, Whitehead speculated, were events that had some degree of experience and agency.

If the most controversial aspect of Descartes' philosophy in the 17th century was his speculation that, with the exception of human minds and God, the universe consists of dead matter, the most controversial aspect of Whitehead's philosophy is his panexperientialism. Modern thinkers have become so accustomed to the idea of dead matter that it is hard to entertain the contrasting proposition: that nothing actual is fully devoid of experience. Given the option of attributing some degree of subjectivity to everything actual (excluding those "entities" such as rocks, chairs, and planets, that Whitehead understood to be aggregates of actual entities) or denying experience altogether, many professional philosophers have concluded that they must deny experience and agency altogether, even their own.

Many contemporary thinkers are also troubled by Whitehead's speculation that there is a universal mind that, like every other actual occasion, exerts some influence on everything. Whitehead called this entity "God."

Whitehead came to the idea of a universal mind relatively late in the development of his philosophy. The fact that the universe has some order, Whitehead believed, means that there must be some universal principle of limitation. If everything were possible at every moment, there would be no enduring patterns, only chaos, indistinguishable from nothing at all. Appealing to a principle of limitation to explain the order of this or any other possible universe, however, violated his own tenant that only actual entities have agency. A principle is not an actual entity. If there is a principle of limitation at work in the universe, this principle must be embodied in an actual entity. Wisely or unwisely, Whitehead chose to name the actual entity that embodies the universal principle of limitation "God."

In addition to providing agency to the principle of limitation, postulating a universal mind solved other metaphysical problems for Whitehead, including the location of possibilities not yet actualized and the locus of ethical and aesthetic norms, as well as true propositions.

Today, the concept of God is so closely associated with patriarchy, super-naturalism, Western imperialism, and anti-intellectualism (including, sometimes, a wholesale rejection of evolution and climate science) that, in retrospect, Whitehead might have been better off employing another descriptor to name the creative force in the universe that houses the principle of limitation, unrealized possibilities, and ethical and aesthetic norms. Trying to assign a new meaning to an existing word that has a long, complicated history is not always the best option.

Whitehead's philosophy is exceedingly complex in its details. The point of this brief overview of his worldview is not to convince anyone of its overall correctness. The point is only to make it clear that there is at least one postmodern alternative to the worldview that is now taken for granted by the modern university—the modern scientific worldview—and to highlight some of the most important differences between these two worldviews. To assume that the modern scientific worldview—a view that, when consistently held, denies human experience and agency as well as ethical and aesthetic values—and Cartesian dualism are not highly problematic, and that there is no credible alternative to these two worldviews, is simply incorrect. Whitehead developed an alternative explanation that some have found to be, overall, much more adequate to the facts of modern science (especially quantum physics and evolutionary biology) and human experience.

***

Unlike the modern scientific worldview that is now widespread in Western culture, Whitehead's postmodern worldview provides metaphysical support for a liberal arts education that, in some respects, resembles the liberal arts education long associated with Western Civilization. Like the Greek and the Christian forms of liberal arts education, a Whiteheadian liberal arts education understands human beings as moral agents in a moral universe. However, unlike its Greek and Christian forebears, it is not anthropocentric. For Whitehead, intrinsic value is universal, not just a property of humans. To be anything at all is to have some value. A Whiteheadian liberal arts education would put humans back into nature, without denying either personal agency or intrinsic value.

In contemporary Western thought, there are basically two ways to understand what it means to be human: either human beings are metaphysically unique (the Cartesian option) or we, like everything else, are simply machines (the position of those committed to the modern scientific worldview). The advantage of the first option is that it allows us to draw attention to our intellectual and moral qualities and to focus on how we treat other human beings. The great drawback of this position is that it separates us from the non-human world. It also lands us in the middle of all sorts of metaphysical problems and ignores the central fact of evolutionary biology — that we evolved from what was not human. The other option is to see ourselves, and the rest of the natural world, as machines, a position that robs us of agency and denies the reality of moral and aesthetic norms, and intrinsic value.

Whitehead's metaphysics allows for a third option. From this perspective, human beings are fully a part of the natural world, but we are not machines — *and neither are other organisms.* This way of seeing the world places humans back into the natural world and requires us to extend moral consideration beyond our species. From a Whiteheadian perspective, everything actual — which excludes aggregates such as rocks and rivers — has some value for itself and is deserving of respect from others. In many cases, the value seems to be trivial. But in the case of complex organisms such as apes, whales, and cattle, the amount of intrinsic value appears to be very significant. This position is, admittedly, speculative, but so is the position that these organisms have no value for themselves. There is no proof that other complex organisms do not value their own lives. Moreover, Whitehead's position accords well with the way humans interact with dogs and horses, for example, and the concern that many people express for large mammals in the wild. It also fits well with evolutionary theory.

A Whiteheadian form of liberal arts education would extend moral consideration to the non-human world in another way. For Whitehead, everything is connected. As William Blake says in *The Book of Thel*, "Everything that lives, lives not alone, nor for itself." From this perspective, a concern for human well-being necessitates a concern for the well-being of the natural world as a whole, as well as concern for our "social environment" — the welfare of other human beings. This is not the Cartesian perspective. For Descartes, there was no reason to care for the natural world because it had no value for itself and it had no influence on the human psyche. Each of us, he thought, is self-sufficient. Our existence is dependent on only one other entity, God.

Scientific materialists see things differently. From their perspective humans *are* a part of the natural world and hence should be concerned about the natural world, if only for our own sake. What materialists cannot affirm, however, is that anything has intrinsic value—either nature or humans. While some of those who otherwise deny the value of human life and the value of non-human life go to great lengths to protect the natural world, their metaphysics works against them. Whitehead's metaphysics, on the other hand, supports both the idea that the non-human world is valuable in itself (and for itself), and that it is valuable for human life, which is also intrinsically valuable.

In addition to putting humans back into nature, a Whiteheadian-based liberal arts education would firmly locate humans in time, which is to say, that it would be profoundly historical. The Greek form of a liberal arts education tended to be somewhat ahistorical, focusing instead on abstractions including logic, grammar, and geometry. A major factor in the Christianization of the liberal arts was the emphasis on history, especially biblical history but also Greek and Roman history and eventually European history. One of the consequences of the decoupling of a liberal arts education from Christianity has been to lessen the importance of historical understanding. A Whiteheadian-based liberal arts education would also stress the importance of history.

John Cobb, the primary organizer of the conference that gave rise to this volume and the author of the first essay in this book, makes this point explicitly in relation to how we think about the natural world and about higher education:

> When physics is studied, there is value in becoming aware of how it arose, developed, and changed. The historical perspective shows that there are alternatives to the presently dominant forms, the reasons they were rejected, and the possibility that the victors are not always the best. The history of higher education shows the particularity of its present form and value of other options. The liberal arts should be liberating, and historical consciousness can serve this end.[8]

Knowing the history of ideas, including the history of science and the history of philosophy, frees us from accepting current modes of thought as "the Truth" and allows us to envision other possibilities. At a time when business-as-usual is destroying the earth and resulting in immense suffering and social disruption, any form of higher education that can liberate us from the intellectual status quo should be welcomed.

From the Whiteheadian perspective, everything actual arises out of the past. The present is not strictly determined by the past, but neither is it free of past. Understanding who we are as individuals and as a culture requires a historical perspective. Without this perspective, we are lost.

***

There is today a great deal of agreement regarding the importance of higher education. Politicians from both major political parties in the United States, business leaders, pundits, and educational experts agree that we will be better off as a nation if only we can increase the number of college graduates. There is, however, very little support for the kind of education that has been historically called liberal arts education, with its twin goals of civic engagement and personal development. In fact, many have explicitly stated that this form of higher education is not worthy of taxpayer support. The only rational purpose of higher education, we are told, is economic.

Whitehead disagreed. A society that does not value the intellectual, ethical, and social development of its young people is doomed. Merely increasing the number of college graduates is not sufficient. In fact, it will only make matters worse. It will, to use the language of Martin Luther King, Jr., produce "guided missiles and misguided men."[9] What is needed are individuals with expert knowledge *who are also liberally educated*, individuals who see themselves as moral agents committed to making the world a more just, sustainable, and beautiful place for all. This kind of education, however, is not possible so long as our society remains committed to the modern scientific worldview. We need another, more adequate metaphysics, one that enables us to make sense out of our lives and provides support for the idea that the world is worth saving. We need a new form of liberal arts education based on a worldview that recognizes the value of life in all of its forms, including but not limited to its human form.

NOTES

1   Alfred North Whitehead, *The Aims of Education and Other Essays* (New York: The Free Press, 1957), 14.

2   Ibid, 1.

3   Marcus Ford, *Beyond the Modern University: Toward a Constructive Postmodern University* (Santa Barbara: Praeger Press), 2–29.

4   Milton Mayer, *John Maynard Hutchins: a Memoir* (Berkeley: University of California Press, 1993), 19.

5   John J. Mearsheimer, "Aims of Education," *Philosophy and Literature* 22, no. 1 (April 1998): 135–55, https//aims.uchicago/page/1997-john-j-mearshimer.

6   Bertrand Russell, "A Free Man's Worship" in *Mysticism and Logic* (London: Allen and Unwin, 1917), 72.

7   William Provine, "Progress in Evolution and the Meaning of Life," in *Evolutionary Progress,* Matthew H. Nitechi, ed. (Chicago and London: University of Chicago Press, 1988), 64–66, 70.

8   John Cobb, Jr. *Spiritual Bankruptcy: A Prophetic Call to Action* (Nashville: Abingdon Press, 2010), 105–06.

9   Martin Luther King, Jr., *Strength to Love* (Minneapolis: Fortress Press, 2010), 73.

4. FIELD-BUILDING, EQUITY, AND TRANSFORMATION IN EDUCATION

WHAT WE CAN DO, HOW TO DO IT, AND WHO WE NEED TO BE

Sheryl Petty, Ed.D.

ABSTRACT: *The chapter indicates that the expanded visions or "promised land" we seek for education, that leads to more compassionate societies, are not possible without a focus on the trio of: systems change, deep equity, and profound inner work. The chapter explores the relationship between: 1) integrative, transformative, ecological visions and values in education; 2) institutional change, systems change, and field change strategies that make the pursuit of such visions and values possible; 3) the role and lens of equity and social justice in such transformation processes; and 4) the "inner" work/ contemplative dimensions that support practitioners and change agents to be our very best selves in pursuing such transformation. The thesis is that transforming educational systems is neither authentic nor sustainable without deep equity; and further, deep equity is neither sustainable nor compassionate without significant inner work on the part of those pursuing educational change. Real equity and real educational change require all three components; anything less is "thin."*

HOW DO WE CREATE the *conditions* for our collective awakening? What structures, supports, approaches, and relationships are required for unraveling the knots to our clear perception, action, and our collective healing? This chapter focuses on three dimensions of change applicable to all social fields, but in this case, directed toward education in its role to support the liberation of all and the development of loving, healthy communities. These dimensions are:

1   The *What* (the "DNA," or "To What End"): including visions, values, and qualities desired for the development of knowledgeable, compassionate, reflective, and engaged human beings, articulated and proliferated in living, breathing, accessible ways;

2   The *How*: encompassing the *components* of and the *processes* that promote transformation and sustainable, deep change in institutions and in the field of education, including developing and moving a *change agenda* in a systematic, flowing, dynamic, and emergent way; and

3   The *Who*: focusing on cultivating who and how we need to be *within ourselves* and *with each other* in order to successfully advance such visions, values, and dynamic change processes. These "inner" dimensions can be thought of as "contemplative" or "leadership" skills, broadly conceived.

INTRODUCTION

There are many in the field now describing various aspects of the "*what*"—the "to what end"—we are striving toward in the transformation of educational systems toward more ecological, holistic, life-preserving visions and values. Sometimes, these are described in terms of *competencies* for human beings—both students and educators. Other times, these aspects are described in terms of the *relationships* that will be required to create the conditions for our collective healing—that is, *who* and *how* we need to be with each other. All of these are critical and necessary components, particularly when some have little sense of what this "promised land" looks and feels like, and how it would actually *be* to be different with one another, as the norm.

In this chapter, I am less focused on the components of the "what"—though I will spend a little time there, if only to give the reader a sense of the terrain and how close or not so close we might be in our understandings of this desired destination. I will spend much more time in this article on the "how"—i.e., the mechanisms and processes that will need to be undertaken both with systematicity as well as with flow, a moment-to-moment discernment of how to evolve our actions in support of the thriving of the many. I will also spend a good amount of time on the "who"—that is, who we need to be in ourselves in order to even undertake this journey with care and with skill. While this "who" is connected to the kinds of human beings whose development we are hoping to support, it is also focused on who we are in this moment, and how we can cultivate, bring out, harness, and direct those qualities and skills that make for the evolvement of our very best selves in relation to one another and this Earth.

I write this chapter as a *capacity builder*, a person who has spent the bulk of my professional life focused on the "how": How do we support organizations, institutions, networks, and individuals to evolve, nourish, assess, discern, and make positive movement in desirable directions? I write this also as a capacity builder with an *equity lens*, a person from multiple marginalized communities who knows the particularities of building capacity for communities, organizations, and individuals whose supports and resources have been severely limited, often intentionally, structurally, and systematically by governments, policies, unexamined systems and processes, and both conscious and unconscious bias. The confluence of these elements has created a very specific set of conditions that has made it exceedingly difficult for particular communities of color, women, LGBT people, and others to access core supports and resources for healthy evolution and growth. The results of such *structural inequity*—ingrained into U.S. education no less than any other institution (healthcare, workforce development, housing, etc.)—have been the generational decimation of whole peoples, where the sheer will, tenacity, and determination of individuals have led to altered outcomes for the few (the exceptions). But for the many, en masse, the deck is most definitely stacked against marginalized communities, coupled with a collective blindness or invisibility to these conditions by most of society.

I say all this to note that our fates are inextricably bound together. We are a global family and community, and we are one nation; what affects one portion of the population affects us all. Limited high-quality education to cultivate the gifts, skills, and wisdom of specific communities leads to disillusionment, desperation, fear, pain, anguish, and needless suffering. The social consequences of such vast, unfulfilled destinies are poverty, addiction (whether to television, drugs, alcohol, or numbness), apathy, social unrest, unkindness, indifference, and various levels of disease. We cannot be obtuse about the effects or consequences of unsupportive, unloving, "thin" education, on us as individuals or on society as a whole. The consequences for marginalized communities are very specific and devastating. And these devastating consequences are *for everyone*, not just for the specific communities being most negatively impacted.

I also write this chapter as a person who has spent a significant amount of time on *systemic* change, beyond the individual level and, in recent years, even beyond the institutional level to the level of *networks, movements,* and *movement building.* These macro dimensions, which often make our collective plight much easier to see and make sense of, help to bring awareness to the *interconnected* nature of our individual and collective choices and decisions, and their impacts. Without this macro view, which includes historical components, we are limited in our capacity to see the *terrain* within which we function, and to make appropriate shared choices to alter our joint course for the better. More will be said on this later, in the substantive discussion on the "how" of change needed to reach our desired goal and destination, which is to support the continued development of humanity.

I want to give an addition to the above discussion on structural inequity, lest some readers draw unintentional conclusions.[1] I have heard it said and often intimated that communities and individuals who lack basic needs (such as healthy food, stable shelter, loving family, etc.) are in danger and less likely to be able to develop and cultivate their inner qualities than those who have such basic needs. I want to vigorously challenge this prevalent, deficit-focused assumption. Indeed, it has been my experience and observation that this correlation does not, in fact, regularly hold.

These observations are important to note lest we fall into a "pity party" for "those poor, unfortunate people and their lot." (I hope the reader is aware that I use the preceding phrases in a manner to provoke awareness, not unconsciously.) As we all know, there are examples of people—including Gandhi, Fannie Lou Hamer, Nelson Mandela, and perhaps those close to us, our friends, family, neighbors and/or strangers—who do not and have not necessarily had the necessities of life, but are mature and refined *to a far greater degree* than those from whom they experience mistreatment (both individually and systemically, collectively termed *oppression*), and who do, in fact, have material security and their basic needs met. Hence, this belies the conclusion that material conditions, in and of themselves, are prerequisite for refined human cultivation. This is not to say that material needs are unimportant. Holistic healthcare, nourishing food, a safe home and neighborhood, loving community, etc. are valuable, important, and beautiful. And yet, as many of us may know, there are too many blatant instances of individuals and communities who are cruel, unfeeling, insensitive, and fear-filled, despite having all the basic needs one could desire; and the contrary, that is, significant examples of people and communities in dire circumstances up to and including those in devastated or war-torn environments, who have experienced significant trauma, and yet who are loving, open-hearted, kind, generous, and compassionate, using their intelligence and gifts for the collective good while also enjoying their individual happiness, even in the midst of material strife. Hence, there is something much deeper that we must be striving for and looking to, something much more fundamental to mature human existence. We need to create the conditions for all individuals to grow into such mature, kind, and skillful human beings. Hence, we have the focus of this book on higher education's role in supporting such cultivation.

Grounded in these thoughts, I turn now to a fuller discussion of: the "*what*," the "*how*," and the "*who*" in institution and field change in education.

THE "WHAT"/ A VISION FOR EDUCATION: THE "DNA" OR TO WHAT ENDS ARE WE STRIVING?

As noted above, the "*what*" includes visions, values, and qualities desired for the development of knowledgeable, compassionate, reflective, and engaged human beings. Such visions have already been well articulated by many, so I will not spend much time here. I refer the reader to other articles, publications, authors, public speakers, and activists including john a. powell (not capitalized), Grace Lee Boggs, Fannie Lou Hamer, Wendy Farley, angel Kyodo williams (also not capitalized), Laura Rendon, and Vijay Kanagala, the authors in this volume, and many others who have written and spoken at length about where we may go as a society.[2] Importantly, these authors, scholars, spiritual practitioners, activists, and academics are multi-racial and otherwise multi-identitied, also cross-sector in their efforts. While international in their outlooks, they are also very grounded in the highly nuanced and complex specifics of a U.S. context.[3]

The components of the "what"/DNA includes articulation and clarification of the *visions and values* we are collectively striving for. From an equity perspective, these components should also include an explicit and deep focus on the "dynamics of difference"—that is, the ways that race, socioeconomics, gender, sexual orientation, and other demographic dimensions profoundly shape experiences and access to *quality* in higher education (and other societal institutions). A focus on the dynamics of difference reflects the value of cultural particularities and also exposes the systemic bias, racism, and oppression by individuals and institutions. These are not trivial matters, and in certain circles I have found that they are often overlooked or given short or superficial shrift in the proliferation of discussions about changes needed in higher education. Such articulations about the "what" should also be conveyed in ways that are accessible to multiple cultural and demographic communities, and that retain their living, breathing essence, the very heartbeat that makes them inspiring.

Further, such articulations about the "DNA" of this "promised land" we are striving toward will also need to be adjudicated and jointly reflected on, in an ongoing process, by widely diverse communities of practitioners who are to embody them. As we grow and change together over time, and as varying communities have sometimes widely ranging ways of articulating values, hopes, dreams, and aspirations—and ways of implementing them—it will behoove us to create structures where we can be in authentic dialogue and continue to learn, grow, and share with one another as we chart and carve the pathway(s) toward a more desirable, healthy, joyful, collective future.

One such articulation of the "what" is encompassed in the following: I spent the last handful of years working with many in K-12 education to develop multiple versions of a shared articulation of the "promised land" that we are striving for. Participants from universities, foundations, non-profits, unions, community organizers, capacity builders, policy advocates, and others worked together to articulate its dimensions. While many versions of this vision have been developed, tailored to each of the constituents of the participating organizations and groups, below is one articulation:

Education is intended to help every person reach his or her full potential, including robust participation in civic life.[4] Education for these ends should build vibrant communities of knowledgeable, reflective, compassionate, engaged community members who thrive, collectively reflect and make decisions together, and who contribute to the well-being of our diverse communities, educational institutions, and world. Preparing youth and adults to prosper and contribute to our collective well-being requires a broad set of skills and competencies: academic, socio-emotional, cultural, linguistic, and political. Acquiring these broader skills prepares people not only to be successful participants in a thriving, mutually supportive economy, but also to lead meaningful and dignified lives in which our strengths and assets are shared in support of one another and society.

A set of *principles* undergirds this vision. When implemented with depth and shared understanding, they can become a "litmus test" by which we can understand how on-target, limited, or potentially harmful content, practices, policies, capacity building approaches, and funding approaches are for students, educators, and communities, toward this vision. Each of these principles has specific operational implications at every systemic level—from classrooms, departments, colleges/universities, and the field nationally. One articulation of these principles is:

1   Ongoing commitment to *self-reflection*, humility, dialogue, and growth (including inner work around presence and awareness from any number of traditions, systems, or approaches);

2   *Investment* in faculty, staff, and leadership learning and growth;

3   Systematic *attention to race, socioeconomics, power, and diversity* (in all its forms) and their impact on policies, practices, and patterns at classroom, department, institution, and field levels;

4   Communities as essential partners that co-create shared visions for *community revitalization* and well-being;

5   Demonstrated commitment to equitable and adequate *distribution and use of resources* in all areas of access to high-quality learning for diverse students and educators; and

6   Focus on collective vision, strategic change, institutional *capacity building,* and use of a wide range of well-balanced, *meaningful data/metrics* for determining impact and success, in ongoing cycles of improvement (where all in the educational community—students, faculty, trustees, staff, and alumni—are in rich dialogue).

When alignment processes are sufficiently developed *within* single institutions to develop a *shared* sense of such vision and values/principles, they can be extended to intentional visioning, alignment, and *field-building* strategy development *across* institutions—extending among and beyond colleges and universities to essential partners such as philanthropic and grassroots communities, and other key influencers in the field. (These alignment processes will be discussed further in the next section on "*how.*")

Specific dimensions of higher education where the "what" typically finds its home are in: 1) *policy*, which articulates what is important to us, and what we commit to one another to put into practice; 2) content and *curriculum*; 3) how "*success*" is measured; and 4) *research* base providing the grounding and "validity" for goals and work. Hence—while not sufficient unto itself—the work in higher education needed to truly embed such visions has to, at minimum, include deep focus on policy, curriculum, how success is measured (in meaningful, heart, head, and hand ways), and the proliferation of an appropriate, multi-method research base.

This is relevant for the current structure of higher education, and there are undoubtedly ways that are being advanced both within and outside of formal higher education institutions to move toward visions and values such as those articulated above. And both *inside* and *outside* work will continue to be needed, so long as the structures of higher education are as embedded and prolific as they currently are. While "the master's tools" may not "dismantle" and transform "the master's house," inside and outside work will certainly be required for such transformation to be deep and thorough, as well as sustainable.[5] That is, the mental models, worldviews, and methodologies that have led to prioritizing and incentivizing a disconnected, atomized, primarily individualistic way of experiencing and engaging with the world, cannot be dismantled and transformed by those same worldviews and methodologies. They need to extend *outside* of themselves, suspending action and perception solely adjudicated from their natal perspectives, in order to change.

Hence, traditional understandings of what is meant by "policy," "curriculum," "success," and "research" will have to evolve and expand, encompassing the broader articulations, approaches, and means of validation that can be found *outside of* traditional and more familiar means. Thankfully, there is no shortage of such expanded articulations and approaches to be found in the prolific, multi-identitied communities working on social justice and social systems change in education.[6]

MOVING FROM "WHAT" TO "HOW"

Once the "what" is clear enough, we then have to move to an exploration of the "*how*"—that is, the methodologies of the process of change itself. Not that these methodologies can be mechanistic. As many in complexity theory and complex adaptive systems theory have recently learned and discovered — (but which was evident for millennia from many feminine-centered, indigenous, earth-based, connected worldviews and approaches)—some problems are *simple*, some are *complicated*, and some are *complex*.[7] Each of these types of challenges requires different approaches; the more one is on the "complexity" end of things, the more "dance-like" one's approaches and strategies must become. "Dance-like" refers to flexible, intuitive, discerning, reflective, engaged, cooperative, responsive, integrative learning — among other adjectives — *as a mode of being, perceiving, and doing.* Such an approach becomes a matter of course, and one can wrap processes around such a flexible, responsive approach, such as multifaceted, qualitative, and quantitative data mining, forums for collective reflection, deliberation and decision-making, plan development, implementation, and cycles of reflection and continuous improvement.

The trick is to know what space we are in: That is, are we in a simple space? A complicated space? Or a complex space?[8] We are undoubtedly in a complex space in the transformation of higher education toward the dreams and visions that many of us have for it; while some subdimensions of the problem remain only simple (i.e., *How do we improve reflection and planning cycles*), and complicated (i.e., *How do we share transformative approaches to curriculum development across departments, colleges/universities, and regions?*). In a complex space, we are seeking to ask and answer questions such as, *How do we support the development of a deeper, expanded, shared ideology and worldview across institutions and a country, given our history, current priorities, and oftentimes financial and structural incentives that have us working against our own and our collective better interests and deepest desires?* This is the space of movement building; and movement building is a science, as well as an art, that can be learned.[9]

So, at minimum, we must collectively (and systematically) consider:

1   What *structures and conditions* (i.e., policies and practices, hiring and retention, leadership, curriculum, messaging, funding, approaches to partnership, etc.) *keep (maintain)* the current visions and values in place?

2   What structures and conditions would serve to *unravel (dismantle)* the undesirable and limiting approaches?

3   What structures and conditions help to *create (build)* the desirable visions, values and approaches?

These are three different functions, and include conscious and unconscious ideology/worldview, values, beliefs, assumptions, norms, habits, organizational culture, and other areas, as well as articulated policies, processes, procedures, and structures. While the full articulation of these dimensions is beyond the scope of this chapter, suffice it to say that the higher education community—by institution and, ultimately, across institutions in alliance with community for an inside-outside, partnered approach—must deliberate about these issues. These are formidable but worthy endeavors, when well-designed and facilitated over time. I have seen many such an institution do great things with committed, dedicated leadership and community partnerships that ground and authenticate the work and its relevance. Nevertheless, institutional endeavors are necessary but entirely not sufficient.

THE "HOW" PART I: SHORT-TERM COMPONENTS OF CHANGE

The components of change attend to the processes that promote sustainable, deep transformation, including developing and moving a change agenda in a *systematic* as well as a *flowing, dynamic,* and *emergent* manner. While not simple (and not an exhaustive list), in the short-term, several areas can be significantly tackled within and across classrooms, departments, and institutions, including very familiar and perhaps less familiar areas: 1) *curriculum* and instructional methodologies/*pedagogy*; 2) faculty, staff and leadership *preparation and on-going support*; 3) institutional *policy*; and 4) *messaging*, framing, and strategic communications. I'll discuss each in turn below.

Curriculum and Pedagogy: It almost goes without saying that the content and methodologies being used to instruct and support students provides a critical foundation for how expansive, inquisitive, reflective, collaborative, engaged, invested, compassionate—and any number of other descriptors—both students and educators may (or may not) be in the learning endeavor. Individual and group work; project-based, real-world application; community partnerships; multi-modal approaches to assessment that allow varied means to demonstrate learning, growth, and capacity in various areas; etc. These are all key and valued methods for supporting students to develop into the sorts of human beings who can heal and continue to advance this world for our collective well-being.

Faculty, Staff, and Leadership Preparation and Ongoing Support: The preparation, supports, collaboration, and resources that faculty, staff, and leadership receive to continue to deepen their knowledge and capacity of *how to educate, reflect, and support growth and learning,* are critical. There is sometimes a notion in institutions of higher education that faculty are teaching *content*, with secondary, tertiary, or no mention of teaching *human beings and students*. Again, this hearkens back to the need for (and potential absence of) reflection on such questions as: *Toward what exactly are we aiming in our educational endeavors? What do we think the purpose, function, role, or capacity of education is to create a successful, shared, prosperous, thriving society?* These are important questions for anyone in any field to consider; to reflect on why we do what we do; what we think it can create in the world; and how closely its current form is to our aspirations. Certainly one can become despondent if there is no notion of the process of change, or no sense of the agency that is possible in our given role. But, *change agency* is a quality in and of itself that can be developed, as a result of and in the context of formal educational institutions as well as (perhaps even more prolifically) outside of them.

In addition to traditional qualities and competencies related to content knowledge and knowledge of pedagogy, management, planning, and other areas, faculty, staff, and leadership can and must also develop a repertoire of "inner" skills and capacities that support deep reflection, compassion for self and others, centeredness in the midst of sometimes raging storms in home and institutional life, and the profound transformations in worldview, ideology, and practice that are undoubtedly called for when such an undertaking toward the values and visions articulated in this chapter are desired. These qualities or "inner" skills are multiply termed and include: presence, awareness, and self-awareness; patience; capacity to process grief and trauma; ability to recognize our historical programming; noticing when we are triggered and cultivating the capacity to remain present and engaged, *responding* from our innate wisdom (instead of *reacting* to situations); releasing tension; opening our hearts more; engaging with others with more compassion; and healing and loving ourselves.

To cultivate these capacities and qualities requires deep tools and support structures — sometimes sacred; sometimes secular — for not only faculty, but also staff, leadership, and community members who would be in partnership to transform educational systems. There are far too many instances of differing visions and values, misperceptions, stalemates, perceived disrespect, misunderstandings and misinterpretations, turf wars, ego trips, and rigor mortis in terms of ability and willingness to see differently and change in relation to our professions, lives, and modes of being and doing in the world. Higher education is no exception to this; quite the contrary, perhaps it (and some approaches to government) may be key models in lethargy and beleaguered ability to change. (This is not finger-pointing; undoubtedly I, too, have been an exemplar of some of these very qualities!) Nevertheless, we have both the capacity and the abundant resources — from meditation; walks in nature; physical practices like yoga, jogging, or martial arts; gardening; spending time with loved ones; journaling; drawing; painting; singing; dancing; and many, many other practices, approaches, tools, and areas that can be formally and informally trained to support our development as more mature, grounded, flexible, receptive, loving beings.[10]

Policy: The third area in our list also won't be a surprise. Transforming institutional policy toward a vision and set of values and principles like the one articulated in this chapter — in partnership with allied trustees and influencers — serves as a basis for creating an *influence agenda*. Coupled with the fourth area below, these set the stage for longer term, more comprehensive approaches to transformation and change across an institution and a *field*, over time. Meaningful, massive, deep, and fundamental policy change is possible, even in entrenched environments, with the right *leaders, partners, allies, champions*, and discernment of the right *timing*.

(It may go without saying, but I will say it anyway: In all of these areas and in *every single aspect of this entire chapter* without exception, there needs to be a *rigorous, brave,* and *committed* focus on equity, including but going well beyond diversity and inclusion, which are noble and necessary but wholly insufficient goals. Coupled with highly skilled and experienced facilitation, the cultivation of the "inner" skills discussed above supports the pursuit of such an equity focus because such skills aid all of us in remaining fully present in the midst of challenging epiphanies and reflections as we work to build our equity muscle.)[11]

Media, Messaging, Framing, & Strategic Communications: The Power of Narrative & Story: Finally, we come to the more public presentation and formal sharing of our commitments and approaches to transformation in education. The methods used and the degree to which single institutions and joint, cross-institution, and community-wide efforts are developing and proliferating (in deeply partnered ways), messaging that reflects and embodies the desired vision and values, and articulates the ways that institutions and fields as a whole are moving toward that vision — providing inspiration and examples — is the degree to which the broader field and the public can be moved and inspired to embrace the new. Many in the movement-building arena talk about the power of "narrative."[12] The power of "narrative" or "story" helps to shape what we can even dream of or envision, even before we have ever tried to enact it. It is what can wake us up in the morning and drive us to continue to learn, grow, share, and be with one another. It may be (in part) what drives creation.

Narrative has the ability to shape public dialogue about visions and values, and the practices or means to achieving these. Stories showcase exemplars and demonstrate what's doable, what's possible, and the actual or potential impact on students, colleges and universities, communities, and society. We are a nation of storytellers. Let us use this method intentionally to shape something new in this arena.

THE "HOW" PART 2: LONG-TERM ALIGNMENT WORK AND CHANGE MANAGEMENT PROCESS

Finally, after laying the groundwork for change, we move to the more intricate strategies around: 1) finding and cohering the "*choir*," and 2) building *power and influence*, and linking with strategic allies. While these are not separate activities—being more like overlapping circles of activities—I discuss them separately here to give texture to their approaches.

Finding and Cohering the "Choir": The "choir" refers to those who are interested in singing the same song; that is, those who have a similar enough vision, values, and principles for the future that they would like to join voices and amplify their approaches. This often begins with finding a handful (or more) of core, like-minded individuals within and/or across institutions or geographic regions (depending on the sphere of influence one wishes to pursue). Beyond this, ad hoc and/or more formal committees or other group structures can be formed to build and shape the shared agenda. Sometimes, these are called "networks," "alliances," "coalitions," or other such terms to signify ongoing, deep investment and joint relationship-building over time.[13]

As many of you know, the work of such groups includes erecting and evolving structures for ongoing dialogue, sharing, collaboration, learning, joint discernment, power analysis, strategy, planning, evaluation, and course-correction. The community building that comes out of such efforts can be quite nourishing, particularly for those who have felt disenchanted and possibly alone in their perceptions, feelings, and endeavors in their departments, institutions, and/or regions. The joining together of voices and visions to develop and advance a shared agenda is the first step in any change process and provides the blueprint for ongoing work. Though the membership of such groupings can and often does change over time, the core of the effort—the DNA or through-line of clarity, continually upgraded and rearticulated by this group(s) to maintain is freshness and relevance—is the thread that holds the effort together, even as inevitable changes and natural evolutions occur.

Such structures are not always easy to erect, nor to maintain. They require skillful design, facilitation, and ongoing reflection, keeping at center a focus on and embodiment of deep equity, the inner skills spoken about above, and the recognition that things will be inherently "messy." The development and cultivation of a movement is no neat undertaking!

This work paves the way for the development of an *influence agenda* within institutions, and a *field-influence agenda* across institutions. Again, coupled with the qualities curated via inner work, such influence development can be humble, loving, compassionate, joyful, discerning, and continually responsive to the moments arising, embodying the very qualities we seek to be cultivating in our educational endeavors.

Expanding the Circle: Building Power and Linking with Strategic Allies: The next phase in the work is to link more broadly with additional key allies and partners, including aligned board members/trustees, community-based organizations and groups, funders, businesses, local and/or state government representatives, and others. This process begins to expand the choir to engage broader circles or spheres of influences, seeking out and networking in broader coalitions within and across institutions and in the community.

Allies in this work can and likely should include those in: 1) the K-*12 educational* arena, in meaningful partnerships to create a seamless relationship between the educational goals of the early years and those of adult education. Such partnership across bureaucracies is no small undertaking, but such a pipeline effort is essential for any notion of success to be achieved with advancing the vision and values at depth, and as early on in our development as human beings as possible. Such relationships are powerful.

Additional allies can and should include 2) those working in the multiple and deep communities of practice who support cultivation of those *"inner" skills* of reflection, mindfulness, contemplation, presence, openness, flexibility, courage, curiosity, etc. spoken about above. By no means an exhaustive list, organizations that are prevalent in this arena, coupled with a focus on social change, include the Center for Contemplative Mind in Society, stonecircles, Movement Strategy Center, the Presencing Institute, the Social Transformation Project, the Center for Transformative Change, the work of Norma Wong, and many others.[14] Most (but not all) of these organizations also include a deep focus on equity, which we have noted as critical in this article.

Thirdly, 3) connecting strategically with *workforce pipelines* to break the frequent binary/bifurcated rhetoric between skills needed for "productivity" vs. skills needed for promoting a just, ecological society, will also be essential. Aligning with like-minded allies and partners who are seeking similar ends and do not see a trade-off or competition between these multiple ends, is an ideal strategy (coupled with the areas above, particularly messaging), to help shift the perceptions and narrative around what is desired for education, for social change, and for communal well-being.

THE "WHO": CULTIVATING "INNER WORK"

Finally, we arrive at a deeper treatment of our above focus on those inner competencies that are at the heart of education and all of our efforts; the very heart of the qualities that make for a healthy society that supports all of its members to find and unleash the gifts and skills we can all share for our collective well-being and happiness. I do not mean to sound Pollyanna-ish; this is not to say there is no strife. It is to say that the ways we *experience* strife (and our *perception* of it) can profoundly change, to be one of resilience, transformative potential and capacity, and caring for others as well as ourselves, in the midst of and even as we learn from challenge. And, further, to the degree we are able, we can seek to transform the structures and conditions that produce needless suffering. We can do this.

From contemplative approaches such as compassion practices, meditation, mindfulness, and body-based disciplines, to centering, connecting with nature, restorative justice, journaling, art, circle conversations, and other areas, these systems and dimensions focus on cultivating who and how we need to be *within ourselves* and *with each other* in order to successfully advance the visions, values, and dynamic change processes discussed throughout this chapter. These "inner" dimensions could be thought of as "contemplative" skills as well as "leadership" skills, conceived broadly. The qualities support us to stay our true course, with clarity and an open-heart, even in overtly or covertly hostile departmental, institutional, or societal environments. This is the notion of *love-based strategy* in the midst of challenge.

Thankfully, there is no shortage of such resources in the world, for every person, of every persuasion and bent, from every walk of life; sacred and secular tools, resources, communities, books, trainings, practices, etc.; for all of our proclivities, no matter where we might find ourselves, and what capacities we may be seeking, currently have, or think we do not or could not possibly ever build! For all of our various interests, strengths, needs, and starting places, there are indigenous practices and traditions worldwide; sacred traditions that are more prevalent and visible in the world; secularized approaches to healing such as somatic disciplines; mindfulness-based approaches; social and emotional learning (SEL) for youth and adults; and restorative justice.

We can utilize systems of learning that are thousands of years old, or the more recent proliferations of teachings and resources from around the world, to help us be our very best selves as we seek to help shape this world further into the most beautiful, vibrant one that is possible, always changing, growing, and re-birthing itself in health.

CONCLUSION AND MAINTAINING A
RIGOROUS FOCUS ON EQUITY

So, we return here to our opening question: *How do we create the conditions for our collective awakening, for unraveling our knots and healing?* This answer was shared in terms of structures, institutions, movements, supports, training, tools, relationships, and inner skills for well-being and cultivating a healthy, global family.

The compilers of this volume write in their introduction, "We need a kind of human development which has not yet occurred on this planet—at least not in sufficient scale to make a real difference." Indeed, this is so. According to this article, such a transformation requires a strong *systems lens*, a rigorous *equity and social justice lens*, and deep *inner work*. Without any one of these, we will fail in our efforts.

Please note: I am writing this section in a very strident way, in the hopes that we can actually become intimates—i.e., those who truly want similar enough things from reality and for our collective life in this world that we are willing to be vulnerable with each other to help create it. If this is the case, then we really do have to be friends, intimates; those who tell each other the hard things, and no longer just smile and nod, and go along our merry ways without ever really having communicated. Let us take off the veil for all of our sakes—for the sake of our collective well-being. Much inner work and much learning about the nature of structural inequity will have to be done in order for this listening and dialogue to be skillful. Without these two skill sets, such pseudo-dialogue is typically fraught with unprocessed tension, pain, guilt, misunderstandings, and accusations. I hope what I write here can be heard, because what follows desperately needs to be said and heard. Without it, we will not really be communicating, and we will fail in our endeavors to heal this world. Many of us do not like to repeatedly have to say these things, after all these years. Let us find a way forward, for all our sakes, and do so with love.

In this essay, I distinguish an *equity and social justice approach* from more *general humanistic* approaches, which tend to *universalize*, and can often erase or lose sight of particularity; the particular and specific conditions of people and communities who are marginalized, and the difference this makes in perspective, vision, understanding, communication styles, priorities, trust, and life experiences, as well as the too-often devastating social, economic, cultural, communal, and environmental conditions such communities can exist within and which inform how we may partner and participate in transformative efforts. In any effort to transform the conditions of education, it behooves us to ensure that we do not have conversations or write about "the promised land" of liberal education and a civil society with relatively monolithic demographic groups talking to, for, with, by, and about one another (unless we are creating intentional, temporary caucuses or affinity groups, which are necessary at times, especially when we are in a mode of healing and/or trying to elevate denigrated and invisible perspectives).

There is no excuse anymore for not engaging intimately and deeply with those who are different from us, and with those who are frequently overlooked, minimized, tokenized, and/or dealt dangerous blows by mainstream, dominant cultures. Higher education is no exception to this. The only excuse for such continued lack of connection and connectivity might be if one *truly does not want to engage, but would rather continue paying lip service to our pluralistic society vs. actually living intimately with others in it.* (These are strong words and sentiments, and in solidarity and sisterhood/brotherhood in our shared fate, my hope is that the reader can hear and see of what I am speaking, if the circumstance applies, and will stay present for it and not check out, using those inner skills spoken about before.)

One does not need to go to another country to deeply encounter the "other," and if that is what we are doing — if we are not engaging deeply with the "other" in our own backyards (in tandem with a global perspective), we are cowering from our duty and responsibility as a human family. "Relationality" as a key concept of this volume requires this kind of intimacy and authentic engagement *at home* and not just abroad. As an example, I was invited (at the last minute) to participate in an education advisory group of a reputable organization. After some hours at the gathering, I asked if anyone noticed that, of the 4 or so people of color in the group (out of about 40 people), I was the only person of color from the United States. No one had noticed: neither the planners nor the invitees. Given the abhorrent conditions of much of public education in the U.S., and the specific egregious conditions that so many students of color (and other marginalized groups) are experiencing, that anyone could plan a meeting 1) in the United States, 2) about education, 3) with dozens of people, and 4) not invite any people of color from the United States, is a gross and extreme oversight that *happens all too often*, and requires some deep reflection and action on the part of those who continue doing it, in order to correct the matter. The deep blockages that this indicates warrant extreme and urgent attention. *What is going on here, and why does it continue in the face of liberal lip service that would belie its existence?* It helps no one to remain silent.

Ways of finding, reaching out to, connecting, networking, and partnering deeply with all kinds of people are abundant and in no short supply for most any of us reading this chapter. So, the choice to not reach out seems to be (on some level, conscious or unconsciously) deliberate — either based in fear and discomfort/unease or a belief that it's simply not that important. We will all have to leave our comfort zones and safety in order to do and be different, for all of our sakes, and for the *full* human family — local as well as global — to be truly, deeply, and authentically included in this articulation, vision, deliberation, and enacting from the outset and not as an afterthought, or at the end, or not at all. We cannot, in good conscience, continue as we have been and wonder why things don't change. I am taking to task those to whom this may apply, and hoping we will all listen.

To my thinking and experience, Whiteheadian philosophy is very indigenous, so much so that I cannot in good conscience refer to intrinsically valuable, interrelated, agency-oriented, interdependent being-ness as something that was "discovered" or "invented" by yet another straight, white man. Pardon me. I just cannot do it. Indigenous traditions that I have practiced, am initiated in, was born and raised in, and am familiar with, have this as a basic, simple, (forgive me) child-like understanding of how the world is — so much so that it almost doesn't warrant mentioning, as in, "Yeah? So? What of it? Did you believe things were some other way? Oh, that's unfortunate or a misperception of reality; a distorted way of viewing the world, that perhaps can be healed." It is not some fantastical, miraculous discovery. It is actually quite ordinary and for many people, common sense.

This reminds me of a very appropriate comment made by the female spiritual elder in the "fictional" film *Avatar* when she says to the protagonist, a straight, white, male, militaristic character (not that there's anything wrong with these characteristics; they just happen to be the predominant demographics that have shaped much of the social, political, and economic conditions of the world for a good long while now): "We'll see if your insanity can be cured." Precisely. This is how most of us — female, of color (most of the planet), indigenous-minded people — feel every day: We hope the mainstream culture's insanity can be cured, and we are vigilant to ensure that we and others hopefully do not drink the Koolaid and get sick ourselves; or that we can purge the sickness or transform the poison, with the help of loved ones, healing ceremonies, meditation, spending time in nature, etc., if we have, in fact, partaken of it. We are in this together, all of us. It is high time that we all behave like it.

It is typically the case that those in non-dominant cultures — in order to move fluidly and become "successful" in society — have to become literate in dominant cultures; but the reverse is not true. That is, those in dominant cultures do not, at all, have to become literate in non-dominant cultures *even if those non-dominant cultures are in the majority in terms of demographic numbers.* Hence, dominant culture community members can remain ignorant of the wisdom present in the non-dominant communities all around them, and not have to do anything about it. They can keep reinventing the wheel on new "wisdom" or keep "discovering" wisdom and knowledge that has been commonplace in non-dominant cultures for centuries or millennia, but has been subjugated, ignored, denigrated, maligned, or co-opted. This is the case now.

It is imperative that the many communities of practice who are now inventing/creating "alternative" visions for the future of education and communities, in isolation, find and join with one another to innovate, connect, and heal. We will no longer get very far alone. We need one another to survive and to thrive. There is so much work already happening. It behooves communities — particularly those well-funded, visible, influenced and informed by dominant communities — to connect with those — often grassroots, multi-identitied — communities of color, who are prolific in their/our movement-building work.

Finally, this chapter was not intended to be an explication of equity. The reader is referred to the prolific resources, articles, books, organizations, people, and trainings in the field on this topic, some of which are included in the resources cited in this chapter.[15] It is important to note that "equity" is not equivalent to "diversity" or "inclusion"; equating equity with diversity or inclusion would be an extreme narrowing. The latter two are *dimensions* of equity, but equity is dramatically broader and deeper than these, and includes the systems and the inner components, (as discussed in this chapter).

Equity without systems change tends to focus on diversity, inclusion, individual and interpersonal "awareness," which are critically important and necessary, but are not sufficient for transforming institutional or structural inequity. Further, equity without inner work often focuses on quantitative metrics and outcomes and can lose the heart and soul of our lives here together, the very essence of compassion, as both sentiment *and* action. Compassion (a core tenet of deep equity), is based in deep relationships and knowing—knowing individuals, as well as viscerally, experientially, and intimately knowing the lived, historical, and current realities of marginalized and dominant communities. Such compassion is beyond book knowledge—articles, theories, assumptions, and stereotypes. Such compassion requires us to leave our comfort zones and (when invited) to respectfully and deeply participate in the communities and customs of those profoundly different from us, both in our backyards and in the global community. Such compassion also requires us to grow, to deepen our comprehension, and to develop the humility to notice what we in fact do not know, and to expand our capacity for change and for loving. This is the work of a lifetime, that, in my professional and personal experience, too few white U.S. residents seem to be undertaking out of perhaps fear, arrogance, guilt, self-loathing, or denial. We can release our attachment to these debilitating states, so that we may actually experience the learning, growth, and compassion that are necessary as well as *inherent* in our capacity to heal ourselves, one another, and this world.

The introduction to this volume notes that, "We need a network of these approaches so we can wake each other up, share resources, and collaborate on the global problems we face." Yes, we do. And may they be deeply representative of both this country, as well as our global family, working in ongoing, authentic collaboration, so that we can truly build our future together, in love.

NOTES

1   See for instance "Systems Thinking and Race: Workshop Summary," *Racial Equity Tools,* published June 2011, http://www.racialequitytools. org/resourcefiles/Powell_Systems_Thinking_Structural_Race_Overview. pdf; Racial Equity Tools, http://www.racialequitytools.org/home.

2   See john powell, *Racing to Justice: Transforming Our Conceptions of Self and Other to Build an Inclusive Society* (Bloomington: Indiana University Press, 2015); Grace Lee Boggs, www.graceleeboggs.com; Wendy Farley, *The Wounding and Healing of Desire: Weaving Heaven and Earth (*Westminster: John Knox Press, 2005); *angel Kyodo williams,* angel Kyodo Williams, www.angelkyodowilliams.com; and Laura Rendón and Vijay Kanagala, "Sentipensante Pedagogy and Contemplative Practice," webinar

posted February 23, 2012, www.contemplativemind.org/archives/214

3   This is an important note since oftentimes efforts to "diversify" or create multi-racial, multi-identitied approaches rely on international students or colleagues, while overlooking the profound impact of difference in this country (in this case, the u.s.). We have a very prevalent legacy of hiding from or downplaying the intricacies and richness of our multiracial-ness, in the hope that we have somehow miraculously "gotten beyond" them, and in an effort to promote a "color-blind" society. And yet, we continue to suffer from this deliberate blindness that impairs our ability to truly see one another in our fullness and to create the depth of change we truly need.

4   Adapted from Sheryl Petty, "Supporting Sustainable Improvement in School Systems: Capacity Building for Equity and Excellence" in *Opening the Doors to Opportunity for All: Setting a Research Agenda for the Future: Select Series Essays from the AIR Research Roundtable on Equity and Opportunity in Education,* 64–74 (Washington, D.C: The Equity Project, American Institutes for Research, January 2015), http://www.air.org/sites/default/files/OpeningTheDoors-EquityProject-Jan2015.pdf

5   From Audre Lorde, "The Master's Tools Will Never Dismantle the Master's House," originally published in 1984, in *Sister Outsider: Essays and Speeches* (Berkeley: Crossing Press, 2007), 110-114, www.collectiveliberation.org/wp-content/uploads/2013/01/Lorde_The_Masters_Tools.pdf

6   Including those previously cited, as well as Tucson, Arizona's (former) Mexican American Studies Department; Gloria Ladson-Billings' work; my own essay, *The New Frontier: An Integrated Framework for Equity & Transformative Improvement in Education,* California Tomorrow, October 2010, www.californiatomorrow.org/media/The-New-Frontier.pdf; Linda Darling-Hammond's work; and many, many others.

7   See "Cynefin Framework," *Wikipedia,* https://en.m.wikipedia.org/wiki/Cynefin_Framework

8   Or a *chaotic* one?—Which is the fourth category, and perhaps less relevant for our discussion here. See for example, "Complexity Theory 101 for Social Justice Leaders," *Management Assistance Group,* published October 2015, www.managementassistance.org/blog/complexity-theory-101-for-social-justice-leaders.

9   See for example *Movement Strategy Center,* www.movementstrategy.org.

10   See for example the "Tree of Contemplative Practices," from the *Center for Contemplative Mind in Society,* www.contemplativemind.org/practices/tree.

11   Field resources include: www.racialequitytools.org; *The D5 Coalition,*

www.d5coalition.org; the Annie E. Casey Foundation's tools, www.aecf.org/resources/race-equity-and-inclusion-action-guide; and many others.

12   See for example, the *Center for Story-Based Strategy*, www.storybasedstrategy.org.

13   See: "Unstill Waters: The Fluid Role of Networks in Social Movements," *Management Assistance Group*, www.managementassistance.org/unstill-waters; and "Nuts and Bolts of Building an Alliance," *Movement Strategy Center*, www.movementbuilding.movementstrategy.org/resources.

14   Norma Wong, "Stance, Energy, Awareness, and Rhythm," *Transform*, published September 20, 2010. www.transform.transformativechange.org/2010/09/normawong/.

15   In addition to these notes, for those new to white privilege and white awareness, there are many resources in these areas, including *White Awake: Developing Race Awareness for the Benefit of All*, www.whiteawake.org (inner work/contemplative practice and white awareness); *Racial Equity Tools*, www.racialequitytools.org; and *World Trust: Social Impact through Film and Dialogue*, www.world-trust.org (films), among others.

5. THE OTHER CONVERSATION

DIALOGUE, MEDITATION, AND SERVICE

Stephen Rowe

ABSTRACT: *The dominant conversation in higher education today is about employments, metrics, markets, and whether a liberal education—or even a general education—is a worthwhile investment. But there is second, less noisy conversation going on as well, one which is concerned with capacities, community and civic engagement, mindfulness, inclusiveness—a constellation of concerns which is quite different from that of the first conversation. The thesis of this essay is that this second conversation can be clarified and focused in terms of three capacities which are also in some respects developmental stages: dialogue, meditation, and service. Further, it is argued that through the influence of these capacities we may be seeing the quiet emergence of a distinctly and positively postmodern form of liberal or civilizing education.*

UNDER ALL THE CHATTER ABOUT EMPLOYABILITY, student debt, market-oriented reform, and whether we really need anything like liberal education, there is another conversation going on in American higher education today. It arises from an expanded vision of adulthood and well-being, focused on capacities and practices through which that new adult state of being and acting in the world can be cultivated, including the (re)discovery of contemplative ways of knowing.

93

This second conversation generates much less noise than the first, and, especially because of its developmental nature, it is more difficult to understand.[1] It could well turn out, however, to be the more powerful and hence more consequential of the two. It could turn out that the second conversation is the medium through which the ancient and ineffable ideal of liberal education is coming to fresh embodiment in our time.

I write in the service of that second conversation and, more specifically, in an effort to help clear up the frequently confusing cluster of terms that appear, often together and sometimes interchangeably, in its discourse: including high impact learning, community-based learning, mindfulness, critical thinking, service learning, diversity, attentiveness, contemplation, transformation, reflection, meditation, otherness, reflexivity, inclusivity, social action, integration, multiculturalism, and dialogue. Part of the problem is that most of these terms, though not newly coined, are quite new to the conversation about higher education, while at the same time it could be argued that at least some of them reach down to the deep roots of the traditional Western vision of full human development (perhaps non-Western as well). So these terms share not only energetic association with importance and possibility, but also considerable confusion as to what they really mean and how they are related.

As a result, many of us who participate in the second conversation stumble along in an atmosphere of both enthusiastic acknowledgment and danger that the discussion can be degraded to high-sounding language which is either empty, cliché, or — worse yet — deflected into the service of purposes that are far from those of their ancient origin. This is the condition I want to address, by proposing a simple distinction between three interdependent developmental practices through which these terms can be understood and advanced, within the rich but frequently muddled second discourse of education in our time. I propose Dialogue, Meditation, and Service as primary practices corresponding to the developmental levels through which a new paradigm of education and adulthood is emerging.

Confusion arises in large part because all of these terms are reflective of the sensibilities and intuitions of a genuinely new era, glimmers

of a way of knowing, relating, and learning that are deeper than can be
envisioned through the modern dichotomous thinking of either idealism
or empiricism, value or fact, objectivity or subjectivity; deeper than the
bundle of unexamined assumptions which constitutes the flooring of
the contemporary research and employment-oriented university[2]; and
beyond the indiscriminate critique, deconstruction, and reductionism
of "postmodernism."[3] Glimmers of a new way arise from the sense that
there is something more than either absolute/ideological Truth or rela-
tivistic personal preference, something all people can be in touch with
and live well by, all the while maintaining — and enhancing — their
distinctiveness. It is precisely the *absence* of sensibilities and intuitions
of this sort — of something deeper and different from what the prevailing modern mindset and its institutionalization in our educational systems could apprehend — that led the great social ethicist, James Luther
Adams, to conclude that absence of "disciplines of the inner life" was
a primary reason for the failure of 1960's activism.[4] It could be that the
second conversation reflects no more than academia's passing interest in
new terminology and in new applications of older terminology — buzz-
words that academia is all too quick to embrace without critical examination and then abandon for the next fad. But it could also be that now,
nearly fifty years after Adam's remark, we are addressing this root issue
through the emergence of the three practices I have identified, and that
they together — in the midst of and through the tumult that surrounds
them — are moving us into a distinctly post-postmodern world, a world
where cultivation of "the inner life" becomes virtually indistinguishable
from a new relationship with the world.

At the center of this emergence, the rediscovery of the contemplative
way of knowing is perhaps the most radical — and necessary — of our
era. It indicates a way of knowing quite distinct from the rationalism
and empiricism which had dominated Western culture throughout
the traditional period, knowing either top down from abstract first
principles, or bottom up from the collected data of experience. Either
way, within this paradigm, knowing is of an objective order of reality
external to the "inner lives" of persons as anything other than thinking
machines. The contemplative, by contrast, represents a way of knowing

that comes from within, from the inside *through* rather than from the outside *to*. It requires renunciation of objectification and intellectualization as prerequisites of knowing, and accomplishes this through cultivation of the inner silence, attentiveness, or the "not knowing" of which Socrates spoke (before his wisdom was eclipsed by the rationalism of Plato, or, rather, by what became the orthodox *reading* of Plato.)[5] It also requires a kind of relationship with the world, other, and self that is beyond dichotomy between self-sacrifice and competitiveness.

In our time, the contemplative is being rediscovered and its efficacy certified not only by the testimony of mystics, but *also* by the contemporary catholicity of science.[6] This has enormous implication for both personal and communal well-being. It holds the promise of liberation from the colonization of human consciousness by the Cartesian world view, which dominated Western — and thereby global — culture since the 17th century. This is a longer story than we want to get into here, but perhaps for now it will suffice to say we are talking about liberation from that package of distinctly modern values that has rather recently been found to be so problematic and/or unsustainable in their addictive hold on the human race: isolated individualism, competitiveness creeping into every dimension of life, materialism, and an ever more "value free" and mechanistic system of both technology, economy — and education.

For higher education, the great rediscovery revolves around the dynamics of cultivating the inner life in a way that does not involve retreat from political life, but its enhancement. The possibility opens up that education can be something much more than acquisition of knowledge and/or technical skill — or, alternatively, withdrawing from the world into isolated self.[7] Now it becomes possible to think in terms of activation of capacities comprising a maturity or form of adulthood that, though not entirely new to the cultural and religious history of the human race, now becomes a democratized possibility for all people — and perhaps, as well, a necessity for our survival. We are talking about an adulthood in which we have greater self-transcendence through calm awareness of our responses in life, that which triggers our defenses and aggressiveness, and greater capacity to live beyond those impulses in a centered presence.

On the contemporary landscape of higher education, in the spaces between the poles of modern dichotomous (or Cartesian) thinking, we see the three practices of both the inner life and deeper relationship being reawakened and engaged—again, dialogue, meditation, and service. The rather long list of terms cited early in this essay, then, can be organized and understood in terms of these three practices or capacities, which are also associated with developmental stages, in a world where the nautilus shell is a more adequate image than the upward sloping straight line.

These capacities and practices, understood specifically in relation to adult development as the ultimate aim of education (and hence also in some respects as "levels"), are richly described by Robert Keegan in terms of those who are longing for "the fifth order of consciousness" which is becoming possible, in part (and somewhat ironically) due to the simple extension of life expectancy afforded by modernity: he speaks of longing "for the recognition of our multiple selves, for the capacity to see conflict as a signal of our [over-identification] with a single system, for the sense of our relationships and connections as prior to and constitutive of the individual self, and for an identification with the transformative process of our being rather than the formative products of our becoming."[8]

The first is *Dialogue*. Moving beyond the dichotomy of rote learning and propositional logic versus assertions of unexamined, unrefined personal preference (the latter being the typical liability of what used to be called progressive, alternative, or experimental education), this level entails opening up the capacity for understanding and "reflection" on a variety of positions—including one's own—on any given issue, as well as the ability to be responsive to emergent truth as an essential quality of full and healthy relationships, democracy, and mature thinking. It indicates the ability to thrive in a pluralistic environment where encounter with the "other" is welcomed as opportunity rather than suffered as threat, where "diversity," "inclusiveness," and "multiculturalism" are not mere concessions to the fragile interdependence of the 21st century, but positive values to be nurtured and celebrated. Is this not precisely what Socrates had in mind when he advocated "the examined life," the

life of examining both self and others on the most important questions
in life — "as the very best thing" a person could do?[9] The life he advocated is associated with contemporary uses of "reflexivity" and "critical
thinking," as something much greater than the ability to recognize
bad logic and/or psychological manipulation: something more like the
exercise of a kind of discernment indicated by such traditional terms as
phronesis (Greek for "practical judgment") or *upaya* (Sanskrit for "skillful
means"). However, echoing the theme of aspiration by Keegan above,
Daniel Yankelovich and others note that the expanded capacity for
dialogue and a new adulthood, one which is more alert, more deeply
responsive, and less ego-driven by aggressive/defensive impulses, is not
one that most Americans are capable of at this time, though it is one
that is being pushed by many efforts at educational reform.[10]

The second is *Meditation.* Moving beyond the dichotomy between
theoretical and applied (or "productive") knowledge, here we are talking
about engagement of a practice that allows us to have access to the
deeper sources of knowing and action, and to cultivate a way of being
we have come to associate with "mindfulness," or the full presence of
"attentiveness." The world and its varied traditions contain many such
contemplative practices, with remarkable similarities and differences.
Essentially, they involve the paradox of clearing and calming one's mind
and thinking nothing, with the aid of a very specific object of mental
focus (or "mantra," such as one's breath). The resulting state of calm
focus then leads to the Socratic "not knowing" which becomes an opening to a more profound level of awareness (more like the *source* of knowing than the objects of knowledge which flow from that source). These
practices are often simple, though never easy. And, while there can be
many arguments about the true nature of this practice, no such practice
can be fruitful apart from the actual experience of entering into it and
then introducing refinements as they are discovered along the path of
actual engagement. On that path — and from the perspective of others
who witness the transformation of those who are walking it — meditation is extremely persuasive in terms of stress reduction, emotional
stability, concentration, compassion, and effective relationships at all
levels. There develops a very significant change in the overall quality

of presence following directly from its engagement. The persuasiveness of meditation is aided by the recent findings of neuroscience, as well as continuing reappropriations of those mystical traditions that had been dismissed in the tempest of modernity.[11]

Third is *Service.* Moving beyond the dichotomy between self-interest and self-sacrifice, genuine "service learning" — sometimes called community-based learning, social action, or even global learning — extends regard for the other, which is necessary for dialogue, to a more active will to engage with the life of that other and the senses in which it is shared with our own, in a broader ecology that is synonymous with affirmation and covenant with life itself as a normative principle.[12]

It is centered on a point that is well understood by the great traditions: that the end of meditation is to stop "meditating" as an extraordinary activity separated and protected from the messiness of ordinary life. In other words, the ideal end of meditation is that it becomes our ordinary way of being. The end is to be meditating all the time, to "return" to caring or compassionate relationships with both other and self. Martin Luther King was eloquent on this utterly crucial point, one that had been excluded from the modern mindset: "From time immemorial men [sic] have lived by the principle that 'self-preservation is the first law of life.' But this is a false assumption. I would say that other-preservation is the first law of life. It is the first law of life precisely because we cannot preserve self without being concerned about preserving other selves. The universe is so structured that things go awry if men [*sic*] are not diligent in their cultivation of the other-regarding dimension."[13] It is this same quality of a life-giving relationship that is indicated by the classical Western love of the world (*amour mundi*), or the Confucian "human-hearted persons establish others if they want to establish themselves."[14] Active caring and creative citizenship become both marks of true enlightenment and sophisticated forms of practice. Service comes to be associated with the wholeness of the person, and hence the "integrative" and "transformational" dimensions of education, through which everything we have studied and become is brought to the essential moment of our authentic being in the world and its ongoing refinement.

As is clear in the great traditions, genuine meditative practices issue not only in a calm and alert state of mindfulness, but also in an actively compassionate presence in the world. Indeed, the great traditions provide perhaps the best explanation for the paradoxical relationship between mysticism and social action, engagement, or civic involvement—to use the language of contemporary higher education. To cite an old Zen saying: Easy to meditate in the monastery, more difficult in the home, most difficult in the world. In other words, the fullness of meditation or enlightenment is not detached purity but the developed capacity to sustain that way of being in the midst of effective presence in ordinary life, exemplified by figures such as Gandhi, Mother Teresa, Martin Luther King, Thich Nhat Hanh, and Sheri Liao. More so, enlightenment is found not only in the ordinary life of the monk doing mundane chores such as cleaning the toilet, but also in the effort to liberate others from suffering in its many forms. In Mahayana Buddhism, for example, the high religious figure, the Bodhisattva, is not the one who drifts off in mystical detachment, but rather the one who *returns* to help others, the one whose embodiment is that of *karuna* (compassion) rather than *karma* (the accumulated consequence of past action driven by fear, ignorance, desire). Note the parallel, for example, with Christianity and its "commandment" (a confusing term, because this seems also to be our best advice as to how to live well) that we "love thy neighbor as thy self." The paradox of "service learning" and its prominence in higher education today is that, in teaching students the value of serving others, ultimately we help students discover where life is rich and vital, the dynamics of "thriving" or "flourishing" (two other key words in our time), which enhance their own lives. When we approach service with awareness of its full significance, we help students (and ourselves) discover and embody the identity between service and dialogue, as well as between meditation and service—in a way of being that is constituted by a complex and endlessly unique pulsing of nonetheless identifiable interdependent aspects.

All this—these three practices and capacities—are simple enough to understand intellectually (and even enjoyable to think about), though by no means easy to grapple with existentially because of the *developmental* aspect, which means that we are stretched beyond our ordinary and inherited ways of thinking, speaking, and acting. For this same reason, this way of being is also vulnerable, as reflected in Alfred North Whitehead's statement that "[g]reat ideas enter history with disgusting alliances, but the greatness remains, nerving the race in its slow ascent." [15] Contemporary programs in American higher education that link meditation and mindfulness to service learning, civic engagement, and social activism, often by way of vague "interdisciplinarity," are therefore especially vulnerable to confusion, incomplete understanding, cliché, and those "disgusting alliances" to which Whitehead refers. Cultivation of the critical linkage is dependent on teacher selection and training that was rare in the past (or unacknowledged, or even at odds with the process of acquiring a Ph.D., let alone becoming an administrator/manager), in the same way that authentic fostering of the value of inclusion, diversity, and otherness require sensibilities and awareness that were also rare among faculty, and certainly no more deliverable in a quick faculty training program—or the artificial order of a "strategic plan"—than they are reducible to managerial protocol. Finding the faculty and support staff (and students) we need in order to embody the new vision of culture and education that is struggling to emerge in our time is probably our most profound challenge. How, in the environment of contemporary higher education, can we identify and then support those who are capable in the development they need, let alone then place them in positions where they can do real good?

Fortunately, there have emerged educational leaders such as the feminist and philosopher of education, Elizabeth Minnich, who are able to "make a case for an overlap of thoughtfulness and mindfulness as arts and ways of being for which we can purposefully educate, not as in some traditions to win release from the world but, entirely on the contrary, to accept our responsibilities as conscious beings affected by and affecting the worlds around us with every breath, action, and word." [16] The work of Parker Palmer and his Center for Courage and Renewal <www.couragerenewal.org> should be especially noted in this regard as well. [17]

On this same question as to whom we can look to for resources and support, there are two other sources I would especially point to as reliable in terms of insight and practice. The first is The Association for Contemplative Mind in Higher Education <www.acmhe.org>. Arising from the emergence of the new interdisciplinary field of cognitive science and a rapidly emerging complementarity between modern scientific rationality and the practical wisdom of the contemplative traditions, the mission of ACHE is "to educate active citizens who will support a more just and compassionate society." This is accomplished through "recovery and development of the contemplative dimension of teaching, learning and knowing," leading to "an ethics of genuine compassion."[18]

The second agency that exemplifies the crucial healthy relationship between meditation and social action is the YESplus Program and its "Art of Living" course <www.YESplus.org>. Arising out of the Hindu tradition and drawing on the resources of contemporary cognitive science, YES stands for "Yoga, Empowerment, and Service." It is distinctly responsive to the linkage between meditation and service—working to a point of merging the two activities into a fully transformed and integrated way of being. Examples of how YESplus has been joined with local programs and initiatives can be seen at Cornell, Stanford, and Brown.

So with this short essay I am proposing simple clarification of some of the more sensitive terminology of our time, and to at least hint at their unification in an emerging, post-postmodern worldview and vision of the educated and fully formed adult. And, as an essential quality of that worldview, I am seeking to illuminate a developmental pathway that some of our more exemplary students travel in the direction of becoming the sort of adults we so urgently need.

However, clarification must be followed immediately by a caution, especially when developmental movement is involved: As we practice the teaching art through which we guide students, we must be careful not to let "levels" and "stages" fall into yet another simple linearity, a risk that runs high in an era that is also characterized by the urge to quantify and standardize. Against these late, more or less desperate assertions of the modern, mechanistic worldview, we need to insist, with all the creativity and persuasiveness we can muster, that the practice of cultivating the new adulthood is *an art*. It is an art that can benefit greatly from science and technique in many forms, especially today through the discoveries of neuroscience. But, insofar as it is humans and not machines we are cultivating, art must be the embracing and integrating quality of education. In what might be the most profound challenge to the technological era, we can only reclaim and develop our humanity through the inherently unpredictable dynamics of human relationship. And yet we have the advantage today of ever greater sophistication as to what this means.

NOTES

1   Stephen Rowe, "The Adulthood We Need: Education and Developmental Challenge in the U.S. and China," in *Reflect, Connect, Engage: Liberal Education at GVSU,* Judy Whipps, ed. (Acton: Xanedu Press, 2013); "Liberal Education as Adulthood: A View from U.S.-China Dialogue," *Philosophical Analysis* (哲学分析) 23, no. 1 (2014): 145–51; In English, *Journal of General Education* 64, no. 1 (2015): 65–73).

2   John Cobb, "The Anti-Intellectualism of the American University," *Soundings* 98, no. 38 (2015): 218–32.

3   Rowe, *Overcoming America/America Overcoming* (Lanham: Lexington Books, 2012).

4   James Luther Adams, "The Changing Reputation of Human Nature," in *Voluntary Associations: Socio-cultural Analysis and Theological Interpretation,* ed. J. Ronald Engel (Chicago: Exposition Press), 31.

5   Jacob Needleman, *The Heart of Philosophy* (New York: Alfred A. Knopf, 1982); Alison Jagger, "Love and Emotion in Feminist Epistemology," *Inquiry* 32, 2 (1989): 151–76; Pierre Hadot, *Philosophy as a Way of Life: Spiritual Exercises from Socrates to Foucault* (Malden: Blackwell Publishing, 1995).

6   Francisco J. Varela, Evan Thompson, and Eleanor Rosch, *The Embodied Mind: Cognitive Science and Human Experience* (Cambridge: MIT Press, 1993).

7   Arthur Zajonc, "Contemplative Pedagogy: A Quiet Revolution in Higher Education," *New Dimensions for Teaching and Learning* 134 (Summer 2013): 83–94; Parker Palmer, Arthur Zajonc, and Megan Scribner, *The Heart of Higher Education: A Call to Renewal* (San Francisco: Jossey Bass, 2010).

8   Robert Keegan, *In Over Our Heads: The Mental Demands of Modern Life.* Cambridge: Harvard University Press, 1994), 351.

9   Plato, "Apology" in *The Collected Dialogues of Plato,* ed. Edith Hamilton and Huntington Cairns (New York: Parthenon Books, 1985), 38a, 23.

10   Daniel Yankelovich, *The Magic of Dialogue: Transforming Conflict into Cooperation* (New York: Simon & Schuster, 1999), 17.

11   Daniel P. Barbezat and Mirabai Bush, *Contemplative Practices in Higher Education* (San Francisco: Jossey Bass, 2014).

12   J. Ronald Engel, "What Covenant Sustains Us?" in *Existence with Ecological Integrity: Science, Economics, and Law,* Laura Westra, Klaus Bosselmann, and Richard Westra, eds. (London: Earthscan, 2008), 277–92.

13   Martin Luther King, Jr. *Where Do We Go From Here: Chaos or Community?* (Boston: Beacon Press, 1967), 180.

14   Confucius, *The Analects of Confucius.* Roger T. Ames and Henry Rosemont, Jr., trans. (New York: Ballentine, 1998), 110.

15   Alfred North Whitehead, *Adventures of Ideas* (Cambridge: Cambridge University Press, 1933), 19.

16   Elizabeth Minnich, "The Evil of Banality: Arendt Revisited," *Arts and Humanities in Higher Education,* 13, 1-2 (2014): 162.

17   Parker Palmer, *The Courage to Teach* (Hoboken: John Wiley and Sons, Inc, 1998); Palmer, Zajonc, et al., *The Heart of Higher Education: A Call to Renewal.*

18   "Mission" and "Vision" statements, *The Association for Contemplative Mind in Higher Education,* accessed February 2, 2016, http://www.contemplativemind.org/programs/acmhe.

6. PRESENT TEACHING: WE ARE CREATING THE FUTURE NOW

REFLECTIONS FROM A PROJECT ON THINKING WHAT WE ARE DOING

Elizabeth Minnich, Laura Gardner, and Brenda Sorkin

ABSTRACT: *Our project has focused close-in on what we actually do as teachers, not as neutral technique that has effect only as it succeeds or fails in conveying subject matter, but as enactment—and teaching—of values, whatever the subject. As we now reflect on our inquiry, we are re-connecting with other thinking friends and colleagues, past and present, toward a fresh articulation of why and how this crucial work of education in a still-aspiring democracy matters so much.*

PREFACE

IN THIS VOLUME, authors are exploring from many angles the possibilities for a regenerating liberal education that takes the living rather than the inanimate—the organic, not mechanistic; relations that are internal, not only external; that which is renewing, not static, dead—as its model, mode, and hope. In this shared spirit, we have here chosen to write about a project that has focused closely on what we actually do as teachers, whatever our subjects. We do this for several reasons, including this belief: If educational changes do not emerge from, rather than being imposed upon, what happens among us as we learn, they will, we fear, finally remain epiphenomenal — or, perhaps, even become dangerous. Values and ideals must also be true to the living process, always interacting, emerging, and subject to attentive consideration in a democracy of beings. This differing locating of our project is, we believe, compatible with Whitehead, and with Howard Woodhouse's paper in this volume (among others, Howard's paper was part of our shared session at the conference). Perhaps, then, keep this in mind as you read the work of an artist/educator, a teacher of somatics/movement, and a philosopher/feminist, who have all found that the values they enact as teachers are profoundly similar, mutually significant, and suggestive for visions of relations on-the-ground and for an alternative world that emerges from practice as well as theory:

> In general terms, the goal of Whitehead's value system is to reenergize university education by enabling "wisdom [as]...the fruit of balanced development."[1] This means that students come to appreciate value as an emergent process in both their own experience and in nature itself; and their education should emphasize concrete experience and action but not to the exclusion of abstract ideas, thereby building a "balanced growth of individuality."[2] He believes that a renewed liberal education should grow from "a renewed exercise of the creative imagination" capable of creating a value system for humankind "to deal with the demands of a modern civilization."[3]

Our concern is always with whether we, those of us with vision, analysis, and theory concerning the ways the world needs to change actually do, or even can, walk the talk. Holding a radically liberating worldview is not, we fear, a guarantee that one will indeed, in class and elsewhere on the ground where we live and have our being, act differently from others who are sure they, too, are right and know what is good for us. So, this one time, we leave the theory to others and instead begin with querying what it is we actually do in class, what we actually teach, no matter the content of a course.

To change the world, it is not enough to change the ways we teach (although this goes a lot further than we may like to think), but it is just as true that, to change the world, we need to keep checking to make sure that how we *are* with others is ever more consonant with how we believe we *ought to be.*

I. WHAT, WHEN, WHERE ARE WE REALLY TEACHING?

"The present contains all that there is. It is holy ground, for it the past, and it is the future." ~A. N. Whitehead[4]

REFLECTING ON ARTFUL TEACHING

For three years now, we have been doing something that only sounds simple: We have been asking ourselves what it is we actually do each time we teach. *How do I start the first class? How do I invite someone to change habits of body/mind that are blocking learning? Have I dealt with a shocking statement? How did I connect a teaching with their lives so they remembered it without even trying? When do I answer a question, when do I ask one back? What does a commitment to equality ask of me in, say, a philosophy class?*

Our project initially seemed interesting, in particular because we are deeply identified with such different subjects that are so often equated with long-divided aspects of human being: philosophy, art, movement—mind, body; reason, emotion, imagination; moving, making, thinking. Working through such old violations of our wholeness was neatly facilitated by our focus on the *how,* and, as revealed through it, the *why* of the teaching to which we are deeply committed. We quickly realized a consequent similarity: We were looking for the art, the highly informed and practiced ways of performing in the moment that, each time a class goes really well, alchemically brings it all together into a unique, memorable, enlivening experience—as when we say, *Now* that *was an experience.* At such times, the aesthetic, cognitive, emotional, and physical come together; we feel as energized and renewed as we do enlightened. Aesthetic experience, and joy, then re-enter education, from which they have sadly been too long banished in our scientist age.

So, we have been in quest of a different grail from generalized, replicable, strictly comparable techniques (and what kind of a world do those values enact? This is in parentheses, but it may be one of our most important questions). We are seeing if we can discern an artfulness that honors the unique rather than the standard—art, rather than science. Trying to capture an art in action is tricky indeed. It flirts with the contradictory. On a very basic level, it does so because, as Hannah Arendt observed, human beings have the paradoxical commonality of being each and every one unique.[5] So, of course, do experiences when we are mindful of and with them.

Throughout, we have observed the characteristics, qualities, and values that are revealed in the choices we actually make in teaching. A through-line of our inquiry: *How do you in your teaching enact, create, and embody what it is that matters most to you and, by your lights, the world?* To run off with Kant's Categorical Imperative: *Could the maxims of the ways you teach be generalized into principles for a more truthful, just and sustainable world?*

NOT JUST TECHNIQUES, NEVER NEUTRAL

Insofar as people have effective experiences something, perhaps not what we intended, has been learned. For example: We could teach democratic theory in a way that actually taught people to scorn their peers while revering an authoritative professor. We could crush art students' imaginations so that what they then teach others is at best technical competence, at worst, the pain of their own creative loss. We could teach people to move in ways that should do them good, but fill them with such self-distrust that they learn only to punish themselves with painful movement. We could teach "philosophy" but actually practice sophistry, the amoral competitive ability to make "the worse seem the better case." We could teach about the land pretending that it is simply objectively there, without intrinsic relation to anything else—a laboratory subject. Or we can teach without contradicting the meanings, and so the values, inherent in our subject, and/or our purposes as educators in and for a would-be democracy, a safe, healthy, and shareable world.

How we purposefully affect other people is never neutral. People remember their teachers.

II. PRESENT TEACHING: CHARACTERISTICS, THEMES, VALUES

WHY "PRESENT TEACHING"?

We are now calling our kind of teaching *present teaching*. It is an odd name. We have thought of it under other headings, including a *practice of attentiveness, relational teaching,* and *artful teaching.* We have dwelled on theatrical aspects: It is *performative,* and each time *improvisational.* It is *close-in, fine-grained, holistic, whole life,* and *personal.* Such teaching does not say, "Leave your life outside." It invites active inter-relation: *How do you understand this? What do you make of it? How do you move with it? How do you feel?* Being close-in, such immediate engagement touches — it is *in touch with* — materials, contexts, and content; the inter-relating of mind, materials, emotions, and our sensate body; and the experiences, interests, and needs of each student.

We like *present teaching,* though, because *present,* and *presence,* have such a rich weave of appropriate meanings and invoke values we find ourselves enacting. Among them: *being present* with and to others mentally, physically, and emotionally; *being in the present* as it holds the past and becomes the future; and *presenting* — and *representing* — ourselves, *knowledge, arts, movements, works, actions.* There was wisdom in having students say "present" when attendance was taken.

SOME GLEANINGS AND REFLECTIONS

First, four basic observations that thread through the others. We read these now and think, *Well,* that's *obvious.* We have observed, however, that, seriously adopted, they would require significant changes. Obvious, then, but more honored in the breach:

It is not only what we say and do in evident relation to conveying our subject matter that teaches. It is not only what we know that we draw on, and not only in discussion that we communicate.

We are embodied minds. Significant learning is not just added on: it is incorporated, it connects with who and how we are or it has no meaning and will not work with us over time. In the words of Moshe Feldenkrais, "I believe that the unity of mind and body is an objective reality. They are not just parts somehow related to each other, but an inseparable whole while functioning."[6]

Each teacher should teach in the ways s/he does best. This is an art; replicable science and technique are there to be drawn on, but teaching well trumps becoming interchangeable.

We create the future by what we do now. We'll let Dewey make this point: "Because the need of preparation for a continually developing life is great, it is imperative that every energy should be bent to making the present experience as rich and significant as possible. Then as the present merges insensibly into the future, the future is taken care of."[7] The present then remains sacred, and not merely a means to securing a particular future. It is a prefiguring of the future, the future in practice, and so entirely worthy of attention unto itself (a crucial point: We are not asking students to "jump through hoops," to do things that will only "pay off" in the future).

DESCRIPTORS, CHARACTERISTICS, VALUES EMERGING IN PRACTICE

Present teaching is relational. We realize this when we observe how important it is to us to be welcoming, respectful, interested, polite, humorous, caring, serious, and gentle, as well as knowledgeable, skilled, and expert. We find how minds/bodies want to move and how each can do so more freely, fully, wisely—the opposite of "rigor," of "no pain, no gain."

It is reflective, and reflexive. We often pause to invite reflection, and we regularly return to earlier comments and movements to interweave or reconsider. More specifically, we think about our own thinking: "The best college teachers," Ken Bain observes, "can think about their own thinking in the discipline, analyzing its nature and evaluating its quality."[8] "Best" or not, we do try hard to find ways to invite students to be reflexive and reflective with us, not only within and about our disciplines but also as they think for themselves more regularly.

It is engaged, active: We do philosophy, make and teach art, and re-find ourselves through movement as individuals, together. There may be lectures and demonstrations in response to a felt need for instruction, and there may be test-like questioning seeking correct answers. But these are tools, techniques; the arts of philosophizing, creating, teaching, knowing, and moving our bodies well make use of them, no more. We prefer questioning, together.

We also observe, in part because of those characteristics and values, that:

A well-taught class is akin to theater and other aesthetic experiences that exist in performance, not in product, including music, running for its own sake, dancing, travelling not only to get somewhere else, and savoring a good book. "Learn and learn and learn," says Ruthy Alon, a senior Feldenkrais teacher, "because this is the entertainment of the nervous system."[9] Teachers are in these senses performers, although only sometimes entertainers. A really good class does not just happen, anymore than a theatrical or symphonic performance does. Sometimes, people even applaud; more often, they just do not want to leave, even after a long, late seminar.

Present teaching is improvisational, not scripted. It is always a bit scary to bring the teacher's loved and very well known subject into conversation with this group of individual students, here and now, afresh each time. Typically, we are highly prepared, but not in ways that block attunement to the people there, then. William James summarizes it thusly: "The advice I should give most to teachers would be ... Prepare yourself in the subject so well that it shall be always on tap; then in the class-room trust your spontaneity and fling away all further care."[10]

The sequencing of learning is not unidirectional. As in life, we may go from the complex to the simple, clear, easy, rather than vice versa. We do not learn any more than we live by the same steps, in the same order, on one flat plane. Different classes invite different narrative ordering.

Thinking, imagining, self-awareness, critiquing, creating, judging, and empathizing are among arts to be practiced with students, whatever the subject — assuredly including the professional and vocational. Otherwise, learning collapses into training that can unfit us for the vagaries and many potential realities that require action, invite relation, and inspire creation. Whitehead stands here too: "The evocation of curiosity, of judgment, of the power of mastering a complicated tangle of circumstances, the use of theory in giving foresight in special cases — all these powers are not to be imparted by a set rule embodied in a schedule of examination subjects."[11]

Present teaching focuses on the unique even as it is grounded in the "sound," the established. It is common to reduce the sound to the standardized, but that is alien to it, and antithetical to the unique. Still, even as we work with students to become informed as others will have the right to expect of them, we observe that we will explore, even at length, a startling insight ("off the wall," some might say), a quirky move, a misinterpretation. You never know where anomalies come from, and as in scientific experiments, sometimes they introduce something genuinely new. Or dissolve when respectfully explored, leaving the sound looking better without even having been defended.

And so:

Lives are engaged. If given a chance, students bring their ongoing worlds with them to class, where we can learn to make connections both immediate and far-reaching. We work with them: "My efforts are centered on enabling people to see that their own ideas are perfectly reasonable and, in fact, are the best starting points," says the teacher of teachers and theorist of education, Eleanor Duckworth.[12] This is why, for example, we usually eschew case studies in favor of real experiences, pressing interests, and problems offered by the students themselves.

With such experiences come changes: "Long-standing habitual action feels right, but our feeling is unreliable until we re-educate our kinesthetic sense to reality-tested norms."[13] Learning is always also updating, reconsidering, and reconfiguring—minds, movement, making. Present learning is antithetical to drilling repetition as to replication rather than rediscovery.

Change, learning, and improvement need not require external motivators. We need the motivators of bribes—grades, status, future "success," and, negatively, of punishments— failure, pain, shame, and anxiety about a future—far less when we are present to each other and the material—when what we do together has come to matter, feels to be a solution, now.

Throughout, present teaching honors and holds the tensions of attention/rest; settled/novel; sameness/difference; disjunction/conjunction;

multiplicity/coherence; disagreement/agreement; disequilibrium/stability; and chaos/organization. In the words of Feldenkrais, "Stability increases the feeling of safety. Instability means risk but easy mobility. Both are biologically important."[14]

It takes time. All real learning is "life-long," whether or not we keep adding to it.

III. OUR MATERIAL: SELECTIONS FROM OUR TEACHING STORIES

These are neither field notes nor transcripts. They are more like professional diaries of teaching lives kept in the present. Although we are focusing *close-in* on what we actually do, we did not purge the reflections; we do not teach without reflection. We now realize that our teaching is an ongoing experiment with enacting values, so these, too, are subject to reflection.

LAURA GARDNER (ART/ART EDUCATION)

I currently teach in the Fine Arts department of a small public university. The majority of my time and attention is in the professional art teacher education program. I am responsible for preparing students to become teachers of art in public and private schools, museums, and arts organizations. I straddle the line of fine arts and pedagogy—teacher preparation. In a world confused about the role of the arts, it can be a sensitive balancing act of heart and mind.

Early arts experiences

I get to know my pre-service students (meaning not yet, but preparing to teach in the classroom) well. I have the privilege of working with them as instructor, advisor, and supervisor over a two-year period as they move through the professional licensure program. We spend many hours together, from an introductory class to a gallery show, final internships, and commencement exercises. I meet friends and family, partners, and children. I have the great pleasure of seeing my students through this liminal stage as they transform from student to emerging artist teacher.

In contrast to the wider world in which my students exist, a world of standards and testing that attempts to rationalize all aspects of the learning, I continue to believe that the teaching profession is essentially a relational one. Teaching provides the venue where we can grow and learn together with others. The tone of the interaction, the being and doing together, is as much the focus as is the content. Both are essential to the curriculum.

We begin — artists / makers

When I work with a new group, I often begin the first day of class by asking them to sit with one another in pairs and introduce themselves. They introduce their new acquaintance to the group. This gives us a way to ease in to the larger group. I welcome them with tea, and sometimes cookies. One way I start to address questions about self discovery is to follow John Dewey's suggestion to "give the pupils something to do, not something to learn; and if the doing is of such a nature as to demand thinking, or the intentional noting of connections, learning naturally results."[15] Eleanor Duckworth summarizes this succinctly: "Engage with the phenomena."[16]

In order to dive into learning about teaching art, we begin by making art, by using materials. We begin as a studio class. The art-making component is the core of the class. What we make each semester varies. One semester I made sewing kits for each student, a small pouch with two needles and thread. On the first day we sat quietly and learned the running and overhand embroidery stitches. That quiet beginning set the tone for the entire semester. Each class we learned new stitches until we had a variety to choose from. We visited a local gallery and area museum to see contemporary and historical exhibits of stitchery. We read articles about "drawing with thread"; we researched stitchery and embroidery from many cultures. And we stitched lovely, colorful samples. We learned how to teach stitchery to preschoolers, and we stitched Chinese characters with middle schoolers. By the end of the semester, our stitchery vocabulary, experience, and muscle memory was rich and deep. As was our artistry and emerging pedagogy.

The making informs the reading, the observing, and the reflecting of the emerging art teaching. All else radiates from it. To be an artist teacher, one must first be an artist and reflect on the why and how of one's art making. My students are artists, makers; they think in space. But they need a way and a place to record what they are thinking about, learning, and making. We capture these actions by making a commonplace book during our first week together. This is a visual verbal journal, a working document in which to collect ideas, observations, reflections, and aspirations. The book is used in and out of class for the entire semester. A commonplace book is different from a sketchbook or a personal journal; rather, it is a visual and textual compilation for learning. Each book is unique. Each student is the author of his or her own, recording notations, snippets, images, and ideas *they* are curious about and want to remember.

As we make art, record our thinking and creating, we spiral out and back again on ideas and observations. Moving away now from self-discovery, we read, discuss, and reflect on exemplars: *Whose artwork do you admire? Who is your teaching exemplar? To whom and where are you going for help? What did these artists and teachers do that you would like to model? How do they do what they do?* Students are asked to think back on who their favorite teachers have been and why. They create a mental collage of what the best teacher might look like, sound like, and do. We discuss positive and negative memories. *What would you say to your 14-year-old self to encourage and support her/him?* Another goal is to help students expand how they think, why and how they make art, in what community, and with what resources. We discuss not only what and how we are making, but also where, and why. *Who is the maker? Who has come before us? Who may come after? Why is it important to situate ourselves?* Questions such as these are interwoven throughout the curriculum.

Before pedagogy

But I am getting ahead of myself. Before thinking about pedagogy, I ask students to begin with that person they know best and yet are always in the process of meeting anew. I invite them to focus on their own artwork and thinking, get to know better who they are as a person, as a maker, before thinking about teaching others. Arthur Combs describes it thus: "A good teacher is first and foremost a *person* and this fact is the most important and determining thing about him [or her]." [17] This is where we begin: *Who am I? What am I thinking about? What am I making? Why? What compels me to become an artist and a teacher of art?* Our classroom is a lab, a place to try things out, tinker with materials and ideas, read, discuss, question, compare, share, to see what attempts at solutions we can come up with. We avoid coming up with "an answer" or "one way"; rather, we approach, think, and observe a multitude of artists and teachers to see the variety, richness, and uniqueness that will become each student's respective approach to teaching: "Looking at art, we learn about ourselves. Comparing views on art, we learn about one another. Disputing it, we shape culture. Where there is no argument there can be no consequentially meaningful art." [18]

Going out into the teaching world

We move from the sublime discussion of art making and artistry, the theoretical, and personal self-exploration, to more practical learning of the developmental, cultural, and pedagogical needs of students we will be teaching. We observe and teach in art classrooms where we get to practice managing groups, talking with parents and colleagues, and planning lessons. Then we come back to our lab and try our hand at resume writing and ordering supplies—skills and attributes that the artist teacher must have.

Generally, we observe at least five art classrooms. Students are asked to take notes on the spatial design of the room, listen carefully to and quote the teacher and students, and interact with students. When we return we deconstruct what we saw. *How does this compare with what we have been reading about pedagogy and child development? What did you see that you would use? That you question? What was a surprise?* By the end of the semester, they have a wide assortment of techniques. One notable example of an observation is how one art teacher addresses her students as "friends." Another teacher addresses her students as "artists." My students leave these experiences with a sense of choice: *How will I address and interact with my future students? Just like my artwork, there is no one "right" way.*

Moving from artist to artist teacher

I tend not to lecture. Rather, I introduce a concept that we read about and discuss and then I hand over the "teaching" to the students. I remind them that the class is a lab, a place to practice, try on new behaviors, and test stepping out of the comfort zone. All—even the shy ones (especially the shy ones)—practice leading readings, presenting a paper, teaching a lesson. We get used to being the facilitator by facilitating. We then relate the concept to our past experience, and our art making and what we are hearing and seeing. Connections, comparisons, and differences are noted. *How are our readings, discussions, observations, and making relative to this idea? Why might I ask you to make a book about your own making and learning? Why do we make art in this class? It's not a studio class. Why would we spend this time researching and making?*

I respond to the students I am with by asking them to begin with their own strengths as we move into this liminal space from artist to teacher: *What do you already know and do? What are you curious about? How do you plan to go about learning? What have you experienced that informs your teaching?* I ask students to listen to themselves and each other, to teach each other, to share responsibilities so they can begin to develop a community where they can rely on and help one another. By asking students to share their stories, we learn from one another, and we learn more fully who we are as individuals. These nuanced exercises and experiences take time, real time.

I continue to see in my work in higher education that, to get to the difficult, one has to be gentle. Deep change in thinking or doing comes with small, patient, calm assistance. Guide, mentor, and coach in this liminal space from student to teacher. Know who is showing up in order to be flexible in the classroom, think and reflect in action, respond to whomever they are with rather than deliver a recipe, a script.

ELIZABETH (PHILOSOPHY)

I'm going to focus now on teaching moral philosophy, drawing particularly on my favorite course, "Contemporary Moral Issues." I want to be teaching individually responsible philosophizing in the world as we sit together in a classroom. In this course, the "we" is more 'worldly' than some; students are 18–65; from rural South Carolina, Somalia, Poland, Mexico, Turkey, New York; veterans and nurses, artists, philosophers, designers, social workers; variously abled. We discuss capital punishment; licensing for parents; abortion; income inequality; civil disobedience; gay marriage; adultery. And that is just a sampler.

Presenting, reflexive awareness

Sometimes I welcome students walking into a first class by introducing myself, asking their name, shaking hands, and introducing them, then, to each other. They find this startling, and funny. I rearrange seating so the most people possible face each other. This leads to odd shapes, which they also think is funny—and unnerving. I have squared a corner for someone who said, *This is weird. I mean, I'm wanting to straighten it out.* I talk about what I'm doing, perhaps, the importance of table shape in diplomatic meetings. Place, spatial relations, order, disorder: these have effects, and we are also starting to pay attention, to think reflexively, reflectively. I bring food. Usually, someone says, *This is great. Shall we all bring stuff?* I say, *I do this because I am in awe of what you are doing, working toward a degree on top of everything else you are carrying. Someone should do something for you, so this is my gift.* For young, more entitled students, I have encouraged contributions.

The primary questions I am raising as we meet and start talking are *What makes something a* moral *issue? How, how far, in what ways, and on what grounds are we responsible to and for each other's acts and our own? What are the moral issues for which we ought to be responsible together today?*

At the beginning, some students want to argue, to use reason to out-muscle the others; some want to convince by their sheer intensity; some are leery of going into these infested waters at all. I work to lessen these maneuvers by questioning whatever is said, careful to do so respectfully, with interest. My intent is to draw out, turn around, and consider rather than correct or reject. Questioning is conversational, then; not one question, one answer, but exploratory and continuing with the same student for a while. That is scary for them until they realize I am not trying to put them on the spot, set them up. It matters whether I smile, lean forward, remember names; ask a question and wait attentively; offer breaks; laugh. I want us to practice listening for the complex lives and meanings each of us, as well as the Official Philosophers, brings.

Engaging, relating

I start with their own thinking so I can invite the Official Philosophers into an ongoing discussion. The students are then not passive, but active; interested, with a stake in what develops; and discovering that philosophizing is not an alien activity only for a few brilliant odd-balls. So, we discuss issues — say, capital punishment. *Do you believe in it?* Yes. You kill my child, I want you dead. *I understand. Who should do the killing? And right away, or after a trial?* And, *Are revenge and justice the same?* "An eye for an eye," sure. *Does revenge require doing the same thing?* Ideally. *Should a rapist be raped?* This brings in one of our readings. The student, unlike the author, doesn't think that's a *reductio ad absurdum*. We consider "an eye for an eye" and modifications, such as being commensurate… but to what? *Should the perpetrator suffer as much, or in the same way? For how long?* Principles and practicalities pull against each other. There is usually some laughter.

Once, a slender, blonde woman in her sixties said, *You're talking about me.* There was a stunned silence. *You are,* she said, *but I might even agree with you. I'm a recovering alcoholic. That I never did hit and kill a child while driving is a flat-out miracle. Maybe I should have been locked up for life. I don't know, but I thought you should know that you're talking about me.* But, said a young man, you changed, you're here, you're not out there driving around drunk. You're making something of your life. *Yes,* she said. *I'm trying. But I feel all the time that I have so much to make up for.* We turned back to *revenge v. justice,* adding both *punishment* and *deterrence value.* What is punishment *for?* I asked. Pay-back? Instruction? Deterrence? Repentance? Do we want people we punish to be harmed, or improved? Could the convicted pay back rather than being locked up, or killed? Everyone was now more careful; more real examples emerged.

I usually bring in readings when a student's comment invites it: For example, on *proportionate punishment,* I have observed to someone that Kant *would agree with you; you may find him compatible.* Later, I have to remember to ask whether she did, and explore how her thinking, perhaps others', has changed since that startling first discussion. We create our own texts, as it were. I might say: *We mostly agreed that requiring licenses to parent violates individual rights, although Jorge, concerned for children, disagreed. He was closer to the ethics of care we just read. Jorge?*

If, when we get to Aristotle's *Nichomachean Ethics* and I ask Tayshawna if she did find him compatible, she looks blank (I remember what they said better than they did at the beginning, although not so by the end), I remind her, and ask her some fresh questions. She had spoken of her mother's amazing goodness, so I mentioned Aristotle's "moral exemplars." I ask, *Were you thinking we should exactly copy our moral exemplar?* Well, no, although I guess I should. Mom is so self-sacrificing. I can't do that. *Are you less good than she?* Oh, yes. *Is it always good to sacrifice yourself for others?* Always? I guess not. Some people way overdo it. *Do you know anyone who is too selfish, the opposite?* Absolutely. *Anyone who needs help being* less *self-sacrificing?* Oh, well, yeah. I mean, unless it's Saint Theresa or something. Sometimes my mom drives me nuts. I tell her to stand up for herself, you know? *Did you find Aristotle's idea of hitting the mean between such extremes helpful?* And then we can explore whether the right balance for Tayshawna might be different from her mother's, and whether it might differ in different situations — say, a mother sacrificing for a child, but not for her boss?

We are not group therapy, we are not just friends, but philosophy, thinking, is also personal if we mean it. When we know each other better, the interweaving happens more. We stop being frightened of emotions as we try to think them through. They do have meanings. A woman in her forties said, *I went to the trial of my daughter's killer this week.* Another student: Oh, my god. I don't think I could look at him! *I went with my other daughter. We wanted to ask the judge for mercy for him.* "An eye for an eye" hovered in the room. A silence, very attentive: still but energized bodies, many expressions. After not too long: How could you do that? *We're Christians. We're just trying to live it.* That seems very, very hard, I said. *No, it gives me peace.* We took a break; we needed to breathe, to re-ground. And there was her choice, her peace with it, when we returned to Aristotle and the idea of acting as we want to become, creating a second nature. Another woman brought her three daughters to class to listen to the next week's discussion, which was quiet, tense, very careful: lives at issue here. They will not let this become sophistry anymore.

Improvising, questioning

Here, in real lives, there is indeterminacy: *This is unlike any other time. Each of these people is unique. Pay attention.* When I attend to students, they reciprocate. Sometimes I have said, *You really don't want to be here, do you? Is it the snow, exhaustion, that you don't want to talk about abortion... ?* Once it was upcoming exams. I asked, *Are tests good for you?*

A good question is the one that needs to be asked of these people entering an inquiry into this subject—and even in, say, this weather through which they travelled to get to class, this news day. I was once ready to start a course called "Women and Violence" with something from the news, but as the women came in (no men signed up) and it grew darker outside the windows that ringed this corner room, I said, *What was it like for you, walking to class just now, in the almost-dark?* These questions aren't trivial: "Interest in learning from all the contacts of life is the essential moral interest." [19]

BRENDA

Feldenkrais: presence in action

The Feldenkrais Method is a unique avenue of self-knowledge attained by discerning how we use our resources of sensing, curiosity, imagination and intelligence in learning through a series of questions that facilitate a process of *experiencing* functional and developmental movements. We begin to think in patterns of relationship. The value is placed on relating rather than abstractions so common in exercise, such as heavy stretching and the idea of no pain, no gain. In experiencing ourselves in this way, we are focusing on how we build awareness efficiently.

Beginning an immersion and training program: improvisational teaching

The three-day Feldenkrais-based Movement Intelligence programs are full 7-hour days held in the quiet, comfortable environment of my private office. It is a diverse group including doctors, artists, various professionals, and retirees, with a maximum number of 18. For those in the training program, we will have 210 hours together and afterwards I offer support through a monthly group mentoring hour. Others in the group will be taking the immersion for their own personal well-being. On the first day, we gather sitting in a circle of chairs as I introduce our subject before I guide them in a movement experiment.

I may begin by having the class partner up and notice each other walk without judgment, or try to mimic their partner in a playful manner. We all have our particular style of moving. Walking in stiff shoes on flat surfaces dulls stimulation to the sensors on the bottom of our feet, as does habitual patterns impeding the transmission of pressure throughout our body. Have you ever noticed wearing your shoes down in one particular area? Try walking on the outsides of both feet. Where do you feel that? In your back? Your shoulders? How is it different if you walk on the inside of your feet, on both heels, or on your toes? If we use our eyes to look down at our feet while walking, we not only compromise our back, we continue the desensitization process as we rely on our vision. These habits are generally obscure — and can come as quite a surprise when a movement experiment is examined in this way. We think we know ourselves because we live in our bodies, yet that sensory aspect that makes us human is often overloaded, dulled or undeveloped. We cultivate our ability to focus and observe through these exercises.

The difference that makes a difference: focusing on the unique

Rather than repetitions and rote movements, which can create boredom and self-alienation, movement sequences are taught in many variations, and sometimes done only in the imagination on the other side for the purpose of enhancing awareness. Any repetition without attention is discouraged.

Developing somatic consciousness: the creative arts

Reading a mastered language requires less attention than learning a new language just as we can unconsciously repeat the same movements. If you tend to walk on the outside of your feet, your entire structure responds and your nervous system is wired for that pathway. In changing these patterns, you are engaging in a process of neuroplasticity by cultivating new connections. Impacting body impacts the mind.

Reducing effort to elicit greater efficiency is another aspect utilized in building somatic consciousness. You may have struggled with a problem only to give up, go to sleep and wake up the next morning with a solution. Engaging in the process of moving with awareness has broad ramifications that can influence every area of our lives. As one participate noted, *"the morning after my third Feldenkrais class, I solved a writing problem I'd been struggling with for weeks. I soon realized that the twenty-four hours after class was often the most creative and productive time of my week."*[20]

Elements of teaching: moving from complex to simple, simple to complex

As soon as the group settles in, I have them lie comfortably on the floor to change their relationship to gravity and have the support that can increase their ability to sense during a movement process, following Feldenkrais's methods:

> I begin by asking people to lie on their backs... and learn to scan themselves. That is, they examine attentively the contact of their bodies with the floor and gradually learn to detect considerable differences — points where the contact is feeble or non-existent and others where it is full and distinct. This training develops awareness of the location of muscles producing weak contact through permanent excessive tension, thus holding parts of the body up off the floor. Some improvement in tension reduction can be achieved through muscular awareness alone, but beyond that no improvement will be carried over into normal life unless people increase their awareness of the skeleton and its orientation.[21]

I strive to moderate the processes of lying, sitting, and standing so as to inform rather than to tire. To aid in these investigations, I may bring out a skeleton for insight into the transmission of pressure through the bones, we may look at pictures from anatomy, art, or images from books that relate to the various themes we are addressing. I use demonstrations to clarify various perceptions of a sequence. Visualizations, stories, or songs may be employed to facilitate a process. Discussion time allows for further insight as another point of view or experience is expressed.

Am I doing this right? critiquing nonjudgmentally

Attending to personal comfort is prioritized in any class or training. We generally don't think of right or wrong movement—yet we may be guiding in a direction foreign to a student and we use the teaching measures described above to bring this into focus rather than emphasizing correcting movements. We use the principles of questioning, focus of mind, greater ease and efficiency to refine what we do in the training and in our lives—whether we want to create the conditions to improve our study skills, work comfortably at the computer, enhance our creativity our sports game or move out of pain. We bring body into the picture, comfortably.

AFTERWORD

This, then, is where we are in our project to *think what we are doing,* and from that reflexive, reflective immersion, to *discern what we are actually teaching,* as subjects, as values, and as modes of being with others and our Earth. As you see, our material is rich, as would be that of any serious teachers and/or activists who spend time together being so attentive not to what they say, to what they believe they mean, or to analysis of what others are doing, but to what they themselves do daily in relation to such claims.

It is true, though, that one could drown in here. It is the realm of con/science, of *knowing-with,* that, turned off, terrifyingly allows us to do anything at all, and turned all the way on, can do exactly the opposite, paralyzing us in a fit of self-consciousness and uncertainty. But midway between lack of awareness and a drowning flood of illumination lies the realm of responsible action, of practice-informed theory, theory-queried practice — of philosophizing in, with, and for the worlds we share. In the face of our times, this is what we are trying to retrieve: a responsible art in which teacher, students, subject, and world are present to each other with full realization of their organic interdependence.

Thus we hope to offer and invite others to join us in what Stephen Rowe has called "a deeper and more relational aspiration" than any focused on "technique, procedure, rules to be followed," one in which an "alternative, a vision of higher education as a kind of relationship to be cultivated" is not only advocated, worked through philosophically and politically, but *practiced here and now.*[22] Such practices, as we have noted, do not suffice to change the world, but without them, our schemes to do so can, against all our desires, lose touch and become yet another ideology to be imposed, rather than ways of being to be tried out in what Gandhi called our "experiments in truth."[23]

NOTES

1   Alfred North Whitehead, *The Aims of Education and Other Essays* (New York: The Free Press, 1967).

2   Ibid, 198.

3   Ibid, 208.

4   Ibid, 167.

5   Hannah Arendt, *The Human Condition* (Chicago: University of Chicago Press, 1958), 8.

6   Moshe Feldenkrais, *Embodied Wisdom, The Collected Papers of Moshe Feldenkrais* (San Diego: Somatic Resources and the Feldenkrais Estate, 2010), 28.

7   John Dewey, *Democracy and Education: An Introduction to the Philosophy of Education* (New York: The Free Press, 1944), 56.

8   Ken Bain, *What the Best College Teachers Do* (Cambridge: Harvard University Press, 2004), 16.

9   Ruthy Alon, lecture, Walk for Life Training Program, New Hampshire, October 20, 2011.

10   William James, *Talks to Teachers on Psychology and to Students on Some of Life's Ideals.* (Cambridge: Harvard University Press, 1983), 23–24.

11   Whitehead, *The Aims of Education,* 5.

12   Eleanor Duckworth, "Teaching as Research," *Harvard Educational Review* (1986): 488.

13   Feldenkrais, *Embodied Wisdom,* 42.

14   Ibid, 39.

15   John Dewey, *Democracy and Education* (New York: The Macmillan Company, 1916), 181.

16   Eleanor Duckworth, *The Having of Wonderful Ideas & Other Essays on Teaching & Learning* (New York: Teachers College Press, 1987), 123.

17   Arthur W. Combs, *The Professional Education of Teachers* (Boston: Allyn and Bacon, Inc., 1965), 6.

18   Peter Schjeldahl, *The New Yorker,* 7 August 2014.

19   John Dewey, *Democracy and Education: An Introduction to the Philosophy of Education.* (New York: The Free Press, 1944). 360.

20   K.S., writer, class evaluation on file with author.

21   Feldenkrais, *Embodied Wisdom,* 35.

22   Stephen C. Rowe, "When Teaching is Good: Higher Ed as Scene of Demise and Hope," paper in draft, September 12, 2015.

23   Mahatma Ghandi, "Experiments in truth," in *Conquest of Violence: The Gandhian Philosophy of Conflict,* Joan V. Bondurant, ed. (Princeton: Princeton University Press, 1958), 17.

7. THE PERILS OF LIBERAL EDUCATION

WHITEHEAD AND THE TURN TO AN
ECOLOGICAL VALUE SYSTEM

Howard Woodhouse

ABSTRACT: *This chapter poses the question of whether or not Alfred North Whitehead's concept of a liberal education provides the basis for a vibrant ecological value system. Having analyzed Whitehead's conception of liberal education and his theory of values, more recent accounts are considered that emphasize the need to inhabit the land rather than reside on it. Such habitation can be strengthened by Indigenous views of land as a source of sustenance for Aboriginal peoples rather than a commodity, where the goal of a land education is to emphasize the ravages of colonialism. The origins of land as private property in the political theory of John Locke are then contrasted with Indigenous views. Whitehead's theory of value as integral to the process of change in the universe coupled with his concept of internal relations enables a critique of the dominant view of land as private property that could be developed further. The chapter concludes with several challenges for an ecologically oriented liberal education.*

INTRODUCTION

T HE GOALS OF A LIBERAL EDUCATION have been identified as "intellectual creativity, a combination of intellectual breadth and specialized knowledge, and the comprehension and respect for diverse ideas and cultures."[1] These goals have great merit and I, for one, strive to uphold them as worthy of integration in the education of future teachers, an activity in which I have been engaged for several decades. And yet it is worth asking, what has liberal education contributed to our understanding of the relationship between the human species and the planet? Can we derive a praxis that would enable us to construct a robust ecological value system?

The historical record is not encouraging. Three examples suffice. The curriculum of the 13th century University of Paris consisted of the *quadrivium* (arithmetic, geometry, astronomy, and music) and the *trivium* (rhetoric, grammar, and logic). While all of these arts drew upon a long tradition dating back to the ancient Greeks and beyond, which formed the basis for the study of philosophy and theology, none addressed the question I have raised directly. Of course, the problems of climate change did not exist in the Middle Ages, and it is unfair to expect a university to have addressed them. But the University of Paris, among others, has been influential in determining what constitutes a liberal education in some modern universities. Take, for example, the Great Books Program introduced by Robert Hutchins when he was president of the University of Chicago in the early to mid- 20th century. Hutchins, together with Mortimer Adler, held an annual seminar of great books, which utilized an interdisciplinary approach designed to foster a community of learning capable of overcoming narrow specialization. The Great Books Program has influenced over 100 institutions of higher learning in the U. S., Canada, and Europe. While some of these texts, like Wordsworth's *The Prelude*, do address questions of ecology, they form a tiny minority. Or consider the more recent, revamped version of the Great Books approach advocated by Allan Bloom in *The Closing of the American Mind* (1987) as a solution to what he saw as the fragmentation of American education.[2] The book was wildly popular; it captured the *zeitgeist* of the 1980s and became a best seller. But despite his objections to a fragmented curriculum, Bloom wrote not a word about how a liberal education could provide answers to the question of how to construct an ecological value system.

WHITEHEAD'S CONCEPT OF A LIBERAL EDUCATION

How, then, can Whitehead help us to answer this question? In *The Aims of Education*, he proposes that the limitations of a liberal education can be overcome by means of a curriculum in which science, literature, and the practical arts ("technical education") are integrated in a seamless whole. This means that craft, involving "headwork and handwork," becomes a central feature of learning for all students in schools.[3] Making things with one's hands is no longer an inferior activity to abstract thought. Similarly, the arts in all its forms (painting, sculpture, dance, drama) are seen as valuable in their own right and as a means to elevating the lives of citizens alienated from society, "herded town populations, reared in a scientific age."[4]

Whitehead has similar ideas for university education, particularly in the final chapter of *Science and the Modern World*. Critical of post secondary education that is narrowly professional, he sees universities producing "minds in a groove... [where] the groove prevents straying across country."[5] Specialization rules out a consideration of the larger questions that plague society; the result is a greater rationality at the micro-level matched only by a dominant irrationality at the macro-level. What is needed is a strong counter balance in which an emphasis on aesthetic education makes possible the rebuilding of our relationship with the natural and social worlds. And, as we shall see later in the chapter, this requires a paradigm shift from scientific materialism to the philosophy of organism as the basis of our worldview. Were the philosophy of organism the basis of university education, an appreciation of the inherent beauty of the sunset would be at least as important as an understanding of its scientific explanation in terms of the rotation of the earth.[6] Such an education would even enable us to appreciate a factory as a living organism, a community of interrelated parts, both human and non-human.

WHITEHEAD'S VALUE SYSTEM

What, then, is a value system? A value system is made up of a set of goods, which are affirmed, and bads, which are repudiated in both thought and action.[7] These related goods and bads may be more or less consciously arrived at, but those who hold them may modify their values on the basis of experience, judgment, intuition, evidence, and argument.[8] Whitehead, for example, tells us that "an essential factor [in my learning to appreciate the value of] beauty... [as] the aim of existence" was his wife, Evelyn, because of her "vivid life."[9] Nor should Evelyn's influence be diminished, since beauty plays an important part in Whitehead's theory of value.

A robust value system should recognize that "we find ourselves in a buzzing world amid a democracy of fellow creatures."[10] Whitehead's use of a democracy among all living creatures is consistent with ecologists' and biologists' concept of "communities" and "populations." And "democracy" in this sense "means understanding how our history and that of everything around us — from, for example, trees to ecosystems — involves exchanges and interconnections."[11] Relatedness among all entities is an essential part of Whitehead's ontology, which conceives of "the creative advance of the world...[as] the becoming, the perishing, and the objective immortalities of those things which jointly constitute *stubborn fact.*"[12] In other words, the creative process of becoming involves the dying and rebirth of all entities in a web of brute fact comprising the world. Beauty is inherent to this entire process and to nature itself, for "beauty...[is] realized in the actual occasions which are the completely real things in the Universe."[13] As the universe unfolds, beauty is revealed in stubborn fact. We find here a series of presuppositions in which nature is understood as an interrelated system imbued with value, a point to which I return later in the chapter.[14]

In general terms, the goal of Whitehead's value system is to reenergize university education by enabling "wisdom [as]...the fruit of balanced development."[15] This means that students come to appreciate value as an emergent process in both their own experience and in nature itself; their education should emphasize concrete experience and action but not to the exclusion of abstract ideas, thereby building a "balanced growth of individuality."[16] He believes that a renewed liberal education should grow from "a renewed exercise of the creative imagination" capable of creating a value system for humankind to deal with the demands of a modern civilization.[17] Alternative possibilities to the dominant ideology of the 19th and early 20th centuries are necessary to meet the profound changes confronting universities and the general populace. Is Whitehead's account of an ecological value system adequate? It may prove to be, if we connect it to the ideas of some contemporary authors, which is the task of this chapter.

A sense of community is being lost in the modern world, where individuals, families, neighborhoods, and nations are engulfed by abstract entities like the market, and there is less and less time for an appreciation of wisdom or of aesthetic experience giving rise to "the full interplay of emergent values" that could serve as the basis for a different framework for living.[18] In place of Social Darwinism, which valorizes war and zero-sum competition, Whitehead advocates cooperation. He recommends that we learn from our own capacity to assist each other by modifying the environment, on the one hand, and the interrelatedness of natural species, on the other. With a certain prescience, he refers to "the trees in a Brazilian forest [that] depend up on the association of various species of organisms, each of which is mutually dependent on the other species."[19] This ecosystem conjoins soil, sun, shade, microbes, rain, temperature, and other living creatures in such a way that "[a] forest is the triumph of mutually dependent species." In other words, an individual tree may lose a certain unique quality, but every tree supports the others in a collaborative effort. In order for humanity to translate this kind of cooperation from nature to society, peace is required among individuals, communities, and nations. Otherwise, further cataclysms like the Great War will ensue, since "The Gospel of Force is incompatible with a social life."[20] Hence, Whitehead links cooperation with peace not simply as the absence of war, but also as the promotion of social justice, as twin aspects of his value system.

Cooperation and peace are only likely to take root when we learn to respect the diversity of humankind. Far from being uniform in the ways in which we think, act, and feel, we are delightfully different and these characteristics should be understood and admired. Respect for diversity is a necessary virtue in a liberal education for life in the complexities of the modern world. Whitehead sees humanity as a creature engaged in "the power of wandering," not simply in the physical sense but "greater still is the power of man's spiritual adventures—adventures of thought, adventures of passionate feeling, adventures of aesthetic experience."[21] This process of wandering, which Whitehead labels spiritual, connects those aspects of our experience that he considers primal: feeling, aesthetic experience, and thought. Those feelings, which enhance our appreciation of the beauty of the natural and social worlds, also give rise to thought, which has its own value, and the promise of future, imaginative action. The spiritual life of human beings is inseparable from the adventure of their life as wanderers; and their spirituality is adventurous to the extent that they learn, feel, appreciate, and think about their connection to reality and how it might be different if their powers of imagination were fully engaged. For example, how would a more balanced relationship with nature look, and how could a systematic approach to climate change be implemented? There is a link, then, between diversity and adventure, both of which Whitehead proposes as twin features of his value system.

Finally, Whitehead recognizes that the twin values of cooperation and peace coupled with those of diversity and adventure may be insufficient to address the problems of a modern civilization. "We must not expect, however, all the virtues," he writes, and this for good reason: "In the immediate future there will be less security than in the immediate past, less stability."[22] In a world that had experienced the destruction of the Great War and the upheavals of the Russian Revolution, the relative tranquility of Whitehead's own upbringing and subsequent life at Cambridge was a thing of the past. While social instability is capable of giving rise to periods of creative growth in the life of civilizations, there is an urgent need to provide a "general education [which] conveys a philosophic outlook…[for a] successful democratic society" in which the values for coping with rapid and unpredictable change are paramount.[23] Only then can the general populace learn to live harmoniously with each other and with nature.

INHABITING THE LAND

How can we build upon Whitehead's insights about the values necessary for a liberal education? Can we remain true to his goal of educating for a "balanced growth of individuality" while recognizing the need to limit those human activities that currently threaten the lives of many species, including our own?[24] And are there ways to strengthen the value system he proposes?

What, for example, are the implications of "the power of wandering," which Whitehead ascribes to the human condition? If we are constant wanderers, what does this mean for our ability to live well in the places we choose as home? David Orr believes that a genuine liberal education would enable persons to inhabit a place rather than reside there. He draws the distinction as follows:

> To reside is to live as a transient and as a stranger to one's place, and inevitably to some part of the self. The inhabitant and place mutually shape each other. [While] residents...become merely "consumers"...the inhabitant is part of a complex order that strives for harmony between human demands and ecological processes.[25]

Whereas residents are alienated from themselves and from the place where they live by their insatiable wants to consume, inhabitants relate to it as a complex system in which they strive for a balance between human needs and ecological processes. Because inhabitants recognize there is a reciprocal relationship between themselves and place, they view "knowledge in the art of living [as a process which] aims toward wholeness."[26] This means that the aim of a liberal education is twofold: the growth of an internal harmony in which feelings, emotions, aesthetic experience, and thought cohere with one another, and an external harmony in which the self is able to appreciate the complex ecological systems that support life and to learn to live in harmony with them.

Orr's account is consistent in many ways with Whitehead's, and he does make reference to the importance of place to the process of education. But, according to Indigenous thought, it is the land that comprises place and shapes the self. Aboriginal author Thomas King makes this explicit as follows:

> Land has always been a defining element of Aboriginal culture. Land contains the languages, the stories, and the histories of a people. It provides water, air, shelter, and food. Land participates in the ceremonies and the songs. And land is home. Not in an abstract way.[27]

Land is home because it is a source of life, not only in the physical sense but also as a participant in the cultural and spiritual ceremonies that sustain Aboriginal peoples as well. The relationship with the land is deeply felt. The Blackfoot in Alberta, Canada, for example, live in the shadow of Ninastiko or Chief Mountain, and "as long as they can see the mountain, they know they are home."[28] This feeling of being at home could not be further from the alienated relationship to place of the resident described by Orr, since the mountain is both a sacred and physical place. And this connection also contrasts with the adventurous wandering that Whitehead believes is integral to humanity's spiritual journey. For the mountain provides a permanent reminder to the Blackfoot of how to live in ways that lead to a balanced harmony between self and place. When they return from wandering, the mountain provides a sense of home and protection. For the Blackfoot, like other Indigenous peoples, practice the art of living well by recognizing land as the source of life.

Dolores Calderon takes up this theme of Indigenous peoples' relationship to the land as the source of their physical, emotional, and spiritual well-being in her recent article "Speaking Back to Manifest Destinies: A Land-Based Approach to Critical Curriculum Inquiry." She argues that land education is necessary in both schools and higher education, because it provides the conceptual space for a critical understanding of the displacement and genocide of Indigenous peoples in North America. Too often, place-based education and social studies select against any critique of colonial history in their narratives of settler domination. In contrast, she writes, "land education is important for environmental educators and students to rethink their relation to land as a dynamic ecological *and* cultural project of recovery and rehabilitation."[29] Only if a process of cultural struggle takes place for the recovery and rehabilitation of land in its full ecological integrity can a challenge be mounted to "the dominant land ethic of a settler society…[which] actively address[es] settler/Indigenous relations."[30] This process involves an understanding of Indigenous agency and resistance tied to Indigenous cosmologies and the recognition that everything in the world, both actual and possible, is intimately related.

LAND, MONEY, AND PRIVATE PROPERTY

How, then, could we learn from Indigenous peoples' respect for the land as inherently valuable and formulate a liberal education for an ecological civilization on this basis? The problem is that we no longer conceive of the land in this way. It is no longer an entity with which we have harmonious, balanced relationships. Rather, "land is primarily a commodity, something that has value for what you can take from it or for what you can get for it."[31] The value of land is what it fetches on the market. A forest, for example, has value only in terms of the trees that can be cut down and sold, not for the food it provides, the animals and humans it supports, nor as a sink for the CO_2 it takes out of the atmosphere, nor for the aesthetic pleasure it provides the beholder. In the abstractions of economic theory, there is no conceptual room for the inherent value of land. As a source of monetized wealth, land has become a paradigm of corporate and individual power and status.

The origins of this theory of land as private property can be found in the work of John Locke. In his *Second Treatise on Government,* published in 1690, Locke begins his theory of private property with the right of the individual to whatever he "has mixed his labor with"—provided there is no wastage of the earth's resources and property by those who appropriate them, and there is "enough and as good left over" for others to work and live from.[32] In other words, there are social, economic, and ecological limits to any wealth acquired through labor. But once Locke introduces the right to money exchanges between buyers and sellers, this expunges any such limits to private wealth. He claims there is "consent" by "tacit agreement" to the value and use of money, which men renew every time they use it, resulting in the following inequality: "Gold and silver," he writes, "has its value only from the consent of men [sic]...[and] *men have agreed to a disproportionate and unequal possession of the earth.*"[33] How, one might ask, can a man—not a woman or a slave as Vandana Shiva points out[34]—consent to the value of money, if he is required to do so in order to sell whatever he has to stay alive? Surely, "it is more accurate to say that after money was historically instituted as the general currency of value, people were compelled to accept its value in exchange for necessities."[35] Compulsion by public law and force is the basis of private property based upon money, not consent. For, as Canadian philosopher John McMurtry states:

> Private property can be accumulated by the medium of money exchanges with no limit to its rightful hoarding and global extent, its rightful inequality, or its rightful dispossession of others by exchanges between lawful owners.[36]

This implication is never openly stated by Locke. But he sets the stage for subsequent market doctrine, according to which the law protects those who not only accumulate limitless amounts of wealth based upon money, then hoard it and create global inequality, but it also justifies the wealthy in using money exchanges to appropriate the property of others since they are the legal owners.

Commenting on these same passages, Herman Daly and John Cobb refer to Locke's "money fetishism" as a prime example of Whitehead's "fallacy of misplaced concreteness."[37] Locke mistakes the abstractions of economics for the concrete experience of human beings and confers upon them a reality which then supersedes every human relationship. Once he introduces money into his account of private property, this abstract symbol and measure of value is mistaken for the wealth produced by the concrete human activity of labor in our interaction with the earth. As a result, money takes on almost magical powers. It supplants labor, land, and humanity as the defining principle of capitalist society. Where market value determines all forms of exchange, human relationships and our connections with the earth are reduced to whatever maximizes monetary profits. This overriding principle of value has become truly global with the growth of free trade agreements and the power of the World Trade Organization to enforce the demands of multinational corporations on national governments.

WHITEHEAD'S THEORY OF VALUE

A liberal education today has the difficult task of challenging the concept of money as the basis of all value. One looks to universities as the very places where a dialogue to initiate this change can begin. A systemic move towards interdisciplinary, problem-posing education is needed, enabling faculty and students to engage in inquiry about how best to become inhabitants of the place where we work rather than transient residents. What better way to educate the young than to start by showing them how neoclassical economics is based on a closed value system, one which does not allow for its assumptions to be questioned? A critical examination of rationality as self-maximization could be undertaken; namely, the assumption that "always more money value for self is good...[and] the yardstick of all worth."[38] This counter intuitive belief expunges dispassionate and empathetic inquiry, normally thought of as constituting reason. An interdisciplinary approach that draws upon the humanities, mathematics, and the natural and social sciences, could also serve as a counterpoint to the power currently exerted by economics.[39] This pedagogical process could be accompanied by a demonstration of how all the major concepts of neo-classical economics from land to the market itself commit the fallacy of misplaced concreteness.

One of the problems here is that Whitehead himself does not have an economic theory to strengthen his philosophy of organism. As a result, a baseline for an ecological economics is lacking, though Herman Daly and others have taken up such work more recently.[40] Nevertheless, Whitehead does provide a critique of scientific materialism as a destructive force that found its apogee in the economic theory of the 19th and 20th centuries:

> Its materialistic basis has directed attention to things as opposed to values...This misplaced emphasis coalesced with the abstractions of political economy, which are in fact the abstractions in terms of which commercial affairs are carried on. Thus all

thought concerned with social organization expressed itself in terms of material things and of capital. Ultimate values were excluded... A creed of competitive business morality was evolved... entirely devoid of consideration for the value of human life. [41]

The abstractions of economics—money, land, labor, the market, capital—now define human relations in general and exclude any consideration of value other than the maximization of private wealth. This misplaced emphasis grew out of scientific materialism, which conceives of the universe as one huge machine composed of inert matter utterly devoid of value and obeying deterministic laws. In contrast, Whitehead asserts that any social organization based upon a mechanistic worldview such as this ignores the intrinsic value of human life. By reducing human beings to units of production, capitalism expunges any sense of their worth that goes beyond the material. What, then, does he offer in terms of an alternative account of the value of life, whether human or nonhuman?

The philosophy of organism provides a quite different narrative, one that recognizes the complexity of nature and the universe. This involves replacing both the monism of scientific materialism and the dualism that conceives of mind and matter as different substances with the concept of events whose energetic flow connects all entities in a web of life. The implications of this claim are many, but one key element is that "nature is alive," a creative, interrelated community of entities whose well-being sustains, and is sustained by, the healthy growth of each one of its members. The value of both individual entities and the systems of which they are a part is integral to the process of change, or becoming, that characterizes the universe. Value is what Whitehead calls "the outcome of limitation," namely the actualization of the potential of any entity. [42] If we think of this in educational terms, the value of every student lies in the fact that they possess the potentiality, or capacity, to learn, which is waiting to be actualized in diverse ways. Value, then, is in the world: In this case, it consists of the self-development of each student. Unlike positivism, which conceives of values as logically distinct from facts, Whitehead regards value as "the intrinsic reality of an event."[43] The beauty of a prairie sunset, for example, permeates the events taking place in distant space, which *we* feel as heat upon our body and we see as the dying embers of the sun.

This account of value is strengthened by Whitehead's conception of internal relations.[44] For example, in order for one species in the boreal forest to survive and thrive, other species must do the same. The brown and black bear populations depend upon an abundant crop of various berries in order to survive the winter and lead a healthy life. Moreover, after feeding the bears leave the seeds of the berries on the ground in their feces, transporting them to places where they fertilize the forest floor. In other words, there is an internal, or deeply reciprocal, relationship between the bears, the berries, and the forest in which the life capacity of them all is increased by the presence of the other. Where human destruction of the brown and black bears' habitat occurs, the life capacity of other species is also threatened. This is why Whitehead refers to forests as "the triumph of mutually dependent species," for the delicate balance of internally related organisms in the web of life can be destroyed too easily by the avarice of capital.[45]

CONCLUSION

The value theory of Whitehead's philosophy of organism strongly suggests that human and natural history are intertwined with the web of life. A liberal education would have to make these interconnections understood in a way that students and faculty can situate ourselves in the midst of a dynamic world of which we are a part. Only then will we learn to live well on the earth. And in order to do so, we need to pay attention to indigenous accounts of metaphysics, which underline what Vine Deloria calls the "[r]ealization that the world and all its possible experiences constitute a social reality, a fabric of life in which everything has the possibility of intimate knowing experiences, because ultimately, everything is related."[46]

For Deloria, the world is an interconnected group of experiences woven together into social and natural life patterns, which enable a process of knowing among all entities as living creatures.

Is liberal education capable of meeting these challenges? First, it needs to recognize the ways in which colonial societies have displaced indigenous relations to the land by both force and legal mechanisms, turning land into a source of private monetized wealth. Second, liberal education should articulate ways in which land can be recovered by indigenous peoples in ways that restore the ecological and cultural equilibrium that has been long been denied. Third, liberal education has an obligation to challenge the process whereby schools and universities are themselves becoming subservient to the demands of the corporate market. These daunting tasks require a *praxis* that has yet to emerge from Whiteheadian process thought, despite its considerable promise.[47] In order to meet these challenges, Whiteheadians need to become allies in the struggles of Indigenous authors and activists. The deep insights of these peoples, especially their cosmologies and epistemologies, can strengthen a liberal education that serves social and ecological justice in the most inclusive sense.[48]

ACKNOWLEDGEMENTS

Earlier versions of this chapter were presented to The Higher Education Track of Section VIII, "Reimagining and Reinventing Education" at a the "Seizing an Alternative: Toward an Ecological Civilization" conference held at Pomona College, Claremont, California, June 4–7, 2015, and to the Sustainability Education Research Institute, College of Education, University of Saskatchewan, November 2, 2015. I wish to thank the audiences and participants for their helpful comments.

I especially wish to thank my colleagues in the University of Saskatchewan Process Philosophy Research Unit—Mark Flynn, Bob Regnier, Ed Thompson, and Adam Scarfe—for their ongoing support and conviviality.

NOTES

1   Paul Axelrod, *Values in Conflict: The University, the Market Place, and the Trials of Liberal Education* (Montreal: McGill-Queen's UP, 2002), 35.

2   Allan Bloom, *The Closing of the American Mind* (New York: Simon & Schuster, 1987).

3   Alfred North Whitehead, *Aims of Education and Other Essays* (New York: The Free Press, 1953), 50.

4   Ibid, 41; Howard Woodhouse, "Mathematics as Liberal Education: Whitehead and The Rhythm of Life," *Interchange,* 43 (2012): 5.

5   Whitehead, *Science and The Modern World* (New York: The Free Press, 1953), 197.

6   Ibid, 199.

7   John McMurtry, *Unequal Freedoms: The Global Market as an Ethical System* (Toronto: Garamond Press, 1998), 7.

8   Janice Newson, Claire Polster, and Howard Woodhouse, "Toward an Alternative Future for Canada's Corporatized Universities," *English Studies in Canada,* 38 (2012): 54.

9   Whitehead, *Essays in Science and Philosophy* (London: Rider, 1948), 11.

10   Whitehead, *Process and Reality: An Essay on Cosmology,* 1929. Corrected edition, David R. Griffin and Donald W. Sherburne, eds. (New York: The Free Press, 1978), 50.

11   Michael S. Carolan, "An Ecological Politics of Everyday Life: Placing Flesh on Whitehead's Process Philosophy in Search of 'Green' Possibilities," *Worldviews* 12 (2008): 71.

12   Whitehead, *Process Reality,* xiv.

13   Whitehead, *Adventures of Ideas* (New York: The Free Press, 1967), 255.

14   Peter A.Y. Gunter, "Whitehead's Contributions to Ecological Thought: Some Unrealized Possibilities," *Interchange* 31 (2000): 221–22.

15   Whitehead, *Science,* 198. For an analysis of Whitehead's concept of wisdom, see Woodhouse, "Whitehead, A.N." in *Encyclopedia of Educational Theory and Philosophy,* ed. Dennis C. Phillips (Los Angeles: Sage Publications, 2014), 851–52.

16   Whitehead, *Science,* 198.

17   Ibid, 208.

18   Ibid, 198.

19   Ibid, 206.

20   Ibid, 206.

21   Ibid, 207.

22   Ibid, 207.

23   Whitehead, *Adventures of Ideas,* 98.

24   Whitehead, *Science,* 198.

25   David W. Orr, *Ecological Literacy: Education and The Transition to a Post-modern World* (Albany: SUNY Press, 1992), 102.

26   Ibid, 103.

27   Thomas King, *The Inconvenient Indian: A Curious Account of Native People in North America* (Toronto: Doubleday, 2012), 218.

28   Ibid, 218.

29   Dolores Calderon, "Speaking Back to Manifest Destinies: A Land-Based Approach to Critical Curriculum Inquiry," *Environmental Education Research* 20 (2014): 33.

30   Ibid, 27.

31   King, *Inconvenient Indian,* 218.

32   Thomas P. Reardon, ed., *Locke's Second Treatise of Government* (New York: Liberal Arts Press, 1956), 27, 31.

33   Ibid, 47, 50 (my italics.)

34   Vandana Shiva, "The Misuse of Science in The Global Crisis," from the Public Plenary Address at the 10th International Whitehead Conference, "Seizing an Alternative: Toward an Ecological Civilization," Pomona College, Claremont, California, June 4–7, 2015.

35   McMurtry, *Unequal Freedoms,* 89.

36   Ibid, 92.

37   Herman E. Daly and John B. Cobb, Jr., *For The Common Good: Redirecting The Economy Toward Community, The Environment, and a Sustainable Future* (Boston: Beacon Press, 1994), 37.

38   John McMurtry, "Collective Life Capital: The Lost Ground of The Economy," *The World Financial Review,* July 30 (2015): 4, 1.

39   See Lee Smolin, *Time Reborn: From The Crisis in Physics to The Future of The Universe* (Toronto: Alfred A. Knopf, 2013) 258–63.

40   See Daly, "Toward Some Operational Principles of Sustainable Development," *Ecological Economics,* 2 (1990): 1–2; *Beyond Growth: The Economics of Sustainable Development* (Boston: Beacon Press, 1996), 90–94; "Ecological Economics for an Ecological Civilization," at the Public Plenary Address at the 10th International Whitehead Conference, "Seizing an Alternative: Toward an Ecological Civilization," Pomona College,

Claremont, California, June 6, 2015; Daly and Cobb, *Common Good,* 4, 362; Jennifer Sumner, *Sustainability and the Civil Commons: Rural Communities in The Age of Globalization* (Toronto: University of Toronto Press, 2005), 88–89; McMurtry, *The Cancer Stage of Capitalism: From Crisis to Cure* (London: Pluto Press, 2012), 1–25; "Collective Life Capital: The Lost Ground of The Economy," 1–6.

41 Whitehead, *Science,* 202–03.

42 Ibid, 93.

43 Ibid, 93.

44 See Whitehead, *Adventures of Ideas,* 181; *Process and Reality,* 58–60, 308.

45 Whitehead, *Science,* 206.

46 Vine Deloria, Jr., *Power and Place: Indian Education in America* (Golden: Fulcrum, 2001), 2.

47 See Cobb, "Beyond Essays," *Interchange* 29 (1998): 105–06; Marcus P. Ford, *Beyond The Modern University: Toward a Constructive Postmodern University* (Westport: Praeger, 2002), 91–92; Woodhouse, *Selling Out: Academic Freedom and The Corporate Market* (Montreal: McGill-Queen's University Press, 2009), 246–47.

48 Margaret See Kovacs, *Indigenous Methodologies: Characteristics, Conversations, and Contexts* (Toronto: University of Toronto Press, 2009), 81–82.

8. CULTIVATION OF HUMANITY THROUGH STRETCHING LIBERAL ARTS EDUCATION

Jiahong Chen & Peimin Ni

ABSTRACT: *Any education has to have an ideal toward which one is supposed to be converted. The main Western philosophical orientation on humanity characterized by the emphasis on rationality has served as the basis of liberal arts education. This conception of humanity has led to great human achievements, yet its narrowness has also led to various deep problems, including materialism, managerialism, and consumerism in education. Inspired by the Confucian notion of humanity along with its gongfu model of learning, this paper calls for stretching liberal arts education on the basis of a broader vision of humanity, a vision of the human as an artist of life, with a heart and the ability to live artistically.*

IN THE OPENING PASSAGE of the *Zhongyong*, a Confucian classic commonly known as the *Doctrine of the Mean*, it says:

> What Heaven commands is called nature (性 *xing*). To follow the nature is called the Way (道 *Dao*). To cultivate the Way is called education.[1]

This famous Chinese thesis demonstrates a vision that puts human nature, the Way, and education in an inherent relationship. It tells people that the ultimate mission of education is to cultivate the humanity (or human nature) that is mandated by heaven, which is therefore sacred, the right Way. That said, what exactly is this heavenly imparted human nature? In other words, what is the ideal humanity that liberal education should pursue? In an attempt to explore this question, this paper discusses some problems derived from using the narrow Western conception of humanity as the basis of liberal education, and concludes with a call for expanding liberal arts education to include that which is inspired by the Confucian notion of humanity along with its *gongfu* model of learning.

I. CRISIS OF HUMANITY AND PROBLEMS OF LIBERAL ARTS EDUCATION

From ancient times to the modern Enlightenment and further into the 21st century, Western liberal education has taken the task of cultivating human rationality to its maximum. However, it has also developed an extreme form of instrumental rationality that ironically turns into an "iron cage" for human beings. Looking back, we see Western intellectual history shifted its central concerns from metaphysically establishing humans as rational beings to theologically articulating that humans, as part of the divine purpose, have a rational role to fulfil in the order of the natural law. Further into the modern age, Western education centered on the conception of humans as thinking beings, rational and autonomous, and capable of being our own moral lawmakers. From such a confidence and uplifting spirit came the libertarian notion of "liberty," according to which every individual ought to be left alone to make her or his own choices and create their own values.

As Carl Schmitt puts it,

> The Enlightened eighteenth century believed in a clear and simple upward line of human progress, which should above all result in the intellectual and moral perfection of humanity; however, ironically, to the extent that... anyone is still interested in moral progress, it appears as a by-product of economic success.[2]

While the Enlightenment has not fully enlightened human beings as promised, a comprehensive reflection is in order. Critical minds such as Hegel, Max Weber, Habermas, Horkheimer, Adorno, and Marcus all criticized increasing instrumental rationality as the destructive characteristic of modern society from a variety of angles.[3] However, as Robert V. Bullough says, "the critique of the Enlightenment seems to imply not simply a retreat from reason, but a collapse into subjectivism and a loss of confidence that we control the future—a new form of nihilism."[4] Postmodern deconstruction of modern ideals heightened the sense of human fragmentation and what Joel Kincheloe calls the "second degree of alienation," a state that is unconscious of the existence of alienation, which further threatens humanity with extinction.[5] While instrumental rationality is rampant, humanistic rationality has been squeezed into an iron cage by the invisible hand and become increasingly vulnerable.

Jacques Lacan first introduced the term "social imaginary," which represents the system of meanings, not necessarily real, that govern a social structure; rather, they are imagined concepts contingent on the imagination of a particular social subject.[6] The term makes us think: Do we really know about our selves and the world in which we live? Whereas French philosopher Paul Ricoeur suggests a hermeneutic way of understanding oneself in the face of reality,[7] cultural theorist Stuart Hall questions the possibility of ever finding a "real me."[8] Ironically, supposed rational beings are not real beings anymore.

We understand subjectivity as prejudice. Many theorists illustrate the reasons. Louis Althusser argues that ideology transforms human beings into subjects, leading them to see themselves as self-determining agents, when they are in fact shaped by ideological processes.[9] Bourdieu, through analyzing concepts such as cultural capital and habitué, seeks to find how objective structures tend to produce structured subjective dispositions. Foucault explores the discursive social practice that enters into the formation of human subjects, the ways in which external forces of control are internalized. Similarly, Ricoeur's "anticipatory structure of understanding," Raymond William's "structures of feeling," and Wittgenstein's "background" all illustrate how and why subjects internalize the socially constructed condition. Examining the "objective world," we understand this as "the precession of simulacra that engenders the territory; It is no longer a question of imitation, nor duplication, nor even parody. It is a question of substituting the signs of the real for the real."[10] Our eyes are "lensed" to see the overwhelming representations that don't reflect a real world but make reality hyper-real. In Martin Buber's diagnosis of the various perceived ills of modernity (e.g., isolation, dehumanization, etc.), he believed that the expansion of a purely analytic, material view of existence was at its heart an advocating of the *Ich-Es* relation — even between human beings. He reminds us that this paradigm devalues not only existence, but also the meaning of all existence, from I-Thou to I-It Relationships.[11]

In retrospect, when Adam Smith as both a moral philosopher and an economist believed that the free and open operation of the market would contribute directly to the common good, he might not have imagined how overwhelming "market-orientations" would threaten the public good today. When Antonio Gramsci developed the classic concept of hegemony, he might not have believed that neo-liberal hegemonic ideology could be so powerful in swinging peoples' consent. When Althusser illustrated the dynamics of educational "Ideological State Apparatuses," he might not have thought that ISA would eventually be distant from the state but very close to the market. Things happen beyond expectation and work together perfectly, making the "invisible hand" tangibly felt. New hegemonic discourse creates new logic. The welfare state coupled with a neoliberal strategy of globalization transformed the imperatives of international competition into a new basis for social control.[12]

In the realm of education, the rhetoric of competitiveness has gained global consent, resulting in what might be called "academic capitalism." To be more specific, educaiton is increasingly threatened by three deadly diseases: materialism, managerialism, and consumerism.

First, in today's world education becomes ever more vulnerable to the dominance of material interest and market economy. As John Hawkins characterizes it, the main formula of today's "dominant educational paradigm" is that "investment in education will lead to economic growth."[13] This formula has spread around the world, reinforcing the specialization, privatization, depoliticalization, and commodification of education, all of which leaves little room for advocacy and development of a humanist education.

Based on two years of research in hundreds of educational and professional journals, studies, books, magazines, and statistical digests published over three decades in the U.S., James Engell and Anthony Dangerfield point out in an article titled "The Market-Model University, Humanities in the Age of Money" (*Harvard Magazine*, 1998, 05) that higher education today is measured by three criteria of "success": 1) whether the field offers *a promise for money*—that it leads to a higher earning; 2) whether the field offers *knowledge about money*, such as business, finance, and markets; and 3) whether the field is itself *a source of money*, meaning that it can receive significant external funding from research contracts, federal grants, or corporate underwritings.

Satisfying none of these three criteria, the humanities all have to follow the whim of the "invisible hand" of the market economy and be penalized with a steady loss of respect, students, and funding. Here is some of the alarming data regarding this crisis that the authors of the article provide:

- Between 1970 and 1994, in 25 years, the number of B.A.s conferred in the United States rose 39 percent. Among them, three majors increased five to tenfold: computer and information sciences, protective services, and transportation and material moving. Two majors tripled: health professions and public administration. Already popular, business management doubled. In contrast, English, foreign languages, philosophy, history, and religion all declined.

- In 1960, one in every 6 faculty members professed the liberal arts. 28 years later, the ratio shrunk to one of 13. In 1960, for every 100 students in college, 16 enrolled in foreign languages. In 1970 it was 12, and by 1995, with a global economy in full swing, fewer than 8.

- Not only did the ratio of faculty and students in the humanities drop approximately 50% in the span of about 30 years, humanists receive the lowest faculty salaries by thousands or tens of thousands of dollars. In the U. S., in 1976, a newly hired assistant professor teaching literature earned $3,000 less than a new assistant professor in business. By 1996, the gap exceeded $25,000!

In his speech at the National Humanities Alliance in 2009 titled *"Humanities in a Time of Crisis,"* Steen Knapp, the President of George Washington University, lists the gap in funding for the NIH, NSF, and NEH, showing the dangerous decline in both absolute and relative support for research across most areas of humanistic scholarship.

2007 NIH: $30 billion	NSF: $5 billion	NEH: 138 million
2009 NIH: $30.3 billion	NSF: $6.5 billion	NEH: $158 million
*2011 NIH: 10 billion	NSF: $3 billion	NEH: 0
*The additional funding for the next two years is the Economic Stimulus bill that Congress has already passed. NIH: National Institute of Health NSF: National Science Foundation NIH: National Endowment for Humanities		

FIGURE 8.1: Steen Knapp lecture, *Humanities in the Time of Crisis,* 2009

As Nussbaum argues, we should have no objection to good scientific and technical education. But other abilities — abilities crucial to the health of democracy, the creation of a decent world culture, and a robust form of global citizenship — are at risk of getting lost in the competitive flurry.[14]

The second deadly disease of today's education is managerialism. Still quoting from the same article in the *Harvard Magazine,* "Administration has been a booming industry," say the authors. In more than 3,000 U.S. colleges and universities, from 1985 to 1990, full-time faculty grew only 8.6 percent, administrative personnel rose by 14.1 percent, and their supporting staff increased by double that, or 28.1 percent.

Along with the growth in numbers of administrators and their support staff, power over personnel, budgets, curriculum, and policies have been shifted away from faculties toward administrative bodies. Professors, now called "service providers," constantly feel the pressure of having to report to the administration, the so-called "management teams." Schools are increasingly managed following the corporate model. The richness of education is watered down and evaluated through standardized procedures against mechanical matrixes. When everything has to be quantified and become "measurable," things unquantifiable such as cultivated intuition, real understanding, moral values, beauty, and spirituality, are ignored and out of the picture. Faculty members are forced to provide data to feed the arbitrary measures and procedures to satisfy the requirements, which chips away their time for doing real work. When they are required to hold x number of office hours, their personal encounters with students are reduced. When they are expected to publish x number of pages every year, they have to pay less attention to the real substance of their research. When they are busy checking the boxes in standardized forms, they have to sacrifice their attention to the uniqueness and integrity of their course materials. Increased paperwork and regulations not only justify the existence of a large body of administrators and their supporting staff, they in turn tend to make those in administrative offices more self-righteous, as they allegedly know the standard procedures better and are entitled to oversee the work of those whom they are supposed to serve and facilitate.[15]

The third deadly disease is consumerism. John McMurtry, professor emeritus of philosophy at the University of Guelph in Canada, reports, "More than ever before, policies, curricula, and salaries no longer follow what an institution thinks students and citizens need to prepare for life,... rather, they increasingly follow the voting feet of students from class to class."[16] When student evaluations are conducted in the form of standard bubble sheets to be read by machines, teachers are forced to bow to the scores. They are discouraged to challenge their students in ways that would disturb their young minds. Whereas Socrates was known as a gadfly who forced people to step out of their comfort zones and whose "teaching award" was a cup of hemlock, our model teachers are now often those who are good at entertaining their students! College students are now like customers in a supermarket, putting whatever they like into their shopping cart. Programs and teachers are provided to satisfy their consumption and help them enter money-making careers, but not to affect and transform them into better people. What new program proposals can be approved? — Those that can demonstrate enough "student interest." Implicitly, we hear the market slogan — "customers are always right." What do business ethics teach? Not how to become a moral person, but rather how to avoid lawsuits or other forms of trouble (in other words, how to get away with whatever you do). What does philosophy teach? Not wisdom, but techniques of reasoning and revealing options for students to choose.

As the 21st century unfolds, it is becoming increasingly clear that technical progress has not necessarily promoted social or moral progress, and that a dramatic expansion and specialization of higher education has not necessarily resulted in a more peaceful and ethical world. This significant problem in education has threatened the very existence of humanity. It is less clear, though, that the root of the problem is, to a significant degree, the narrow conception in the West of what is ideally human in the first place. The conception of humans as rational autonomous thinkers and choice makers has played a significant role in the development of science, technology, human rights, and democracy, but it has also nurtured the culture or the social imaginary of the modern age, according to which education should simply provide service for rational autonomous individuals to make their free choices but never their actual transformation. The very maturity of such individuals is now measured by their ability to utilize the resources around them, including educational institutions and programs, for whatever purposes they happen to choose.

This then brings us to the main thesis of this paper: that we need to stretch the idea of liberal education itself! It is vital for us to realize that the dominant notion of humanity in the West must be expanded, modified, and enriched by encountering the Other, which includes the resources from non-Western cultures as well as the resources of the West marginalized by its mainstream culture! The dominance of the mainstream Western culture in liberal education is not merely politically incorrect; it blocks its own way to go beyond its limitations, and it is fatal to humanity.

Up to today, liberal education is still mainly about Western culture.[17] Since the very beginning of its conception, reading classics has been the central concern or pedagogical approach of liberal arts education. Following this tradition, Western education in the humanities has, since the end of the 14th century, developed a canon of scholarly disciplines: grammar, rhetoric, history, poetry, and moral philosophy, and a set of canonic works has been identified as the most essential readings for such an education. In the U.S., there are models of classical liberal education such as Robert Hutchins' General Education or Great Books program, started at the University of Chicago in the 1930s; the Harvard Core Curriculum of the 1970s; the General Education Curriculum, Humanities A, with Jaques Barzun at Columbia University; and the H. Adler, Great Books Curriculum at Johns Hopkins University.

In 1936, Robert Hutchins wrote *The Higher Learning in America*, with a chapter dedicated to the topic of *General Education*. He emphasized that the essence of a university is to share common spiritual and cultural foundations among all students. He suggests that general education in the university should be a permanent study that is not about the specific or special problems encountered by people in modern society, but rather about the fundamental question of common human nature, the attributes of the race, and what it means to be a human being. Ten years later, in 1945, James Conant, President of Harvard University, published *General Education in a Free Society*. According to him, the crisis in Western civilization after the two world wars was the most significant reason that called for the promotion of general education. Conant asserted that all development, from information, technology, math, physics, and science couldn't offer a sufficient and solid foundation for education, because all these together still cannot answer the question as to what our cultural pattern is and what the wisdom of the ages is. For him, the core value of general education is to maintain the Western classical humanistic tradition.

Clearly, they all take reading classics as a good method of dialogue with the past, a good way to pass on Western civilization and to keep it growing. However, their thoughts also reveal some problematic moments when their conception of general education is solely restricted to Western civilization, leaving other civilizations virtually blank. May we ask, is "general education" really general? Is "common spiritual foundation" really common? Is the "dialogue" really dialogic among cultures? The reading lists in *Harvard University Literature Humanities, Columbia University's Classic Readings,* and *Yale's Directed Studies* all contained mainly Western classics. When "West" means the "world,"- the reality of those students exposed only to Western civilization, in fact, has not been expanded but "narrowed." Professor Willliam Theodore de Bary keenly observed this problem:

> Western writers recognized that Asian traditions had classic thinkers who spoke to the same issues and concerns, though perhaps in somewhat different terms, but as the twentieth century, though the most creative minds were already extend- ing the Great Conversation to Asia, it had as yet little effect on Western education at the base level. Asian classics did not become part of the Great Books program. They were not among Mortimer Adler's 100 Great Books; nor did his 100 Great Ideas include any Asian concepts.[18]

When people in liberal education blame others for downplaying the importance of liberal education, it is time for us to critically reflect of the narrowness of liberal education itself, and expand it in order to revitalize it.

II. STRETCHING LIBERAL ARTS EDUCATION: ENGAGING THE CONFUCIAN *GONGFU* APPROACH

Although we have seen how narrow liberal education came to be con- ceived as education of the Western perspective, we still see some Western scholars questioning this Western-centric model, such as de Bary, a scholar whose life was marked by more than fifty years of unrelenting pursuit of cross-cultural dialogue. In suggesting the establishment of the "Classics for an Emerging World," he says,

> Every major tradition has its own canon or canons, and in considering what texts might be worthy of global attention we

Harvard University Literature Humanities

N° Author and Works
1   Homer: The Iliad, The Odyssey
2   Aeschylus: The Oresteia Trilogy
3   Sophocles: Oedipus the King, Oedipus at Colonus, Antigone
4   Euripedes: Alcestis, The Medea, Hippolytus, the Bacchae
5   Plato: The Republic, The Symposium
6   Aristophanes: The Frogs
     The Bhagavad Gita
7   Thucydides: The Peloponnesian War
8   Aristotle: The Nichomachean Ethics, The Poetics
9   Tacitus: Agricola, Germania
10   The Holy Scriptures: Hebrew Bible: Genesis, Exodus, Psalms
11   The Holy Scriptures: The New Testament: Matthew, Romans,
     I Corinthians
12   Virgil: The Aeneid
13   St Augustine: Confessions
     The Lotus Sutra
14   Abu Mansur al-Ghazali: Deliverance from Error
15   Dante Alighieri: The Divine Comedy 1: The Inferno
16   Giovanni Boccaccio: The Decameron
17   Michel de Montaigne: Essays
18   William Shakespeare: King Lear, The Tempest
19   Johan Wolfgang von Goethe: Faust, Part 1
20   Jane Austen: Pride and Prejudice
21   Leo Tolstoy: The Death of Ivan Illyich
22   Fyodo Mikhailovich Dostoevsky: Notes from the Underground
23   T.S. Eliot: The Wasteland
24   James Joyce: Dubliners: "The Dead"
25   Virginia Woolfe: To the Lighthouse
26   Vladimir Nabokov: Pale Fire
27   Mikhail Bulgakov: The Master and Margarita

FIGURE 8.2. *From* Classics for an Emerging World: Proceedings of a Conference on Liberal Education and the Core Curriculum 2008. *Edited by William Theodore de Bary, Shang Wei, and Rachel Chung. New York: The Columbia University Committee on Asia and the Middle East.*

start first with the idea that their classic status has been confirmed over time by the respect they have continued to receive in their own tradition. These are works that have commanded attention, been appreciated or contested, and have survived scrutiny over the ages. We do not read them because they conform to our own ideas or norms, but to show respect to what other human beings have valued. We are looking for common ground, but respect for differences is part of the process.[19]

Similarly, with decades of his life devoted to cross-cultural understanding and dialogue of civilizations, Fred Dallmayr calls upon each culture to actively participate in this constructive endeavor:

> Under the impact of globalization, civilizations are steadily pushed closer together, and a dialogue among cultures is emerging at least as a possibility. In this dialogue, each culture has to ask itself, what are the basic teachings or insights that we would like to bring to bear on the global interaction?[20]

Having immersed themselves deeply into non-Western cultures, these scholars have profound understanding of the value of stretching liberal education beyond its Western borders. They realize that the deep reason for seeking a true dialogue among civilizations is because each civilization has embodied spiritual wisdoms and core values that are invaluable for human beings to survive and flourish. In his influential analysis of the Axial Age, Karl Jaspers depicts the original co-emergence of major civilizations in the history thusly:

> Confucius and Lao-tse were living in China, all the schools of Chinese philosophy came into being, including those of Mo-ti, Chuang-tse, Lieh-tsu and a host of others; India produced the Upanishads and Buddha and ran the whole gamut of philosophical possibilities down to skepticism, to materialism, sophism and nihilism; in Iran Zarathustra taught a challenging view of the world as a struggle between good and evil; in Palestine the prophets made their appearance, from Elijah, by way of Isaiah and Jeremiah to Deutero-Isaiah; Greece witnessed the appearance of Homer, of the philosophers — Parmenides, Heraclitus and Plato — of the tragedians, Thucydides and

Archimedes. Everything implied by these names developed during these few centuries almost simultaneously in China, India, and the West, without any one of these regions knowing of the others.[21]

For Jaspers, this axis is "situated at that point in history which gave birth to everything that, since then, man has been able to be, the point most overwhelmingly fruitful in fashioning humanity." It is a time in which "man becomes conscious of Being as a whole, of himself and his limitations... By consciously recognizing his limits he sets himself the highest goals."[22] Now, after more than two millennia, we come to the realization that these civilizations might have co-emerged at roughly the same period of time out of coincidence, but the "everything" that spun off from the axis reflects part of the human wisdom that may have to be eventually complemented by the other parts. We seem to be facing a new axial age in which these cultures must come together as a common resource for the entire human race to re-examine ourselves and reset our highest goals.

While we are advocating a culturally pluralistic liberal education, we do not want to fall to the relativist cliché that every culture is equally good and valuable. Nor do we want to be mistaken as simply advocating a politically correct liberal education program in which each culture is allowed to have a seat. We are advocating it out of the confidence that each civilization has its own perspective that can serve as a spiritual resource for cultivating humanity, although the richness and the value of each culture may vary. Following Dallmayr's suggestion, here we would like to offer some insights from a cultural tradition of our own Chinese origin, Confucianism, as a more concrete example of how a different culture can help stretch our predominantly West-oriented liberal education, with the awareness that Confucianism has its own limitations and will, in the process of encountering its Western counterparts, have to stretch itself for its modern transformation. Let us repeat the opening passage of the *Zhongyong*:

> What Heaven commands is called nature (性 *xing*). To follow the nature is called the Way (道 *Dao*). To cultivate the Way is called education.

Similar to its Western counterpart, this Confucian approach also brings to our focal point the question about what the heavenly endowed human nature is, or what we are supposed to be, as humans. Yet immediately from here, we see a profound departure from the more intellectualist Greek philosophy. For Confucius, to be human is not equivalent to being rational, but instead it is to be *"ren"* or human-hearted, which amounts to being loving and caring. The classic Chinese lexicon *Shuowen* says, *"ren* means affections." Confucius says ren is to "love people" *(Analects,* 12.22), and the method to be ren is *shu* 恕—reciprocity, or comparing one's own heart to other hearts with compassion *(Analects,* 6.30). Confucius' most prominent late followers, Mencius and Xunzi, provide us with more specific articulations. According to Mencius, humans all have "four incipient tendencies" — the heart of compassion, the heart of shame, the heart of courtesy and modesty, and the heart of right and wrong. Humans have these four incipient tendencies just like we have four limbs *(Mencius* 2A6). They are what differentiate humans from animals and plants, *(Mencius* 6A3), and must be conceived as what we are supposed to be (7B24). Even though Xunzi has a different view about human nature, he also holds that the ability to develop moral sense is what makes humans different from everything else. He says,

> Water and fire have vital energy, but not life; plants and trees have life, but no consciousness; birds and beasts have consciousness, but no sense of appropriateness/rightness. Humans have vital energy, life, consciousness, and, in addition, a sense of appropriateness/rightness. This is why humans are the most valuable beings under the heaven. *(Xunzi* 9:16a)[23]

In other words, both Mencius and Xunzi hold that it is this sense of appropriateness rooted in love and care that makes humans distinct from, and nobler than, animals and objects. For Xunzi, who believes human nature to be evil, humans nevertheless have the ability to develop their sense of morality through learning; for Mencius, who believes human nature to be good, the incipient tendencies still need to be cultivated and developed. Both believe that humans possess the potential to be morally excellent, which is what they should strive to be.

This understanding of human being defines what the Way is for Confucians—to follow the vision and manifest the ideal humanity, which the Confucians call "sagehood." Since the ideal in humanity is fundamentally in loving and caring, starting from one's immediate family and extending outwardly with no limit, to be an ideal human is also to bring harmony to the world. This understanding of the Way further determines what would be considered by the Confucians as the proper pursuit of liberal arts education—a process of cultivation that transforms a person beyond the biologically given and into the state in which one can "follow one's heart's wishes without overstepping the boundaries" (*Analects*, 2.4). It is a process summarized by Confucius as, "to aspire after the Way, hold firm to virtue, lean upon human-heartedness, and wander in the arts" (7.6).

This process is liberal, or liberating, not in the sense of making one an independent rational choice maker, but in the sense of achieving a cultivated spontaneity and relational virtuosity that would allow a person to lead a good life. Normally we consider freedom as either a state of having no constraints (the so-called "negative freedom" or "freedom from") or the ability to make choices (the freedom of the will, "positive freedom," or "freedom to"). But the above statement by Confucius entails that, for Confucius, freedom does not mean the lack of any "lines" of conduct that serve to constrain what one can and cannot do, nor does it suggest the freedom to deliberate between alternatives and act freely on what one chooses. Confucian freedom is a cultivated spontaneity that frees one from making choices in the first place, because as a result of cultivation, one naturally knows the proper lines of action and has no inclination to overstep them! From this perspective, the "lines" of proper action mean no more than what "No smoking" signs mean to a non-smoker, or what surveillance cameras mean to those who have no intention to rob a bank. Just as any decent human does not deliberate whether or not to kick a child for fun, a well-cultivated person will be free from the need for deliberation in most cases.[24]

This kind of freedom is not "freedom of indifference" (having no inclination toward anything), either. The so-called "freedom of indifference" is in fact not only impossible, since we are never totally free from inclinations, but even undesirable if it were possible. One who is totally indifferent to alternatives would be like Buridan's fully rational ass, which starved to death between two equally good piles of hay because it could not find a reason to go to one pile and not the other, or a novice chess player who knows not what to do in light of many available options.

The freedom of cultivated spontaneity is not a natural state that people are simply born into and can enjoy without having to earn it, nor is it merely a matter of knowing all the relevant facts of a situation and making deliberate choices. One has to develop proper inclinations or dispositions. Like learning *gongfu*, the art of life that is exemplified by (but not limited to) the martial arts, one gains the freedom by acquiring and embodying skills and abilities. The fundamental Confucian "*gongfu*" for freedom is to develop *ren* and practice ritual propriety. "Those who know are not perplexed," says Confucius. But that is not all. Confucius also says that one must be *ren* to be free from worry, courageous to be free from fear (9.29), and know the ritual to be able to establish oneself in a society (16.13, 20.3).

Not having the person cultivated to a certain level of maturity, the availability of alternatives could even endanger oneself. Certainly one can choose to walk with closed eyes, or choose not to follow traffic laws, but by doing so, one does not practice the freedom to walk or to drive; instead, one gets into the danger of getting injured or killed, making it impossible for one to ever walk or drive again. In general, before one can know and understand what is really good, the availability of some bad options can do no good for the person except for giving painful lessons. Prior to reaching the stage of cultivated spontaneity, one needs to be constrained by "the line," and the line is a necessary guide for one to reach the stage.

For Confucius, freedom is also a socio-political matter. In this regard, however, Confucianism also differs from the modern Western Enlightenment ideas. For Confucius, the proper socio-political environment for personal freedom does not simply leave people alone to do whatever they like. Instead, it is an environment that provides community support. Just as water is a necessary condition for swimming, and proper adjustments of one's bodily movements in water increases one's freedom in it, adjusting one's relationships with others is a necessary condition for an individual to be free within a given social environment. Not only is the degree of one's freedom affected by one's relationship with others, one's domain of alternatives from which to choose is itself defined and transformed by one's interaction with others.

From such an understanding of freedom, the traditional Confucian liberal education program consists of learning the six arts—ritual, music, writing, arithmetic, archery, and charioting. Among the six arts, Confucius took rituals and music most seriously. Rituals can be considered social grammars. They define the meaning or even meaningfulness of social actions. They are also effective means of moral education, as childhood is the most important stage that shapes a person's character. During this stage, it is not the moral reasoning of Kant's categorical imperative or utilitarian calculation but rather simple ritual practices such as saying "thank you" and "I am sorry" that transform one into an educated and civilized human being.

For Confucius, music is far more than merely a means of entertainment, as it is commonly perceived today. If to be human is to be *ren*, and *ren* is more an affective disposition than an informative state, then naturally music can play a big role in cultivating one's sentiments and sensitivity. In addition, music can help creating harmonious social relations.

In such a liberal arts education there is certainly a place for reading the classics. But even reading the classics are taken to be more a training than acquisition of intellectual knowledge. Furthermore, the training program is more aimed at transforming a person than merely allowing the person to obtain some skills. As Song dynasty Confucian Cheng Yi says, "Nowadays people no longer know how to read. When they read the *Analects*, for instance, they are the same kind of people before they read the book and after they read the book. This is no different from not having read the book."[25]

The Confucian learning is indeed the learning of liberal arts. The word "art" fits well here for two important reasons. First, as it aims at creating artists, and not merely technicians, of life. As Confucians would say, learning arts typically begins with emulating masters. Real mimesis is not mechanic duplication; it is rather "doing-after," as Heidegger puts it, which is the very process through which one gains the ability to be creative on the ground of the greatness of the exemplar.[26] In contrast, by overly emphasizing the importance of free choices, our current liberal arts education tends to produce more self-proclaimed innovators than real masters.

More importantly, the word "art" serves us well in that art has no single absolute right form or style, and yet it does not mean no better or worse either. Indeed, one would get closer to the real spirit of Confucianism when one takes its teachings as *gongfu* instructions rather than absolute truths or principles one must adhere to universally, regardless of concrete situations. Talking about different stages of learning, Confucius deemed "wandering in the arts" and using one's discretion (*quan* 權, which is defined as "the goodness resulting from transgressing well-established canons"[27]) to be the highest (*Analects*, 9.30). The instructions of Confucian masters are recommendations, based on their concrete life experience and their perception of what is an excellent life. Of course, one may disagree with the Confucians about these values. But this would be like competing visions of beauty in art appreciation, where one does not have to have one definitive answer, and there is no singularly good answer either!

With this conceptual framework, Confucius presented us with a vision of liberal education that connects human life with heavenly endowed *xing* (nature), and thereby anchored sacredness right within the secular. Since this *xing* is the very possibility of becoming *ren*, something that everyone can easily find within oneself and experience its effectiveness in leading toward a good life, it does not need to rely on any transcendent being for justification. This feature allows it to be a great way of re-enchanting the world with spirituality without getting into religious conflict. It opens the lofty ideal of aiming at perfection, which goes far beyond the minimalist aim set by liberalism and enters the realm of the unification of heaven and human (天人合一), and yet it is utterly worldly in that the implementation of the ideal is right within the reach of everyone as it is practiced in the most ordinary life activities.

Although *ren* is a virtue that may be possessed by an individual, it is by nature relational, so much so that some even translate it as co-humanity.[28] From such a basis, to be sincere to one's genuine selfhood and to manifest love and care for others become one and the same. It is this foundation that allows the Confucians to claim with confidence that their liberal education (or in their own words, "learning") starts from what is personal, but will end with global peace. We will let the words of the Confucian canon *Da Xue*, or the *Great Learning*, speak for themselves:

> Things being investigated, knowledge became complete. Their knowledge being complete, their thoughts were sincere. Their thoughts being sincere, their hearts were then rectified. Their hearts being rectified, their persons being cultivated. Their persons being cultivated, their families were regulated. Their families being rightly regulated, their states were rightly governed. Their states being rightly governed, the whole kingdom was made tranquil and happy.[29]

NOTES

1   Zhongyong 中庸, in *Shisan Jing Zhushu* 十三经注疏 [*Commentaries and Subcommentaries of the Thirteen Classics*] 1625 (Shanghai: Shanghai Guji Chubanshe, 1997).

2   Carl Schmitt, "The Age of Neutralization and Depolitizations," *Telos* 96, no. 2 (1993): 131.

3   Max Weber, *The Protestant Ethic and the Spirit of Capitalism* (Glencoe: Free Press, 1951).

4   Robert V. Bullough, "Introduction" in *Toward a New Enlightenment* (London: Transaction Publishers, 1994), 3.

5   Joe Kincheloe, "Critical Pedagogy in the Twenty-first Century: Evolution for Survival," in *Critical Pedagogy: Where Are We Now?* Peter McLaren and Joel L. Kincheloe, eds. (New York: Peter Lang Publishing, 2007).

6   Jacques Lacan, "Principe de réalité" in Écrits (Paris: Seuil, 1966); in 1936. Lacan developed his theory of the "Mirror Stage" and published a number of articles about its importance in the development of the subject. Imaginary is one of these articles.

7   Paul Ricoeur, *Hermeneutics and the Human Sciences,* John B. Thomson, ed. (Cambridge: Cambridge University Press, 1981).

8   Stuart Hall, *Introduction to Representation: Cultural Representations and Signifying Practices* (Thousand Oaks: SAGE, 1997), 1–11.

9   Louis Althusser, *Ideology and Ideological: State Apparatuses* (New York: Monthly Review Press, 1971), 86–127.

10 Jean Baudrillard, "The Precession of Simulacra," in *Simulacra and Simulation* (Ann Arbor: University of Michigan Press, 1994).

11 Martin Buber, *I and Thou*, prologue and notes by Walter Kaufmann, trans. and ed. (New York: Touchstone Editions, 1996).

12 Raymond A. Morrow and David D. Brown argue about this point of view in *Critical Theory and Methodology* (London: Sage Publications, 1994).

13 John N. Hawkins, "The Intractable Dominant Paradigm," in *Changing Education,* Peter Hershock, Mark Mason, and John N. Hawkins, eds. (Hong Kong: Comparative Education Research Center, 2007).

14 Martha C. Nussbaum, *Cultivating Humanity: A Classical Defense of Reform in Liberal Education* (Cambridge: Cambridge University Press, 1997), 6–13.

15 For more detailed articulation of the problem, see Stephen Rowe's article "A Humanities Response to Managerialism: Diversity, Democracy, and Liberal Education in the Shade," *The International Journal of the Humanities* 5, no. 8 (Dec. 2007): 95–102

16 John McMurtry, "Education and the Market Model," *Journal of Philosophy of Education* 25, no. 2 (1991): 214.

17 Leo Strauss, *Liberalism Ancient and Modern* (Chicago: University of Chicago Press, 1995).

18 William M. Theodore de Bary, "The Great 'Civilized' Conversation: A Case In Point," in *Classics for An Emerging World: Proceedings of A Conference on Liberal Education and The Core Curriculum,* William Theodore de Bary, Shang Wei, and Rachel E. Chung, eds. (New York: The Columbia University Committee on Asia and the Middle East, 2008), 11.

19 de Bary, "A Shared Responsibility to Past and Future," in *Classics for an Emerging World,* 6.

20 Fred Dallmayr, "Revisiting the Classics," in *Classics for an Emerging World,* 15.

21 Karl Jaspers, *The Origin and Goal of History* (Westport: Wood Press Publisher, 1953), 2.

22 Ibid, 2–3.

23 Xunzi 荀子, *Xunzi Jijie* 荀子集解 [Collected Commentaries on the Xunzi], annot. by Wang Xianqian (Beijing: 北京: Zhonghua Shuju 中華書局, 1988), 164.

24 Joel Kupperman, *Learning from Asian Philosophy* (New York: Oxford University Press, 1999), 102-114.

25 Zhu Xi, *Lunyu Jizhu* 论语集注 [Collected Commentaries of the *Analects*] (Shandong: Qilu Shushe, 1992), 4.

26 Martin Heidegger, *Nietzsche* vol. 1 (Pfullingen: Neste, 1961), 215.

27 See *Gongyang Zhuan*公羊传, Duke Huan, Year 11, in *Shisan Jing Zhushu*, 2220.

28 It is suggested by Peter A. Boodberg, and endorsed by Tu Weiming, in his *Humanity and Self-Cultivation: Essays in Confucian Thoughts* (Berkeley: Asian Humanities Press, 1979), 18.

29 *Great Learning*大学, in *Shisan Jing Zhushu*, 1673, James Legge, trans. *Confucian Analects, The Great Learning, and The Doctrine of the Mean* (New York: Dover Publications, 1971), 358–59.

9. "LIBERATING THE CURRICULUM" BY INTRODUCING TRANSDISCIPLINARITY AND HUMAN VALUES

INTO UNDERGRADUATE EDUCATION AT THE UNIVERSITY OF TASMANIA

Mark R. Dibben

ABSTRACT: *This chapter explores the challenges of civilizing education in terms of two initiatives implemented at the University of Tasmania, Australia: breadth units and a unit in philosophy of management. The chapter first discusses Whitehead's concerns regarding civilization as a result of the growth of business and Cobb's concerns regarding the effect of disciplinization on academia. It then considers what sort of education will render the curriculum relevant to the future by moving us beyond the passive acquisition of discipline-specific knowledge and toward a grappling with the central issues of our time. It then considers the importance of value-laden intellectual discussion for civilizing management education, and whether, how, and with what success such an approach can be embedded within the fabric of a "capstone" third-year class. The chapter concludes by arguing that a philosophical questioning mode of inquiry, not a scientific answering one, is central to equipping students for the realities they will face as citizens.*

[I]deas which are not utilised are positively harmful. By utilising an idea, I mean relating it to that stream, compounded of sense perceptions, feelings, hopes, desires, and of mental activities adjusting thought to thought, which forms our life.

I can imagine a set of beings which might fortify their souls by passively reviewing disconnected ideas. Humanity is not built that way... [T]heoretical ideas should always find important applications within the pupil's curriculum. This is not an easy doctrine to apply, but a very hard one. It contains within itself the problem of keeping knowledge alive, of preventing it from becoming inert, which is the central problem of all education... (3)

[W]e should not endeavour to use propositions in isolation. Emphatically I do not mean, a neat little set of experiments to illustrate Proposition I and then the proof of Proposition I, a neat little set of experiments to illustrate Proposition II and then the proof of Proposition II, and so on to the end of the book. Nothing could be more boring. Interrelated truths are utilised en bloc, and the various propositions are employed in any order, and with any reiteration... (4)

The mind is never passive; it is a perpetual activity, delicate, receptive, responsive to stimulus. You cannot postpone its life until you have sharpened it. Whatever interest attaches to your subject-matter must be evoked here and now; whatever powers you are strengthening in the pupil, must be exercised here and now; whatever possibilities of mental life your teaching should impart, must be exhibited here and now. That is the golden rule of education, and a very difficult rule to follow... (6)

It is in respect to the activity of knowledge that an over-vigorous discipline in education is so harmful. The habit of active thought, with freshness, can only be generated by adequate freedom. (32)

The solution which I am urging, is to eradicate the fatal disconnection of subjects which kills the vitality of our modern curriculum. There is only one subject-matter for education, and that is Life in all its manifestations... The pupils have got to be made to feel that they are studying something, and are not merely executing intellectual minuets. (6)

~A. N. Whitehead, *The Aims of Education*

I. INTRODUCTION

N O ONE CAN DOUBT the *potential* positive benefits for society of the majority of its young people continuing into higher education, such as has been witnessed since the 1980s. However, the anti-intellectualist revolt of Modernism that brought about the discipline-structure,[1] and thus the inherently value-free nature, of the contemporary research university has deeply affected *what sort* of higher education has been brought to that wider audience. As the leading ecological thinker Vandana Shiva notes, "most universities are either teaching two hundred or three hundred-year-old irrelevant stuff, or are only creating skills for exploitation, destruction, and serving an empire over the Earth; we need to have teaching for giving service to the Earth."[2] The experts the research university in particular produces, and "the way the university has socialized them to see the world" is deeply at odds with the needs of the 21st century,[3] in which humanity's impact on the biosphere is all-too obvious. Whitehead's philosophy of education's "first importance lies in ridding education of the dreary thought that science has the only answer to its questions and the only satisfaction of its hopes."[4]

This chapter explores some of these arguments against research universities through two case studies of initiatives that I have been intimately involved with at the University of Tasmania: so-called "breadth units" and a unit (i.e., a 12-week, semester-long course) offered in the Business School entitled Philosophy of Management. I take the opportunity to write about Philosophy of Management in a book about civilizing education not least because of course Whitehead took "special interest at Harvard in the development of the Graduate School of Business Administration."[5] Indeed he noted:

> It is not enough that [business men] should amass fortunes in this way or that and then endow a college or a hospital. The motive for amassing the fortune should be in order to use it for a socially constructive end... It is time to teach business its sociological function; for if America is to be civilised it must be done by the business class, who are in possession of the power and the economic processes. I don't need to tell you there is a

good deal of sniffing on this, the Harvard College and graduate school's side of the Charles River…at the new Harvard School of Business Administration on the opposite bank. That strikes me as…unimaginative…Universities…[should] be taking business in hand and teaching it ethics and professional standards.[6]

Whitehead is here arguing that the intellectual environment of the university (as existed prior to the "Chicago School" reforms that shepherded in the disciplinization effect), in which "issues of fundamental importance were discussed in a context in which all opinions were heard and criticized,"[7] was fundamental if the effects of business economics were to be guided by human values and thus rendered positive. Noting both a trend towards individualism and a growing reliance upon employment, creating a freedom of choice heavily constrained by the need to work—what he termed "iron-bound conditions of employment and trivial amusements for leisure," Whitehead was concerned that the uninformed, unfettered, value-less progress of business "will go hard with the civilization that we love."[8] The ecological crisis we face, caused by the principles of economism—of economic growth through business as the universal panacea, is a powerful illustration of his fears.[9] Management needs civilizing more than any other subject.

In short, in this chapter I attempt an answer to the following question: Is it possible for research intensive, value-free universities to create intellectual educational opportunities that "support students coming to their own convictions, as long as they [are] prepared to defend them in open discussion?"[10] That is, despite their disciplinarity, can they engage even in some small way, in civilizing education? I begin with a discussion of the problem of disciplinization before exploring whether and how disconnected science research can be brought together to reveal interrelated truths. Through the case study of breadth units, I then explore what sort of education is required to move beyond the passive acquisition of discipline-specific knowledge, and instead move towards a focus on subjects that grapple with the central issues of our time to render the curriculum relevant to the future. I then address the question of whether and how value-laden education can be enabled through the case study of the unit in Philosophy of Management.

I conclude by arguing three things that appear to arise directly from our experience at the University of Tasmania: 1) Students are *yearning* for the opportunity to think holistically about the central issues of our time; 2) units designed from their outset as genuinely transdisciplinary bring staff from multiple faculties together, with similar positive responses from the students and even the recognition of shared research opportunities that would not have been possible otherwise; and 3) that Whitehead's speculative philosophy has a central role to play as a civilizing force in education, because it helps to equip students with the intellectual wherewithal to produce an ecological civilization.

II. DISCIPLINIZATION AND "THE GREAT CLEFT" OF "POSITIVELY HARMFUL IDEAS"

It is natural for us, as thinking human beings, to think broadly; to take in information from a variety of sources from what have become known as academic disciplines; and to put this information together to draw informed conclusions. And yet, the reductionism inherent in the science axiologies does not make this easy. It even trains the professional mind of the scientist or social scientist to avoid it. That is, it forces her to live in what John Cobb has described as "the great cleft." Namely, to live between, on the one hand, her natural existence as a human being, intimately cognizant of both her mind-body co-relation, her existence as part of and in Nature, and, on the other hand, her professional existence as a scientist, forced, to a greater or lesser extent, to deny that very human existence she experiences.

In the 1950s, the explorer Thor Heyerdahl observed during his Kon Tiki expedition that "Modern science digs in its own holes. It is not usual for anyone to take what comes out of the holes, and try to put it together."[11] It is a worse problem even than this. At the end of editor Paul Arthur Schilpp's volume for the Library of Living Philosophers (1941), Alfred North Whitehead concluded a lifetime's work with these words: "My point is the final outlook of Philosophic thought cannot be based upon the exact statements that form the basis of special sciences."[12]

The exactness is a fake.

As John Cobb has again said, "disciplinization has been forced upon us by the academic mindset. The separation of academic fields from each other involves considerable loss."[13] We might reflect on the considerable loss of the necessary Planetary perspective to see the crisis *Homo sapiens* has brought to the biosphere, through its cherished economic growth narrative of economism. That is, the production of more and more goods, services, even (dare we say it?) more and more academic journal articles measured by a quantified assertion of "quality," as the sole signal of prosperity. Even the word "productive" has come to be analogous with "making a contribution."

III. "INTERRELATED TRUTHS" VS. "BORING SETS OF EXPERIMENTS"? TRANSDISCIPLINARITY VS. DISCIPLINOLATRY

The Manifesto of Transdisciplinarity in 1994 sought to prevent the people of tomorrow from being imbued with scientism-economism.[14] Amongst other things, it asserts, "life on earth is seriously threatened by the triumph of a techno-science that obeys only the terrible logic of productivity for productivity's sake." Obviously this is entirely in accordance with the auspices of an Ecological Civilization. As an Australian research university, the University of Tasmania is required to operate within the constraints of a federally and competitively funded value-free disciplinary science research reality — a reality applied across not just the sciences and the social sciences, but increasingly the humanities and even parts of the arts as well. The starting premise of the Manifesto, that "the proliferation of academic and non-academic disciplines is leading to [an] exponential increase of knowledge which makes a global view of the human being impossible" is perhaps a little beyond its reach!

Nevertheless, since the overall Manifesto so powerfully rings true to the human being, it is fair to say that the approach to transdisciplinarity taken by people of the university is in fact not very far away from it.[15] For example, we would find no one involved in the breadth unit program in disagreement with the Manifesto's argument that "[t]ransdisciplinarity complements disciplinary approaches." Nor that it "occasions the emergence of new data and new interactions from out of the encounter between disciplines," that it "offers us a new vision of nature and reality." Nor even that "[t]ransdisciplinarity does not strive for mastery of several disciplines, but aims to open all disciplines to that which they share and to that which lies beyond them."

We should note that Tasmania is not alone among leading research universities in this. Many around the globe are appreciating the need for graduates to have a rounded perspective. Like its counterparts, the University of Tasmania, the only university in the State of Tasmania (Australia), is keen to provide all its students with the opportunity to view these broad global challenges. In other words, there is a growing recognition not just among liberal arts colleges but even among some scientific research universities — I don't mean to say all, or even many; just some — that we need to pass on to future generations an appreciation of the world that is more than that found within the confines of just one discipline. We need somehow to ensure that our young people become genuinely aware of other points of view, other ways of seeing, appreciating, and thinking about topics than what is covered by any one discipline.

The value-free research university, with its steadfast reliance on disciplines as not just the "keepers of the keys" to knowledge but the only means by which legitimate knowledge advances, has been accused of a particular kind of idolatry that John Cobb calls disciplinolatry.[16] This is the sacrosanct placing of the disciplines beyond any real critical debate as to the need for their existence, in a peculiar kind of belief, a faithful but *false* worship of their capacity to provide the answers to all things. Whether or not this is a fair criticism, there is no question that the disciplines are the starting point for academic discussion and the very basis of academic life at research universities. It so happens that this is none more so than at the University of Tasmania, which has only recently restructured itself into disciplines and placed them at the heart of academic life.

IV. "PASSIVELY REVIEWING DISCONNECTED IDEAS"?
INTERDISCIPLINARITY AND MULTIDISCIPLINARITY

In attempting to bridge the cleft between disciplines and to connect students to multiple perspectives, the focus on discipline specialism has led some research universities down what we might call an interdisciplinary path. By this we mean having an academic from one discipline give a lecture on the topic of a unit of study being taught in another discipline. Superimposing a different point of view, a different body of knowledge content, has a tendency only to confuse the audience and enrage the course coordinator. Taken in combination, these two effects commonly result in the assertion that the lecturer concerned clearly doesn't know what she is talking about. The experiment in interdisciplinary study of this kind often ends in dissatisfaction on all sides.

Another way of attempting to focus on the broader topic and its significance for the world is to adopt a multidisciplinary approach. That is, multiple perspectives — multiple discipline knowledge contents — used to develop research projects, and also presented to students in chunks in such a way that they are brought to bear upon topics traditionally isolated from each other. New insights are then arrived at by critical analysis *inter alia*. There has been some success in this endeavor, since it is generally recognized that the mainstream of any scientific or social scientific discipline rarely yields much by way of new discovery except in the most iterative incrementalism. Rather, it is at the interstices of the disciplines that most new discoveries are made. Of course, the discovery tends only to create a new subdiscipline.

Worse, for the student, it can be difficult to discern the connection between the chunks, precisely because they are presented by discipline experts in isolation from each other. This problem can be explained in process philosophical terms by thinking about what is happening. We admit immediately that the capacity to synthesize contrasts into a *consciously* discerned whole is reserved only for higher occasions of experience. While we may intuitively appreciate the connections, it is hard to integrate "the many" together so that we are appreciative of the harmony inherent in "the one," let alone pursue the implications that might follow from such a concrescence! Still, at least this second approach begins to move the focus away from an individual discipline's body of knowledge towards a focus on the wider topic and its impact on the world.

V. "ERADICATING THE FATAL DISCONNECTION OF SUBJECTS WHICH KILLS THE VITALITY OF OUR MODERN CURRICULUM" AND THE GOLDEN RULE OF THE "HERE AND NOW"

There is a third way, the way the University of Tasmania has approached the issue. This is not only to start out with the topic and its impact on the wider world, but also to frame this in terms of a "wicked problem." Despite the growth of a considerable literature around this phrase, I prefer the phrase "complex challenge" particularly since "wicked" retains certain traditional religious connotations. Complex challenges are those conundrums that students will face as they enter society as adults, and that they will have to comprehend and contribute to solving as active, informed, and engaged citizens. Not only this, the units of study are then built from scratch to deliver particular graduate attributes. These include: highly regarded professional; culturally competent citizen; and socially responsible individual. We do note in passing the individual focus of these attributes, a signal perhaps that the University of Tasmania remains a place of bifurcation!

Only once the complex challenge that is the topic of study and the graduate attributes to be attained have both been agreed upon does any discussion of material content begin. In this way, the units are not superimposing multidisciplinarity, but are turning the design of the unit upside down; ideally, content is the last thing to be worked out, *not* the first thing. The purpose of content is now to deliver an understanding of the particular complex challenge such that the students, on completion of the unit, shall have met the university's graduate attributes that have been selected as appropriate for the complex challenge under study. In this transdisciplinary model, one does not start out with the specific content of the discipline. It doesn't drive the design of the unit.

It is brought in, but only insofar as it contributes to exploring the complex challenge and delivering the graduate attributes—when seen in mutual relation to the other relevant disciplines' appropriate contents of knowledge. This approach requires a team of academics from more than one faculty (let alone one discipline) to be involved from the outset in designing the unit. Not only this, but, in addition to approving special funding for each breadth unit's development, the University's Academic Senate has mandated that breadth units can *only* be developed this way.

It is for these reasons I describe the University of Tasmania's new breadth units as "built from the bottom-up." In breadth units, knowledge content is not superimposed but genuinely integrated to deliver a rounded understanding of the topic that is, itself, intimately connected to the wider world. Some of the units that have been and are right now being developed include: Human Rights and Global Justice; Global Food Security; Developing Resilience in the Face of Emergencies; Confronting Sustainability; Asia and Australia: Bound by Sea; Indigenous People of the World; and War: The Moral and Legal Limits of Political Violence. It is clear from this list of units and others like them that there is a fair degree of seriousness about preparing students for lives that, however unfortunately, coincide with what John Cobb has called "the ending of an Age."[17]

Breadth units are compulsory for students commencing the majority of undergraduate degrees on offer from the 2015 academic year. This fact alone is quite an achievement for a science (or might we say perhaps a little more critically, a scientistic) research university focused on disciplines! More than this, however, is another principle that has governed our thinking, and that is the principle of student choice. Whereas a number of universities have addressed the question of preparing students to be "global citizens," they have approached the task by making a very small number of units, two or three at most, compulsory for all students. Tasmania has taken on the yet more difficult task, as will already be apparent, of developing a suite of, we hope in time, around thirty such units for students to choose from. This is so that, while they must study breadth units, they can take units that are of most interest to them, i.e., they can tailor their breadth units to their specialist degree. This renders breadth units relevant to the immediacy of their disciplinary study and their disciplinary study connected to the central challenges of our time.

VI. DEMONSTRATING HOW "AN OVER-VIGOROUS DISCIPLINE . . . IS SO HARMFUL . . . [TO] THE HABIT OF ACTIVE THOUGHT"

A second aspect of Cobb's (2015) argument concerns the way in which the modern research university constrains the capacity of its students to think beyond the confines of the taken-for-granted norms of the discipline in which they study, which is taught by academics who themselves are trained and expert in a narrow field of inquiry intended purposefully to advance the knowledge of the discipline in question. A good example is management, a very young academic discipline. It is characterized by either borrowing bits here and there from other disciplines, or by sticking rigidly to a narrow management literature that forsakes the knowledge of others, hard-won over many centuries. Neither approach gets the discipline very far in terms of the extent to which it is or is not respected by other disciplines within a university.

Furthermore, management is unlike any other practice-based discipline in that it is not respected for what it produces as graduates. Medicine is legitimate in that it produces doctors, law in that it produces lawyers, accounting accountants, divinity clergy, and so on. But management? Everyone's a manager. And, in any case, management practice is about ensuring people leave their brains at home, because brains are the very last things they'll need at work. I am not alone in worrying that our contemporary experience as "knowledge workers" delivering "diverse product packages" to "differentiated market segments" of "discerning learning consumers" reveals the brain to be nothing but a mischievous impediment to daily life...

In management-as-science, knowledge is advanced as it is in many other disciplines, namely by focusing on a narrow range of so-called top-tier journals recognized by business school deans as legitimate and appropriate for academics in business schools to publish in. However, a pause for thought reveals that such focus in fact leads to a very narrow understanding of the topic. It also assumes that the double-blind peer review processes at work in these journals operates with the distanced objective rigor of the equivalent hard science journals. Even assuming the latter do engage in objective review, the reality is that the former do not. It is a game, and if one is on the inside of the system, one's work will be published. If one is not, it won't be.

This is charades: relying on this game for the purpose of an objective demonstration of quality is not credible. Nor will it guarantee that the central issues in management are exclusively and wholly contained in these journals. More than this, the scientific axiology of knowledge advancement, as "witnessed" by and in such an approach to publication, forces the academic to only concern him or herself with what can be published. This is not the same as what is publishable and *should* be published. Some colleagues and I have recently contributed a chapter to a book whose expressed purpose was to publish material on ethical leadership—an entirely worthy topic for serious thought at the ending of an age—that was intentionally radical and thus not publishable in the mainstream journals.[18]

The importance of this point should not be lost, for it bears two significant implications. First, the misunderstanding of the academy that the mainstream is the location of valid ideas and that ideas are valid precisely because they are published in the mainstream produces "a celibacy of the intellect... [in which] the specialized functions of the community are performed better and more progressively, but the generalized direction lacks vision."[19] Second, from this, any discussion of the development of an ecological civilization by its nature requires radical rethinking and re-envisioning of important topics; radical ideas cannot be published in the mainstream.

VII. "STRENGTHENING POWERS IN THE PUPIL" BY "IMPARTING POSSIBILITIES OF MENTAL LIFE" THROUGH PHILOSOPHY OF MANAGEMENT

This problem of fresh thinking being constrained by inadequate freedom is a serious problem in and of itself, but—worse—it extends inexorably to the teaching of students.[20] If they are only exposed to the mainstream ideas in the discipline, as presented through the top tier mainstream journals, by academics trained to think that only ideas in those journal are worthwhile (by dint of their publication therein), then not only will the topics of their thinking be constrained by the reductionistic scientific mode of modern thought, but what they are *allowed* to think in the classroom will be so constrained. Of course, the scientific method will also preclude other *ways* of thinking; it "restrains serious thought within the groove."[21] In sum, much management education, as an example of much social science education, is concerned with, to paraphrase Whitehead, the packing of content into the minds of the students coupled with the expectation of a regurgitation of the same content onto the exam page to demonstrate the student's mastery of the discipline.[22] The art of business is such that the leaders of companies must be capable of independent thought; it follows that mainstream management education is highly unlikely to produce good managers. It only produces good employees if the leaders of companies want unthinking people, but at the interstices of epochs when robots are taking much unthinking employment away from human beings, opportunities will exist only for those who can think for themselves.

Of course, management education must at the very least provide students with the opportunity to learn content about management, and learn how to provide answers to practical management issues. For civilization at the ending of an age, however, it must move beyond this, to provide students with the opportunity to question, to think for themselves, to discern their own ways of being. In other words, it must expose students not only to a scientific mode of inquiry focused on the search for objective facts and answers, it must also allow students the opportunity to experience a philosophical mode of inquiry focused on the development of subjective questions, the comprehension of values, and the discernment of truths with which to navigate one's way through management as a personal experience. A manager who is not true to her or his own values is quickly "seen through" by the employees of today. It is difficult to be true to one's own values if one is not aware of them. Which is to say, "the type of generality which above all is wanted is the appreciation of the variety of value"[23] such that ultimate values are not merely "politely bowed to and then handed over to the clergy to be kept for Sunday."[24] Values are fundamental to a constructive postmodern education.

How might one then engage students in the study of management in such a way that they are freed from the expectation to learn the content of management and given the wherewithal to think about management in terms not of science but of art? How can we "strengthen habits... of enjoying vivid values"?[25] The first step is to start out purposefully with a mode of inquiry different from the scientific, answer-driven approaches adopted in most other units in the curriculum by introducing students to a philosophical questioning mode of inquiry.[26] This allows them to rethink material already learnt in a different way, to shed light on core issues in management practice, such as leadership, ethics, management knowledge, the nature of management itself, and the question of organization. Each of these topics and more are dealt with through the application of topics central to philosophy, such as ontology, epistemology, philosophy of mind, and philosophical ethics (as opposed to "Corporate Social Responsibility" and "Business Ethics"). The focus is on the development of active and purposeful thinking and the questioning of taken-for-granted understanding as a practical managerial resource.

The second step is to approach the delivery of the unit purely as seminars in which it is stated and repeated that each seminar group will take the discussion of whichever topic moves the discussion forward in quite different ways to any other group, and that this is perfectly fine; no discussion is to be regarded as definitive and "right," and other discussions thus "wrong." Furthermore, each individual in the group must be reassured that there are no pre-set outcomes or destinations that she is expected to arrive at; each student's journey through the unit is their own, their destinations are each their own, and this is fine and proper. Taken together, these two reassurances allow the individual student and the collective seminar group to feel safe to ask questions, safe to explore topics as the ideas come to them. Over the duration of the unit, the professor's role changes from instigator to co-participant in what becomes genuinely practical philosophical discussion. In seminars of this type, philosophy of management is not studied, it is practiced.

VIII. "YOU CAN STUDY PHILOSOPHY, BUT STUDYING PHILOSOPHY IS QUITE DIFFERENT FROM . . . *SAYING* IT" [27]

Doing philosophy of management in the classroom, encouraging students to be ones who say it, almost from the beginning, does require they study the work of philosophers beforehand. Within the first fortnight, students are given early passages of Heidegger's "What is Called Thinking?" (1976) to read at home along with a series of questions to consider by way of supporting them as they read. Of course this naturally encourages them to see thinking as an important topic, which they have never thought about, and, eventually through the seminar conversations, they begin to learn how to think purposefully and actively, rather than passively. They begin to be able to use their thinking as a tool of inquiry; they drive their own thinking, rather than being led by it. The realization not only that this is possible but that, having made the transition from passive to active thought, they can then meaningfully inquire about management *for themselves*, is a joy to behold.

At this point, Whitehead's thought is introduced to show how, as managers, it is not what happens to them that counts but rather more what they make of what happens for themselves and others. In Whiteheadian terms, this is about rendering the internal relation of constructive postmodern thought as primary over the external relation that dominates even so-called process thinking in modern and deconstructive postmodern thought.[28] In other words, that they, as *human becomings*, can positively shape the world around them as managers in a world that is not pre-determined but is instead open, internally connected, fully relational, and ever-evolving. Being released from the three combined tyrannies of a) pressing for answers; b) feeling a profound separation from people and nature (not least because the taken-for-granted understanding of coercive, externally imposed power is one of the mainstays of traditional management thought and practice); and c) the demand for pre-defined content knowledge is a profound experience!

The resulting freedom of mind allows the fresh thinking necessary for questioning to really begin. Here, as Moore notes, "learning concerns asking hard questions and then . . . search[ing] in unexpected places for lost and neglected traditions" of thought.[29] The insights thereby arise from the seminar conversation — from the thinking of the students themselves. Instrumental economistic judgments — Management as Object — are soon left behind and replaced by a discussion of personal values. Even love, understood as meaning "to act intentionally as sympathetic response to others (including God), to promote overall wellbeing becomes a legitimate topic of discussion."[30] The only interjection occasionally necessary is "Okay, having thought about this philosophical topic, how can that thinking be turned to the reality of being a manager, be applied to management?' Soon, even this interjection is not necessary. One example of the insights that arise is the understanding that, when the mainstream management literature argues super-efficiency just precisely *is* effectiveness, the two can be meaningfully distinguished using process thought.

This yields an appreciation that a focus on efficient causation leads to a constrained, and entirely unnatural emphasis on fully determined happenings, whereas effective causation yields a self-supporting inherent freedom of perpetual creativity. Using Whiteheadian process thinking, effectiveness can therefore be understood as quite different from efficiency, a distinction of immense importance for the mid-21st century when resilient, resourceful, and ecological regenerative communities must replace the delicate, dependent, and ecological depletive ones of today. A second example is an appreciation that business ethics as practiced by most businesses is the expedient use of ethical arguments to justify business growth; it has little, if anything, to do with moral philosophy. Most particularly, as Cobb notes, the significance of truth as correspondence is revealed.[31] Through application to management, the insight that modern business has done remarkable damage to the biosphere and to civilization soon becomes apparent, not by having been externally imposed but instead by becoming internally revealed.

More broadly, the students now own the unit, making of it what they wish, co-creating new personal understanding of what it means to experience managing as subject by doing applied philosophy — and even occasionally applied process thought! The professor now becomes the student, witnessing philosophers of management at work, i.e., young people able to use their new capacity for real thoughtfulness to change management practice away from profit towards human value, away from the growth of economy as primary and towards the growth of society as naturally connected civilization. The final task of the professor at the conclusion of such a unit is simply to encourage students not just to practice their newly learned active, serious-minded, hard-core, thoroughgoing thinking—what I describe as "capital-T" Thinking—in their future management roles. In other words, they can Think beyond economism. They can also enjoy Thinking as a pastime, as an active leisure activity rather than an "iron-bound trivial amusement."[32] There are surely few greater pleasures in the art of life.

IX. FINDINGS AND CONCLUSIONS: "ERADICATING THE FATAL DISCONNECTION OF INTELLECTUAL MINUETS"

In respect of breadth units at the University of Tasmania, they are presently designed largely for first year undergraduates, to provide students at the beginning of their university experience with an understanding about what is going on in the world *as primary*, as they embark on the study of disciplines and what goes on in them.[33] We have found breadth units to be doubly genuine. That is to say, they are genuinely transdisciplinary and focused on a problem of world significance, and they can, if the student chooses, genuinely inform, ground, and locate her particular study of a special discipline. The response of students when first faced with the reality of having to take breadth units was to argue against the need on the grounds they had come to the university to study their chosen subject and that alone. Having experienced breadth units, however, the response has changed to a genuine enjoyment and appreciation for their need and a recognition not least of the value inherent in studying with students not just from their own individual faculties but from across the university. Students are yearning for the opportunity to think holistically about the central issues of our time.

Another benefit has been that the design of the units has brought staff from multiple faculties together, with similar positive responses and recognition, even, of shared research opportunities that would not otherwise have been possible. It seems even academics trained and socialized by their training into science will recognize and grasp the intellectual opportunity for "the interchange of ideas."[34] In the cases of both the students and the staff, disciplinary boundaries are beginning to break down. The university is slowly ceasing to be a silo-ity and is gradually becoming a universe-ity, to the benefit of all. This approach to integrating transdisciplinarity into the curriculum does not deny the reality of disciplinization in the research university, but it does seek to ground it in the problems of the crisis we face. In some small way, therefore, breadth units can help to overcome the tendency of producing experts who "contribute more to leading the world to catastrophe" and instead can fasten in the mind of the student and the graduate the need to "steer it away" from catastrophe.[35]

In respect of Philosophy of Management as a third year "capstone unit" in the Business School, we have found the students quickly see the value of it and have said so most emphatically in official student feedback. Here are some examples, each quote being from a different student: "This is one of the most enjoyable units I have undertaken in my degree. The philosophical approach to management is refreshing and thought-provoking"; "I really enjoyed the unit as it was very different to the standard teaching approach. I also feel as if I have learnt a lot and that I have found a new perspective on management"; "there is no right or wrong answer while doing this unit, it is the way we think, it is about inspiration and innovation"; "this subject was extremely helpful in making me think deeply about organizations and my perceptions of them. I thoroughly enjoyed [this] way of teaching and found [it] very engaging"; "at first I was a little hesitant as to the structuring around this unit, as all other classes have theory you must know. This course was all about asking the appropriate questions and thinking about why I'm asking them"; and "the [seminars] were brilliant as [we] put the questions out there [and although] at times it was awkward thinking about the questions [...] this type of tutorial environment was very beneficial and after a few tutorials the thinking process started to occur naturally. This course is a must for any management student."

As the lecturer, what am I to make of this feedback? At minimum, I am confident that (once they realize it is possible) even management students thirst for the opportunity to arrive at their own properly thought-through convictions. From the perspective of the wider business curriculum, at the very least other staff recognize the inherent worth of giving students an opportunity to revisit topics they have covered previously with a fresh eye and a different approach, for this is understood to embed learning. Overall, this is to suggest that a speculative philosophical inquiry is required for us to grapple with the implications both of what lies ahead of us, and how humanity will need to respond if it is navigate its way towards a more ecologically sound and connected civilization.

This is particularly the case for management. Unlike any other academic discipline, perhaps with the exception of law (which creates its own reality in the legislation), management is almost uniquely concerned with how to use that knowledge to change reality. To offer but one example, an environmental scientist who ceases to be interested in measuring environmental degradation and instead wishes to act to change and arrest it is no longer engaged in environmental science but environmental *management*. More than this, of course, management is in and of the mind; the arguments and actions managers make and take arise from often thoughtless consideration of the need for profit alone. For a constructive postmodern civilization, thoughtful consideration of the fundamental interrelatedness of ourselves as part of nature is imperative. We need to civilize not just higher education in general but management education in particular. Perhaps the foregoing suggests that it is possible.

By way of a conclusion, what I have hoped to show in this chapter is that for all their problems, research universities can create such opportunities without losing sight of what they — and I purposefully use the term — value, if such education can be worked into and be seen to contribute towards the teaching that is carried out in the disciplines. It is amazing what students can think when — with just a little help from Heidegger — they are first shown what Thinking is and then encouraged *how* by Whitehead's speculative philosophy. This tells us that the way to Think about the central issues of our time does exist, both in the general as well as in the particular case of management and its impact. But it is not the scientific way. The science disciplines of the research universities do not provide a universal panacea. Far from it. As John Cobb rightly notes, through their deeply Cartesian approach to knowledge and understanding, they cause at the least as many problems as they solve.[36]

In this, however, I do not mean to say that the liberal arts college, or its modern equivalent such as the thoroughly ecologically oriented and excellent Schumacher College in the UK, is not necessary. Rather, I suspect that as research universities come under increasing pressure to produce graduates who can genuinely and meaningfully contribute to business and society, their curricula may become more like liberal arts colleges of old. This is indubitably the way the University of Tasmania is inexorably and intentionally — if slowly; there is much resistance — moving. It seems clear, therefore, that intellectual modes of thought can at least be used *alongside* the scientific in a research university, and students can have access to the sort of value-laden education required for the transition to an ecological civilization.

My point is that a philosophy concerned with enabling speculative, questioning Thought in and by the student as the citizen of the future is not just a practical subject. For those of us faced with the task of bringing — and I will use the phrase now — thoroughly wicked problems to the attention of future generations, it is *the* practical subject for a civilizing education.

NOTES

1   John Cobb, "The Anti-Intellectualism of the American University" *Soundings* 98, no. 2 (2015): 219; Alfred North Whitehead, *Science and the Modern World* (Cambridge: Cambridge University Press, 1925).

2   Vandana Shiva, *Introduction to Inspired by Schumacher College: a Film,* 2013.

3   Cobb, "The Anti-Intellectualism of the American University," 232.

4   Henry Wyman Holmes, "Whitehead's View on Education" in *The Philosophy of Alfred North Whitehead,* ed. Paul Arthur Schilpp (La Salle: Open Court, 1941), 626.

5   Ibid., 632.

6   Alfred North Whitehead, *Whitehead's American Essays in Social Philosophy,* ed. A.H. Johnson (New York: Harper and Brothers, 1959), 63–4.

7   Cobb, "The Anti-Intellectualism of the American University," 224.

8   Whitehead, "The Study of the Past — Its Uses and Its Dangers," *Harvard Business Review* 11 (1933).

9   Cobb, *Spiritual Bankruptcy* (Nashville: Abingdon Press, 2010), 107–124.

10 Cobb, "The Anti-Intellectualism of the American University," 224.

11 Thor Heyerdahl, *Kon-Tiki: Across the Pacific by Raft* (New York: Pocket Books, 1984).

12 Whitehead, *The Philosophy of Alfred North Whitehead,* ed. Paul Arthur Schilpp (La Salle: Open Court, 1941), 700.

13 Speech delivered at the American Academy of Religion Special Symposium, 2014.

14 Nicolescu, *The Manifesto of Transdisciplinarity* (Albany: SUNY Press); also <http://inters.org/Freitas-Morin-Nicolescu-Transdisciplinarity>.

15 It should be noted that the word transdisciplinary is not used at the university, for fear of it creating the impression we mean "beyond" discipline. Instead, a refinement to the meaning of inter-disciplinary has been adopted, to mean not "between" but instead "across".

16 Cobb, *Spiritual Bankruptcy,* 92–97.

17 Introduction to this volume, part of the Toward Ecological Civilization Series.

18 Mark Dibben et al, "Rethinking Ethical Leadership Using Process Metaphysics," in *Radical Thoughts on Ethical Leadership,* ed. R. Giacalone and C. Jurkiewicz (Charlotte: Information Age Publishing, 2016).

19 Whitehead, *Science and the Modern World,* 245.

20 Mary Elizabeth Moore, *Teaching from the Heart: Theology and Educational Method* (Harrisburg: Trinity Press International, 1991), 147.

21 Whitehead, *Science and the Modern World,* 245.

22 Whitehead, *The Aims of Education and Other Essays* (New York: The Free Press, 1967), 33.

23 Whitehead, *Science and the Modern World,* 248.

24 Ibid., 252.

25 Ibid., 24–28.

26   Paul Griseri, *An Introduction to the Philosophy of Management* (London: Sage, 2013); Griseri is the Managing Editor of the journal *Philosophy of Management* (Springer Verlag, Holland). My Philosophy of Management unit is—with his permission—essentially Paul's University of Middlesex (London) unit of the same name, which he turned into the textbook I use; we work together in developing the two units and comparing student performance, which interestingly is near identical.

27   Cobb in conversation, American Academy of Religion Symposium, 2014.

28   David Ray Griffin, *Unsnarling the World-Knot: Consciousness, Freedom, and the Mind-Body Problem* (Berkeley: University of California Press, 2008); *The Re-Enchantment of Science,* ed. (Albany: SUNY Press, 1988.)

29   Moore, *Teaching as a Sacramental Act* (Cleveland: The Pilgrim Press, 2004), 109.

30   Thomas Jay Oord, *Defining Love: a Philosophical, Scientific, and Theological Engagement* (Ada: Brazos press, 2010), 29.

31   Cobb, "The Anti-Intellectualism of the American University," 228.

32   Whitehead, "The Study of the Past – Its Uses and Its Dangers."

33   For more information on the arguments that have been developed to demonstrate the importance of breadth units to students, as well as access to approved units and their descriptions see: <http://www.utas.edu.au/dvc-students-education/introduction/breadth-units>. For more information on the breadth unit proposal and financing process, as well as the incentive measures established by the Deputy Vice Chancellor, Students and Education, see: <http://www.utas.edu.au/students/breadth-units>. Both of these websites are in the public domain.

34   Cobb, "The Anti-Intellectualism of the American University," 223.

35   Ibid., 232.

36   Cobb, "The Anti-Intellectualism of the American University."

10. LIBERAL EDUCATION AS A COUNTER-HEGEMONIC MOVEMENT

Vandana Pednekar-Magal

ABSTRACT: *Higher education has responded to economic and cultural globalization; nevertheless, it has largely ignored the disruptions and discontents of globalized society. Inspired by the "Seizing an Alternative" theme of the 2015 Whitehead conference, this paper observes that higher education, particularly liberal education, should be attentive to the full gamut of human experience and address the needs of global civilization.*

OVER ROUGHLY THE PAST TWO DECADES, higher education—predominantly in advanced, but also in emerging economies—has responded to two societal trends. First, universities have adjusted to the progression from a post- industrial to a "knowledge society." Knowledge is considered as a resource—vital, at that, and regularly produced for application in industry and economic growth. Second, higher education has adapted to the transition from national to post-national or global society. Globalization is highly evident in the academy in terms of foreign students, international faculty, and curriculum content. In fact, universities promote these developments as their "relevance" credentials.

And yet there is a dark side to globalization. The hegemonic forces of globalization are the source of untold difficulties for the fragile economies of developing countries, causing destruction of the environment and native cultures and deepening the poverty and isolation of the poor across the globe.[1] Particularly, globalization undermines traditional societies by generating the cultural chaos that results when thousand-year old cultures are expected to modernize/Westernize within decades. We are indeed in the throes of "reflexive modernization,"[2] "world risk society," a "post" postmodernity, facing the consequences of the success of modernization and techno-economic development. In this condition, as Roland Robertson has argued, the local and the global are not mutually exclusive.[3] The breakdown and disruption of globalization can be grasped only when we consider its particular effects on the "local," as in the politics of cultural difference, cultural homogeneity, ethnicity, race, and gender. In other words, the risks of globalization are experienced at a local level, much as a devastating local conflict can be experienced globally—think of refugees fleeing a conflict and the crisis of migration across countries.

Higher education has, for the most part, been blind to the discontents of globalization. In this essay, I argue that higher education, especially that type of higher education commonly referred to as liberal arts education or, more simply, liberal education, should be attentive to these aspects of globalization and yet be local, diversified, and grounded in a specific cultural tradition. Further, a greater emphasis should be placed on what Nussbaum has called *cultivating humanity* as distinct from training workers.[4] Institutions of higher education around the world need to disentangle themselves from the logic of market globalization and become deeply attentive to the full gamut of human experience. Education must address the needs of global civilization, rather than the needs of the global economy. I refer to examples from India (a country I am most familiar with), where such efforts are under way.

HIGHER EDUCATION AND RELEVANCE

While the definition of a knowledge society is contested (which type of knowledge?) there is a general agreement that we are in the midst of a time where knowledge is acquired, created, disseminated, and applied in various fields for economic and national development.[5] This discursive definition has received large-scale endorsement of knowledge understood as scientific, technical, and with a potential for innovation and application in the development of the material advancement of society. National governments in advanced as well as developing economies have increasingly considered knowledge as an adjunct of national policy, particularly of economic growth. Universities pressured by politicians, business leaders, and pundits have appropriated this definition. Indeed, universities now claim their relevance in these very terms of creating knowledge useful for business and the economy. The argument is more straightforward to make for the teaching of so-called STEM subjects: science, technology, engineering, and mathematics; although academic departments such as sociology, psychology, communications, hitherto protected from the imperatives of economic development, have lately begun to claim relevance for being useful to business and society.[6]

University research, too, has responded to the pressures of relevance as acquiring funds becomes much more competitive. For example, research grants proposals need to specify how the results would directly apply in social contexts. Indeed, "scholarship of discovery" has less currency. It's not hard to see that in light of mounting competition for state resources, rising tuition costs, and the fact that national policy diverts resources towards more utilitarian areas of education, universities have shifted towards enhancing their utilitarian credentials.

GLOBALIZATION

While there are many perspectives about the nature of globalization, there is a general agreement that we are in the midst of, as Rosenau has described, a *polycentric world.*[7] Communication and transportation technologies have diminished geographical and social distances, moving ideas, people, and goods across space and time as never before. Consequently, we experience globalization through internationalization of organizations (Apple Inc., World Bank, even drug cartels). Corporations have been at the frontier of this process as they deploy production, marketing units, and labor across several countries (as cost- and tax-saving measures). Problems are increasingly global (climate change, ethnic conflicts, currency crises); structures flow across borders (forms of work through outsourcing, banking, and financial flows). This context of new density of international ties of dependence has created a compelling argument that the globalized economy necessitates an internationally and inter-culturally competent workforce. The argument gathered much currency in the academe.

Universities and colleges have responded actively with making campuses more international. They vigorously recruit international students (some of this is self-serving, as universities expand markets for tuition-paying students) as well as faculty and staff. Nearly every campus in the U.S. and other advanced economies invests in cross-border partnerships for study-abroad programs. Students are encouraged to travel and take courses in a foreign country. Universities have availed themselves of various programs funded by the state, as well as by such private foundations as the Fulbright Foundation and the Carnegie Mellon Foundation, which encourage student-exchange as well as faculty-exchange programs. While these funds (particularly government funds) have been granted as part of wider public diplomacy programs, universities have nevertheless utilized them and broadened their curricula with foreign language studies, international studies, and cultural competence or cultural awareness programs. Universities support their faculty's collaborative research with scholars and scholarly communities across borders. Such connections are in any case made possible with new, emerging technologies. Indeed, many universities and colleges have added the concept of internationalization to their mission statements.[8]

It is worth pointing out that higher education's alignment with internationalization is, yet again, underlined by the dominant discourse of economic globalization. It is predominantly conceived in utilitarian relationship with productivity and economic development. This notion of higher education as closely tied to economic growth is now prevalent across the globe, particularly in nations that have emerged out of the "development" stage in material measures (per capita income, GNP) and are competing with advanced economies; India for example.

CULTURAL TURBULENCE: PARADOXES OF GLOBALIZATION

I revert here to Beck's notion of world risk society and the arguments that refer to globalism's discontents.[9] Beck points to the larger economic and cultural turmoil, the macro-level crises that come with globalization, as the "bad" side of the "good": ecological destruction and technological industrial dangers caused by the very forces that bring us prosperity and material advancement; the capricious consequences of genetic engineering that assures food self-sufficiency in developing countries; the depletion of tropical rainforests; and weapons of mass destruction created by states for state use, yet available to private individuals and organizations as a means of exerting political threats, among other issues. These are dangers that result from a context of modernization, but individual countries lack the institutional and political means to ward off the threat of destruction. The other kinds of crises are at micro-level, or localized threats that are nevertheless experienced globally. Beck suggests that these publicly discussed dangers constitute a kind of "negative currency": "Coins that no one wants but find their way in nevertheless, compel people's attention, confuse and subvert. They turn upside down precisely what appeared to be solidly anchored in everyday normality."[10]

Indeed, implicit in much of the current discourse on globalization as we experience it today is the "natural" or inevitable consequence of exogenously determined technologies of communication and transportation. Beck sees these consequences as "threats to civilization" that may be faced as a result of scientific-industrial decisions, yet he asserts that they are really the result of "human decisions." In that, Beck and others effectively argue for immense possibilities for change, an alternative paradigm of globalization through countering these discourses.[11] The thwarting of these market discourses is played out in the quotidian struggles for dignity and economic security, as well as in the recent social movements across the globe that bring these impending threats into sharp focus in the global public sphere.

In the past few years, a number of social movements have transfixed the world: thousands taking to the streets of Tunisia demanding freedom and democracy; the struggle over urban green spaces in Turkey; waves of protestors calling for educational rights in Spain and Chile; Occupy Wall Street and the heightened attention it provided to economic inequities; and the waves of protests over racial injustice in the U.S. These movements are indicative of a new era of social action and a call for reform in the wake of failures (a breakdown, if you will) of economic and political institutions. The protesters in many ways underscored that the growth of transnational connections can potentially be harnessed in the service of sustainable ecological practices, equitable distribution of wealth, basic rights of dignity, and equal opportunities. These are urgent issues of our time, even when they are very much rooted in human history. These movements signify a shift, a clamoring to change the dominant social paradigms. Universities need to respond to this shift and not remain mesmerized in shortsighted focus on economy and profitability and its utilitarian relevance.

Here I offer as a case a particularly significant social protest that erupted following a horrific incident of crime in India. The protest shot into the public debate facets of an endemic malaise that exists in modern India. Features of this case offer remarkable insight into the critical role of education in society.

On December 16, 2002, a 23-year-old female psychotherapy student was violently raped on a moving public transport bus in Delhi and died of horrific internal injuries a few days later. She had been to see a film, *Life of Pi*, with a male friend. At 8:30 PM they boarded an off-duty bus with six men on board, five adults and a juvenile. The men beat the woman's friend and each raped the woman in turn before assaulting her viciously with an iron instrument.

Leslee Udwin, a British filmmaker who made a documentary based on interviews with the convicted perpetrators and the lawyers of the defendants, (and she echoes Hannah Arendt's "banality of evil,") said this about the convicted men:

> The horrifying details of the rape had led me to expect deranged monsters, psychopaths. The truth was far from chilling. These were ordinary, apparently normal and certainly unremarkable men.[12]

In the film, Udwin documents the comments of one of the attackers:

A decent girl won't roam around at nine o'clock at night. A girl is far more responsible for rape than a boy... Housework and housekeeping is for girls not roaming in discos and bars at night doing wrong things, wearing wrong clothes. About 20 percent of girls are good... People had a right to teach them a lesson... When being raped, she shouldn't fight back. She should be silent and allow the rape. Then they'd have dropped her off after doing her and only hit the boy.[13]

Clearly, any remorse was absent. In fact, the man was affirming his actions as aligned to some distorted cultural context that in his view bestowed a right to the brutal atrocity.

A collision took place on that bus—of two worlds in one country. One India, the beneficiary of the modern global economy, was embodied by the woman, who had found imagination, freedom, and opportunity to better her life. She had moved from a humble home in the rural outskirts of the big city, enabled by a family that valued education and saved enough to send her to a college in the city.[14] The path of progress that modernization promises evidently inspired her. The men who committed the crime were marooned in the opposite world, the other India, where modernization and urbanization are a source of chaos with no gain except low-wage employment in the city and a dead-end life. They were of a class of men, also from rural India, who come to the city as young boys for subsistence work, and who stay on for mere daily wages, living with throngs of other men in makeshift tenements. These men are trapped in a loop of, to use Appadurai's phrase, fractured deterritorialization; dislocated, and disconnected from all social institutions—family, traditions, and polity—and unaware of their role or ties to society, the nation, and its democracy.[15] They were men with no introspection, who were never made to think or reflect. With no useful reference for moral guidance, they tend to fall back on the distorted clichés they have gathered in their vapid world. It is not hard to see the contradictory meanings of globalization and modernization as they play out at the local levels.

Of course, it is true that not all those deprived of opportunities buckle under the strain of poverty and revert to violence. There are many who do live noble lives in the face of hurt. In fact, it is certainly the case that success does not assure a life of thought and reflection. Consider the interview excerpts of the lawyers who defended the convicts in this case:

> In our society we never allow our girls to come out from the house after 6:30 or 7:30 or 8:30 in the evening with an unknown person... You are talking about man and woman as friends. Sorry, that does not have any place in our society. We have the best culture. In our culture there is no place for a woman.[16]

Another lawyer, A.P. Singh said this:

> If my daughter or sister engaged in pre-marital activities and disgraced herself and allowed herself to lose face and character by doing such things I would most certainly take this sort of sister or daughter to my farmhouse, and in front of my entire family, I would put petrol on her and set her alight.[17]

Indeed, dousing young new brides with petrol to burn and kill, whether its called "dowry death" or "honor killing," along with female infanticide and child marriage, are endemic practices perpetuated by unthinking men (and in some cases supported by women) whose "obtuseness and ignorance," to use Martha Nussbaum's phrase, seldom gets examined or questioned. Social institutions, both economic and political, in India (as in many other parts of the world) have ignored this distortion as they employ armies of men who are needed either as cheap labor or a "voter bank." Religion, too, has failed, with spiritual traditions such as self-realization through meditation and learning from the scriptures being replaced by blind faith, the building of monumental temples by self-serving groups, and engagement in grand rituals that are disconnected with the "inner life." The fact that the lawyers, who earned a law degree at a university, could so casually voice those shockingly violent thoughts against women reveals an alarming disconnect between a university degree and education.

Following the horrific incident in Delhi, protests erupted in all parts of India—in cities as well as small towns across the nation. The protestors included university students, housewives, young urban profes- sional, and women working as domestic help. These protests discursively launched against the failures and inaction of the state (police apathy towards gender violence, weak laws) yet they also were a plea to social institutions—to become attentive to these challenges of modern India.

As Udwin recalls in an interview with BBC News:

They [the protestors] braved a freezing December and a ferocious government crackdown of water cannons, baton charges, and teargas shells. Their courage to be heard was extraordinarily inspiring.[18]

Many nations today are concurrently successful and unsuccessful—affluent and imaginative as well as mired in desperation and deprivation. Consider the rich and poor people in regions of the United States or France. Zygmunt Bauman's important 1998 argument about globalization points to the polarization of rich and poor on a world scale. Yet the First World is contained in the Third World and Fourth World. They cannot be identified as the North and South or, to use Wallerstein's terms, as Center—advanced economies, or rich countries—and Periphery—backward economies due to colonization, or poor countries. In the globalized world, both conflict with each other in a variety of "hybrid relationships" and are contained inside a nation.

It is the moral challenge of our times to acquaint the two nations within the nation; to pay attention to the ills in order to rehabilitate and renew. In this project, higher education needs to urgently engage in that counter-hegemonic project to challenge the privileging of utilitarian pre-professional education and become attentive to education for the mind; to, in the words of Martha Nussbaum, *cultivate humanity* in that humans create ties of recognition and concern with each other, see themselves as citizens, but beyond that also empathize with each other. These are some of the basic tenets of a liberal education that have new urgency in every national society.

I use the phrase *counter-hegemonic* to draw a parallel between social movements aimed at countering dominant practices, and institutional power structures known to perpetuate marginalization, exploitation, and, often, violence. For examples, women's movements, environmental movements, or struggles for sustainable development across the world are efforts to transfigure dominant practices and effect social change. These efforts begin at a local level, within a given cultural context, are varied in their strategies and yet, due to their solidarity with similar struggles across the globe, magnify their power. I suggest that reform and reconstruction in education should be, similarly, local, pluralistic, diversified, and grounded in specific cultural traditions—opening up cultural spaces that are closed up due to the totalizing effect of utilitarian techno-economic Western-style education. There is, in fact, a long history of such movements.

Consider an example: *Gurukul Kangri Vishwavidyala,* a university near New Delhi established in 1902. In 1922 it extended education to women on two campuses in the region. The university's ideological foundations are rooted in the discourse of resistance to the hegemonic Western education of colonial India. The institution's aim was to preserve the ancient *Gurukul,* also known as *Guru-Shishya,* or teacher-disciple system wherein scholar teachers, learned men and women, or eminent artists, accepted disciples with whom they shared an everyday life of learning and work in an *ashram*—a spiritual hermitage, a Hindu monastery. Here the scholar, teacher, or artist would impart specialized knowledge and simultaneously, through meaningful interactions in daily life, provide guidance on moral, spiritual, and religious matters. At the end of their term as disciples (typically ten to fourteen years), the disciples become practitioners, as well as teachers.

This system was the locus of education in the arts, humanities, metaphysics, and physical sciences. During colonial times in India, under the stewardship of Lord Babington Macaulay (the British Secretary of War and a historian), the English language and mass education in classroom settings were imposed via the English Education Act of 1835.[19] While the Western system took hold due to massive funding and mandatory training of teachers in English, many Indian scholars resisted this mass-education system; consequently, the *Gurukul* system, rooted in the pluralistic traditions of multi-lingual India, continued and survived, especially in the performing arts, until the mid-20th century.

Gurukul Kangri Vishwavidyala is an acknowledged institution that continues to emphasize teachings of the primary texts of Indian philosophy and ancient and modern literature, along with a modern science and technology curriculum.

A newer institution emblematic of a counter-hegemonic movement in education is Swaraj University near the city of Udaipur in India. The institution emphasizes *Shiksha*, loosely translated as "education," which is rooted in the idea of individual growth through interaction with nature and fellow human beings. It was founded as *Shikshantar Andolan*, a Hindi phrase that again loosely translats as reform in education. The subjects of study, pedagogy, and teaching philosophy are all grounded in the idea of self-directed learning (students are called a "Khojis"—seekers of knowledge), with the help of a mentor or friend. Instruction is in Hindi, the regional language, and so maintains a connectedness with local culture and the seeker's living and learning community. Students chart out their interests and design their own learning paths.

A statement of Swaraj University's beginnings spells out a scathing criticism of the state of university education in India:

> growing threats to our ecology, disruption of local communities and the rise of global consumerism have made it necessary to question many basic assumptions that have shaped the modern world. We are left with a worldview of society as a great machine whose purpose is to extract and convert natural and human resources like commodities for concentrated profits. As a result today's youth find themselves at a crossroads, not sure of their own ideals and values, or of their identities. Alien and alienating institutions like schools and colleges, the mass media and government promise a successful life but in reality drain their labor and energy and leave them cynical and dependent. The education system has not prepared them to understand their needs, strengths or dreams. Rather, it has urged them to become standardized products designed to fit into techno-industrial molds.[20]

The two universities have different strategies in countering the current education system with effective, local, and relevant alternatives. Yet both seek the goal of transformative liberal education. Such ideas are being realized in many universities around the world. Quest University in British Columbia, for instance, offers an unconventional university administrative and teaching structure for integrative, experiential deep learning.

These efforts reveal that a movement is afoot, and there are possibilities to reconstruct education that are relevant for marginalized groups, communities that are neglected, left behind, or alienated by the crushing force of the needs of a global economy.

Here I offer that innovations and reform in higher education should be further explored with the new tools of our times.

"The world we live in today is characterized by a new role for imagination in social life," Appadurai suggests.[21] He considers the links between the increasing density of media-generated images that surround us and human agency, or individuals defining possibilities. People now imagine a range of "possible lives" from the supply of images available through global media. Yet, this imagination is fabricated by the culture industry and simply refracts from real life, in enticing consumerist forms, a "possible life." My point is to draw attention to the tools and technologies that are appropriated by the global culture industry: contemporary and emerging art forms that use technologies, such as photography, film, video, multimedia or digital storytelling. These are tools of our times but are fundamentally and actively employed in the hegemony of the market (think about advertisements). These technologies instead should be engaged to shape an imagination for alternatives, for social introspection. Take, for example, what Walter Benjamin wrote about the camera:

> By close-ups of the things around us, by focusing on hidden details of familiar objects, by exploring commonplace milieus under the ingenious guidance of the camera, the film, on the one hand, extends our comprehension of the necessities that rule our lives; on the other hand, it manages to assure us of an immense and unexpected field of action. Our taverns and our metropolitan streets, our offices and furnished rooms, our railroad stations and our factories appeared to have us locked up hopelessly. Then came the film and burst this prison-world asunder by the dynamite of the tenth of a second, so that now, in the midst of its far-flung ruins and debris, we calmly and adventurously go traveling.[22]

Technologies are indeed a double-edged sword. "Technologies of freedom," to use So la Pool's phrase,[23] need to be in the purview of liberal education and should be utilized to foster thought, to explore coherence, unity and diversity of cultural meanings, to draw attention to silenced voices and oppositional discourses in society.[24]

I reiterate my point: Our world is defined by dizzying contradictions of global economy, culture, and politics: connection and fragmentation, unification and dislocation. The brutal incident in Delhi I described earlier is symbolic of one of the multiplicity of risks of the society we live in. In this milieu, universities around the world would serve well to disentangle from the logic of the market and become deeply attentive to the full array of human experience.

NOTES

1   Joseph Stiglitz, "Globalism's Discontents," *The American Prospect*, 13, no 1 (2002).

2   Ulrich Beck, "The World Horizon Opens Up: On the Sociology of Globalization," in *What is Globalization?* (Cambridge: Polity Press, 2000), 22–63.

3   Roland Robertson, "Globalization: Time, Space, and Homogeneity-Heterogeneity" in *Global Modernities,* Mike Featherstone, Scott Lash, and Roland Robertson, eds. (London: Sage, 1995), 22–44.

4   Martha Nussbaum, "Liberal Education and Global Community," *Liberal Education* (Winter 2004), <www.aacu.org/libeducation>.

5   John Brennan, "The Academic Professor and Increasing Expectation of Relevance," *Key Challenges to the Academic Profession,* UNESCO Forum on Higher Education Research and Knowledge, <http://portal.unesco.org/education/en/files>.

6   Ibid.

7   James N. Rosenau, *Turbulence in World Politics: A Theory of Change and Continuity* (Princeton: Princeton University Press, 1991).

8   May Hser, "Campus Internalization: A Study of American Universities' Internationalization Efforts," *International Education* 35, no.1 (2005).

9   Beck, "The World Horizon Opens Up"; Stiglitz, "Globalism's Discontents."

10 Beck, "The World Horizon Opens Up," 37.

11 Ibid, 26; also see Peter Evans, "Counterhegemonic Globalization: Transnational Social Movements in the Contemporary Political Economy," *The*

Handbook of Political Sociology: States, Civil Societies and Globalization, Thomas Janoski, ed. (Cambridge: Cambridge University Press, 2005), 655–68.

12   *BBC News Magazine,* March 3, 2014.

13   *India's Daughter,* directed by Leslee Udwin (2014; London: Assassin Films), DVD

14   *BBC News Magazine,* March 3, 2014.

15   Arjun Appadurai, "Disjuncture and Difference in Global Cultural Economy," *Public Culture,* vol. 2 (Durham: Duke University Press, 1990), 1–24.

16   Excerpts from Interview with lawyer M.L. Sharma, BBC News.

17   Ibid.

18   *India's Daughter.*

19   Stephen Evans, "Macaulay's Minutes Revisited: Colonial Language Policy in 19th Century India," *Journal of Multilingual and Multicultural Development.* 23, no. 4 (2002).

20   *"Why Swaraj?"* Swaraj University, swarajuniversity.org.

21   Appadurai, "Disjuncture and Difference in Global Cultural Economy," 5.

22   Walter Benjamin, "The Work of Art in the Age of Mechanical Reproduction," in *Illuminations* (New York: Schocken Books, 1969).

23   Ethiel de So la Pool, *Technologies of Freedom* (Cambridge: Harvard University Press, 1983).

24   Wimal Dissanayake, "Issues in World Cinema," in *World Cinema: Critical Approaches,* John hill and Pamela Gibson, eds. (Oxford: Oxford University Press, 2000).

11. HUMANITIES ENTREPRENEURSHIP

Abigail Dehart & Joseph Hogan

ABSTRACT: *It is no mystery that the humanities are in crisis and in need of a new defense. Regularly cited causes of the crisis are the dominance of STEM, the anti-intellectualism of university administrations, and so on. This paper argues that working scholars in the humanities are partly to blame, for they often fail to produce a convincing account of the worth of their disciplines that engages students' imaginations or allays their immediate (and very real) concerns about economic well-being after graduation. This paper examines some of the historical underpinnings of this alleged crisis, engages with one aspect of its development in the academy, and proposes a solution: "Humanities Entrepreneurship," or a method of doing the humanities that engages deeply, creatively, and entrepreneurially with the world. It details the historically recent divide between economics and the humanities, ending with the rising tendency of humanities scholars to distance themselves from the economic world in reaction against the perceived need to prove "marketable." The authors argue that in order for the humanities to thrive in the 21ˢᵗ century, humanists must engage deeply and creatively with the economic world.*

I F THE PRESENT ACADEMIC PARADIGM is truly oriented toward "inter-disciplinarity," as one so often hears, then it should make little sense why only one question seems to draw the immediate and vigorous attention of humanities scholars from all disciplines: whether, that is, the humanities are in "crisis" and in need of substantial reform. Then again, paradoxical as it may seem, the situation should not be surprising—after all, the question applies equally to literature professors as to philosophy professors, historians as to classicists. Indeed, the crisis is one of broad "institutional legitimacy," as Louis Menand characterizes.[1] Why can't humanities scholars in general convince a critical mass of incoming freshmen—to say nothing of university administrations, Congress, or the general culture—that their disciplines are worth significant intellectual, social, and financial investment?

Anxiety about this crisis has been an interdisciplinary phenomenon; it has raised, and continues to raise, serious questions about the future of a number of disciplines. Classics and art history professors must wonder whether there will be enough incoming students interested in Sappho or Rembrandt to justify, at least for administrations, the maintenance of their typically small programs.[2] Scholars and culture critics rightly see trouble ahead if enrollment does not increase; they are certainly justified in thinking, as they often do, about why the majority of students don't consider majoring in the humanities to begin with.

But what of the students who *do* decide—whether out of passion, a sense of vocation, or on the off chance of inheriting a fortune someday—to major in the humanities? As recent humanities undergraduates, we can attest to the fact that most of our peers, from third-year undergraduates to fifth-year doctoral candidates, do, in fact, know that the disciplines they hope to enter—more importantly, the disciplines they intend to commit their lives to—are in crisis. How could they not? Any Google search of "the humanities" unleashes an avalanche of books and articles attempting to prove or disprove, bemoan or dismiss, this crisis. Often, these articles have the tone of a funeral dirge: titles such as "Who Ruined the Humanities" and "The Death of the Humanities" are, though certainly grim, all too common to shock or offend.[3] In fact, as early as 2003, *The New Republic* had already committed a webpage, "Humanities Deathwatch," to the discussion of whether this crisis might, in fact, be lethal.[4] Such articles and forums, so often authored by working humanities scholars themselves, hardly inspire in young humanists any sort of *joie de vivre* or professional optimism. After all, these young scholars' apparently parlous career choice has already been met with everything between incredulity and reproach from outsiders.

The ubiquitous concern of a generation of aspiring scholars — indeed, our generation — is that we may very well inherit a crisis even larger than the one presently at hand. To be sure, humanities professors today face a crisis of *institutional* legitimacy — on the line is, as Menand suggests, the opinion of the public, as well as of university administrations and scholars in other disciplines, about the social value of the humanities.[5] But if the current professoriate does not take real steps to address and alleviate this problem, the next generation of scholars will inherit not just an institutional crisis, but, in the worst cases, an existential one. That is to say, every aspiring humanities professor currently in her second or third year of undergraduate study would not be out of bounds in asking herself: will the discipline I've chosen exist at enough universities for me to expect any work out of graduate school? The answer to this question has a direct bearing on whether or not she will be able to live a life committed in any meaningful sense to her field of study. It is clear that, to our generation, the necessity to seize an alternative to the current model of teaching, studying, and promoting the humanities is of existential importance.

But to properly seize this alternative, we need to know the root of the problem. Many readers will of course be familiar with this or that explanation of the crisis in the humanities. It might be best, at this point, to summarize the highlights. Martha Nussbaum's immensely popular 2010 book, *Not for Profit: Why Democracy Needs the Humanities*, puts the blame for the decline of the humanities largely on our government and the leaders of our educational institutions for, on one hand, placing undue emphasis on technical training and STEM education, while on the other, becoming slave to the profit motive and to a hopelessly utilitarian model of education.[6] Nussbaum's diagnoses are likely right; nevertheless, it is unclear whether the defense of the humanities she provides will hold out in the eyes of policy makers and, more importantly, students. It is entirely possible, in other words, that Nussbaum is, like so many other humanists who publish defenses of the humanities, preaching only to the choir.

At the same time, Nussbaum and many like her do not fully address another important and persuasive account of the "fall" of the humanities. This alternative account is best summarized by the National Humanities Scholar and long-time tutor at St. John's College, Eva Brann, who writes that Nussbaum's book "nowhere acknowledges that this quietus may be less a sudden garroting than a slow-motion suicide."[7] Brann's autopsy identifies as lethal both "the German mania for specialized research and the French disease of sophisticated un-intelligibility," as well as "our own betrayal of literature to ideology."[8] In other words, humanities professors, by adhering to nineteenth-century German notions of hyper-specialization, as well as by allowing their language to become abstruse and their ideas obscurantist, have caused the crisis themselves.

These divergent but not mutually exclusive accounts represent much of the conventional finger-pointing that has gone on since the culture wars took hold of the academy in the Nineties: the academic left blames the fall of the humanities primarily on anti-intellectual policymakers and corporatized administrators who operate as CEOs rather than edu-cators; the (significantly smaller) academic right places all blame on neo-Marxist and Foucauldian ideologues who, while masquerading as traditional humanists, sap the humanities of any human meaning. Such finger-pointing quickly proves counterproductive if it is not followed by reasonable plans of action. Admittedly, such plans would be compli-cated. It's quite likely both sides, the left and right, are in the first place mostly correct in that the confluence of the major trends they identify— the corporatization of the university, the hyper-departmentalization of academic knowledge, the inability of most scholars to write in a manner intelligible to anyone outside their discipline or school of thought, and the reduction of the humanities to ideology—reveals just how serious is the threat currently facing the humanities in universities and the public, as well as how hard it would be to imagine and implement a solution.

But none of this is new. The problem, that is to say, is not one of diagnosis. Every humanist, having read a number of apocalyptic prog-nostications about the death of the very thing they have committed their lives to studying and teaching, has surely considered the crisis as well as its possible causes. What is so frustrating and demoralizing about the present situation, however, is that few humanists seem willing or capable to do anything about it except write the occasional op-ed. For all their talk about interdisciplinarity, many humanists can hardly engage other disciplines effectively or constructively, and thus certainly cannot dialogue constructively with policymakers, university administrations, or, for that matter, incoming freshmen. Meanwhile, small humanities departments face discontinuation, student enrollment maintains its low plateau, recent PhDs take adjunct jobs and consign themselves into exploitation, and tenure-track faculty are forced to produce monographs of increasing sub-field specificity and decreasing relevance to the real-life problems they and others face. In short, the prognostications appear, as of now, quite accurate: the humanities are simultaneously being eaten, and are eating themselves, alive.

As two young humanists cautiously considering different graduate school and career choices, we believe we have enough critical distance from this crisis, or at least enough professional and personal incentive, to ask an uncomfortable question: why can't humanities scholars, on the whole, address and alleviate the problems they face?

Having posed the question directly, we should now leave some room for qualification. Perhaps it is not that humanists simply need to become better at explaining to the public what they do and why it's valuable. We might suggest, further, that they ought to think more seriously about how this valuable and honorable undertaking remains responsive to the demands of life in the twenty-first century. Committed humanists should in fact be doing more than producing monographs on topics of increasing specificity and specialty—or, if their work is definably special, perhaps its specialty should amount to more than placing a mere brick in the massive mortar edifice of the academic enterprise.

To be clear, our point is not that humanists should abandon academic research and all journal publications (in fact, that would be rather hypocritical of us). Rather, it is that the conventional work of the humanities scholar should not necessarily be the only constituent of what they have to offer to society, nor should it represent the sole social or intellectual value of the humanities in general. Young humanists in particular need to start thinking about alternative models of "doing" or "teaching" the humanities now. In fact, they should realize that ignoring important questions about the future of their disciplines might simply not be an option.

So, one potential alternative to the current paradigm would involve the development of a new ethic, a new way of being a humanist. We have in mind one such ethic, which we've termed "humanities entrepreneurship." This concept will, we understand, elicit different readings and reactions from scholars. On the one hand, to say that humanists ought to be "entrepreneurial"—in the sense that they should "think outside the box," and attempt to apply their thought in creative, interesting, and institutionally disruptive ways—is precisely what it will take to seize an alternative model for higher education in the 21st century. At the same time, the term "entrepreneur," with its intimations not merely of "instrumentalization" but outright venture capitalism, will offend the sensibilities of many academics. So why not bypass this offense altogether and use neutral words such as "creativity" to imply the kind of spirit we hope humanists adopt? We suggest there is something essential contained in the term "entrepreneur" that helps locate a tension between what humanists ought to embrace and what many are currently fighting against.

To this day, we are convinced the term "humanities entrepreneurship" came to both of us independently—or perhaps, subconsciously; neither of us wants to have been the sole mastermind of a concept that, if put into practice, would drive yet another nail into the coffin of an academic era we both hoped one day to inherit. Whatever the term's origins, we have been using it for the past year and a half. In that time, we quite unintentionally conducted a sociological study of humanists simply by asking what they thought of our term, "humanities entrepreneurship." We were surprised to find, in an almost uniform manner, most scholars recoiled at the suggestion that humanists might benefit from becoming more entrepreneurial in the most original sense of the term, i.e., one who undertakes an enterprise of some scope, complication, or risk.

Resistance to the notion of "entrepreneurship," in our view, has its roots in an aversion to business, and more generally to the "instrumentalization" of the humanities in any sense, among academic humanists. This aversion is, in our view, often counterproductive, and is to some degree a relatively recent phenomenon. There has not always been such a clear schism between humanists and the market, and we can't help but wonder whether, in reaction against the need to prove "marketable," humanities scholars have, on the whole, become too absolutist in an attempt to separate themselves from the economic world. In so doing, they may have moved *too far away* from the expanding global economic world—a tendency that we argue has resulted in dry theory devoid of 21st century content with which to apply it.

Today, with few exceptions, it is clear that topics of business, marketing, and economics are not found within Colleges of Arts and Humanities. Yet historically, economics (or political economy) was considered well within the realm of a humanist's proper inquiry.[9] Economics was, and still in some sense is, a study of what is human, as opposed to its now common mathematical and purely rational bent. Encouragingly, there have been movements to "reclaim" thinkers like Adam Smith as first and foremost humanist thinkers (a task made particularly easy in Smith's case, as he was Professor of Moral Philosophy at Glasgow.) Movements like these need not only to reclaim thinkers like Smith, but in so doing must also revisit early modern interest in concurrent social and political events. Eighteenth-century humanists lived and worked in a time of unprecedented economic expansion: they witnessed the rise of the global commercial society in which, for the first time, it was conceivable and, perhaps more importantly, feasible to trade goods around the entire planet. Compounded with a rapidly changing social order in which individuals were increasingly able to own property and manage small businesses, this uniquely modern commercial society certainly provided no end of phenomena to study. One need only look at pieces from writers like Condorcet, Hume, or Rousseau to see their careful observations of economic issues drove them to produce serious pieces—not fully analogous to policy recommendations—that interweave economic matters with ideas about political personhood and even philosophical reflections on what it meant to be human in light of such rapid changes.[10] But importantly, these humanists were not merely studying these changes; they were, in a large sense, setting the terms for subsequent debates, discussions, and analyses of modern commercial society. The use and misuse of "Smithian" terminology—invisible hand, division of labor, unintended consequences—is a standout example of such influence.[11]

Why, with the rise of this relatively new phenomenon (the past 300 years), has the inquiry and fascination with the changing economic world around us not continued within the humanities? Partially, we suggest, because of some real tensions between liberal arts education and the economic world. One tension that needs acknowledging is how the spread of the humanities, and liberal arts education for that matter, does have a clear relationship with economic considerations: Whether it be patrons commissioning artists in the Renaissance, or the Industrial Revolution's unique economic factors that gave rise to the feasibility of compulsory education in the U.S., there is a relationship, albeit awkward and undefined, between the wider spread of art, philosophy, and education and economic interest. To ignore this relationship, to pretend it does not or should not exist, disallows us to contribute meaningfully to modern debates about the purpose of education in a modern commercial society. And let's be clear: we, as humanists, have the whole "purpose of education" bit down. The contextualization of this purpose, however, is not as readily apparent. What it takes to be a humanist—that is, one who constantly re-examines humanity in its myriad contexts—must, by necessity, change. Indeed, as modern commercial society changes, so should at least some of the methodologies and functions of the humanities change. For example, a humanities scholar with an entrepreneurial spirit might consider how social media can be a new frontier to engage the humanities, and at the same time realize it is an area teeming with new content to explore ageless questions—fittingly, it also allows for new expansions of the market (consider Amazon, or even the ideas behind the Bitcoin movement). By the same token, an entrepreneurial humanist might consider ways in which the methodically conservative mode of teaching the humanities—i.e. the fifty-minute lecture—might be revised to work more compellingly on digital platforms. Though platforms like Coursera.org have made clear that access to content is not, in itself, enough to replace live classroom experiences in a humanities classroom, the entrepreneurial spirit behind the open online course movement is undeniable.

Though it might be painful to admit, we are in the business of the humanities. Nevertheless, it is essential for disciplines within the humanities to be, in numerous ways, separate from market interests. A certain degree of separation is necessary in order to have the space and occasion to offer critical assessments without fear of institutional pushback, defunding, or the like. Indeed, intellectual life in universities must (or rather, should) fundamentally be different from that of privately funded research institutions and think tanks. After all, one of the central if oft-neglected purposes and functions of the university is rigorously to pursue truth for its own sake—not, that is, in service of any ideological end or in pursuit of any "return on investment." This uniquely important scholarly vocation, protected by academic freedom and tenure, allows critics in the academy to perform the duties of the Socratic gadfly—that is, to pester the authorities, to challenge the status quo, to hold truth above all else. Important though it is, many scholars' preoccupation with their role as gadfly often distracts them from another Socratic aim: midwifery. While it is true Socrates was a gadfly, asking crucial and unnerving questions, he was also known for his pedagogic midwifery by aiding others in giving birth to their ideas. This Socratic purpose is fundamentally connected to entrepreneurship and innovation, to venture capitalists and to garage-based start-ups, to government officials and to college students preparing for their futures.

The cognitive dissonance we observe between resistance to a term like "humanities entrepreneurship" and the crucially connected Socratic aim of midwifery is as curious as it is worrisome. Yet before we provide more detail about what, exactly, we think movements of humanities entrepreneurship can look like today, we want to first clarify what it is not.

Humanities entrepreneurship is not, in our usage of the term, yet another expression of the "corporatization" of the university. In fact, we imagine pushback to this notion will come because we give up "too much ground" to market interest and in so doing reduce the role of humanities education to no more than a handmaiden to capitalists' needs. But we are not advocating an entrepreneurial approach to help students get more lines on their resumes, to land sexy jobs at a firm, or to become more marketable. In fact, an ideal outcome would be that merely having the line on a resume indicating one's college major would carry enough weight to indicate a thoughtful, aware, and engaged applicant. That said, to reach the day when one spends more time in an interview justifying the choice of a marketing major over a philosophy degree will take work.

So what do we mean by humanities entrepreneurship? We mean that humanists, in order to carve a new space for themselves to thrive intellectually and politically, and to convey the worth of the humanities to the wide world, ought to cultivate a kind of *savoir faire,* savvy, and willingness to both specialize and generalize — to see the forest and the trees. They need not only to be able to critique the status quo, the institutional apparatus and fixed centers of power, but they need to actively challenge them into better forms, and be involved in the grueling work of reform. To do this, humanists need to be in dialogue, not argument based on mutual suspicion, with "the other" — in this context, "business types" such as the leaders of "start-ups," even the economics professors down the hall. To work with such people will, for many humanists, require some social and intellectual exertion — the development and employment of new vocabularies, new ways of thinking.

We have had an eye out for humanists who engage with the world entrepreneurially. Our discoveries have been, on the whole, encouraging; it seems there are many humanities scholars already working as entrepreneurs (in the sense we've laid out) in their disciplines, even if they themselves would not describe their actions as such. At a meeting with the National Endowment for the Humanities in the summer of 2015, we learned about a new initiative, the Public Scholars Program, which is designed to help scholars render their academic knowledge accessible to the wider public. Such programs bolster the many pioneering efforts already undertaken by professors who, for instance, emphasize community engagement in their syllabi. At the June 2015 conference, "Seizing an Alternative: Toward an Ecological Civilization," we met

other humanists who, out of concern for the future of higher education and the liberal arts, had already been conducting the sort of work
of which we hope to see more in the future — work that shows more
than tells about new, methodologically innovative forms of value a
well-trained humanist, as Socratic midwife, can bring into the world.
One of the many exemplary humanities entrepreneurs at the conference was Professor Robert Neustadt, who sees his role as a professor of
Spanish near the U.S.-Mexico border as necessarily including different forms of pedagogy than classroom language instruction. He has
been a vigorous proponent of campus dialogue about immigration
and human rights — a subject that, given the location of his campus,
requires discussion. Professor Neustadt sometimes takes his students to
the border, where they see first-hand the dynamics between immigrants
and border patrol.[12]

In similarly entrepreneurial fashion, Professor David Helfand,
president and vice chancellor of Quest University, has designed and
spearheaded the implementation of an independent university that
provides a rigorous liberal education and small, integrated intellectual
communities for students and faculty alike.[13] Helfland, for his work, is
rightly considered to be on the vanguard of movements away from the
modern, hyper-departmentalized and bloated research university. The
work of scholars such as Neustadt and Helfland will only continue to
increase in value: if scholars are going to seize an alternative model of
higher education, they are going to have to innovate their pedagogy
and take risks.

Still, it may turn out to be that the present crisis of the humanities
is not all that unique but, rather, simply one crisis in a string of many. A
longue durée perspective on the history of liberal arts education reveals
many strikingly similar moments of "crisis" in and among communities
of humanists.[14] Though the humanities truly are, in Nussbaum's terms,
"on the ropes,"[15] the fact that humanities departments still attract students, and that these students still express commitment to their disciplines, ought to inspire some optimism about the future. Nevertheless,
hope for the future ought not release humanists from shaping, in
innovative and entrepreneurial ways, what their disciplines look like

in the future. An immortal subject may imply infinite opportunities for application, but it does not also imply the methods for doing so. The question is not a matter of if but *how* the business world engages with the tradition of the humanities. Because these discussions are happening, it is essential for humanists to take part in deciding how their tradition can interact with the modern world in new, yet still anciently transformative ways.

Let us conclude by returning to the concept of Socrates as a midwife. The analogy is rather subtle, for a midwife is not merely interested in the end goal (or bottom line, if you will) of producing a baby. Midwifery is an art that sets as its aim the preparation of the mother both for the birthing process and for life after the birth. Midwifery is a holistic practice that does not view birthing as a single act with a single product at the end, but rather as a process that begins well before labor and ends well after birth. Socrates was a midwife of *ideas*, not simply concerned with the initial production of the idea or its dissemination in a small community of thinkers—rather, he was concerned with how ideas come to lead lives all their own. A 21ˢᵗ century Socratic approach to the humanities ought to look the same.

NOTES

1   Louis Menand, *The Marketplace of Ideas: Reform and Resistance in the American University* (New York: W. W. Norton and Company, 2010), 13.

2   Irony defined: Michigan State University, home of the Spartans, discontinued its Classics program in 2009. See Matthew Miller, "Final Classics Major at MSU Gets Diploma," *Lansing State Journal* (Lansing, MI), May 2, 2014. In fact, as we write, the administration at Calvin College is moving to cut their theater, art history German, Greek, and Latin programs. See "Calvin Makes Cuts to Humanities Programs," *Inside Higher Ed,* September 30, 2015 <https://www.insidehighered.com/quicktakes/2015/09/30/calvin-makes-cuts-humanities-programs>.

3   Lee Siegel, "Who Ruined the Humanities?," *The Wall Street Journal,* July 12, 2013; Victor Davis Hanson, "The Death of the Humanities," *Defining Ideas: A Hoover Institution Journal,* January 28, 2014 <http://www.hoover.org/research/death-humanities>.

4   "Humanities Deathwatch," *The New Republic,* 2003 <https://newrepublic.

com/tags/humanities-deathwatch>.

5   Menand, *Marketplace of Ideas,* 62.

6   Martha Nussbaum, *Not for Profit: Why Democracies Need the Humanities* (Princeton: Princeton University Press, 2010).

7   Eva Brann, "Liberalism and Liberal Education," *Claremont Review of Books* 6, 3 (2011).

8   Ibid.

9   The term "political economy" signifies an old area of intellectual interest, but its emergence as a distinct discipline is relatively young. Its traces are found about four hundred years back in intellectual groups like the French Physiocrats. Today there are a number of initiatives at work to bring more attention to this earlier history of economics and to question the assumptions taken as given in some prevalent strands of economic scholarship. This effort has come in many forms: journals, research centers, organized conferences, and even novels. A leading example of such initiatives is the Center for the History of Political Economy at Duke University, which has as part of its mission the revival of economic history in undergraduate curricula. This center hosts scholars, produces a leading journal, and holds seminars and conferences to actively promote the study of the early days of economics. For a lighter (but nonetheless scholarly and historical) introduction to some economic history, one can usefully turn to Robert Heilbroner's *The Worldly Philosophers: The Lives, Times, and Ideas of Great Economic Thinkers* (New York: Simon & Schuster Inc), 1953.

10   Some examples: David Hume, *Political Discourses* (Edinburgh: A. Kincaid and A. Donaldson, 1752) <http://www.econlib.org/library/LFBooks/ Hume/hmMPL24.html>; Jean-Jacques Rousseau, "Discourse on the Origin and Foundations of Inequality Among Men or Second Discourse" in *Rousseau: "The Discourses and Other Early Political Writings"* Victor Gourevitch, ed. (Cambridge: Cambridge University Press, 1997); Marquis de Condorcet, *Outlines of an Historical View of the Progress of the Human Mind,* translated from the French (Philadelphia: M. Carey, 1796) <http:// oll.libertyfund.org/titles/1669>.

11   Amartya Sen, "Uses and Abuses of Adam Smith" *History of Political Economy* 43, no. 2 (2011): 257–71.

12   See Robert Neustadt, interview by Joe Harting, The Big Talker 105.1 KBTK FM, April 3, 2014: <https://www.youtube.com/watch?v=dI9-_ VgUfr8>; See also Neustadt's chapter, "Encountering the Other: Case Study in Applied Liberal Education" in this volume.

13   See Helfland's profile by *The New York Times:* Tamar Lewin, "David

Helfand's New Quest," *The New York Times,* Jan. 20, 2012 <http://www.nytimes.com/2012/01/22/education/edlife/david-helfands-new-quest.html?_r=0>.

14   See Menand's discussion of humanities scholars' tendency toward "crises" in chapters 2 and 3 of *The Marketplace of Ideas.*

15   See final chapter of Nussbaum's *Not for Profit,* titled "Democratic Education on the Ropes."

12. EDUCATION FOR CITIZENSHIP:

ENVIRONMENTAL THOUGHT

Mark Stemen

ABSTRACT: *This essay answers John Cobb's call for faculty to cut against the anti-intellectual trends of university culture and shift toward an ecological civilization through civically focused curriculum. Working within the emerging field of sustainability, I have designed my Thought in Action course to give students the tools and space they need to create positive change on their campus, with effects that ripple out into their community. I discuss the logistics of the course, the most effective template I have found for creating change (campus elections), and the many successful initiatives we've launched, which included Chico State's decision to divest completely from the top 200 fossil fuels companies within four years. This type of active learning echoes Alfred North Whitehead's belief that theoretical ideas need to be paired with practical applications if they are to have any lasting impact*

I AM NOT A WHITEHEADIAN BY TRAINING. Nevertheless, I agree with the editors of this volume that the "present state of affairs is ruinous and that a pervasive culture shift is necessary."[1] I also believe that colleges and universities can help bring about that cultural shift, but faculty will have to cut against the grain to do it.

Like John Cobb, I am critical of modern research universities that have divided intellectual activity into separate disciplines housed in individual departments. Problems like climate change demand a trans-disciplinary response. I have had the pleasure of teaching in a geography department where my colleagues "continue to seek holistic answers to broad questions," and where I have had a lot of flexibility in exploring the emerging field of sustainability.[2] My training as a historian gives me further permission to wander the academic landscape. As one of my advisors once told me, "a PhD in history is like an intellectual hunting license; everything has a history."[3]

Sustainability is a new academic buzzword; colleges and universities are building "programs" in sustainability as they did with women's studies and ethnic studies a generation earlier. By its very nature, sustainability transcends any one discipline in the academy with a broad focus on environment, economy, and equity. Cobb writes that topic-based programs "often encourage intellectual reflection"; however, these "approaches" cut against the general trends of university culture. Despite the need for faculty to step outside of their own disciplines to comprehend problems like climate change and offer solutions, Cobb points out that these types of border crossing explorations are seen as "speculation, and…discouraged" by administrators and the faculty tenure process. I would add that such expeditions inspire students and feed faculty souls, and that is enough reason to press on.[4]

At Chico State, I teach a 4/4 load. I have around 135 students a semester cycle through three sections of my general education course, where they learn all the terrifying things some of us already know about the state of the environment. Lecturing on all of this destruction can get pretty depressing, for both students and faculty. To counter that, I teach one course each semester where I have created an opportunity for students to enact positive change. In December 2014, Chico State became the first public university in the U.S. to pledge to fully divest from fossil fuels investments within four years. Students used my GEOG 440's student-directed format to campaign for fossil fuel divestment. Their student government election victory the previous April testified to the success of their efforts. But the victory came after years of cultural work on campus by previous classes as students used their "liberal education…to bring about this cultural shift." In other words, the course has turned civic engagement into a subject, and my students study how to act.

Marcus Ford, co-editor of this volume, writes in an essay for the conference,

> "if colleges and universities are to become a force for bringing about the kind of cultural change that is so urgently required, they will need to rethink their educational mission, their curriculum, and their worldview. They will need to see themselves...as institutions committed to wisdom and to passing along the values and *skills* of responsible citizenship and ecological stewardship."[5]

Many of the submissions to this volume talk about incorporating much needed values into the classroom. But none discuss the skills needed to move toward an ecological civilization. I agree we need a pedagogy that "aims much higher than training for careers" and "education which is concerned with maturation and transformation into the kind of adult we so urgently need," but what would such a class look like? What would students read and what would they write about? In the following pages I will describe a class I created a decade ago in one of my "better moments of teaching, community engagement, [and] curriculum design" that is transformative for students and the campus as a whole. I will also describe in greater detail my class's 2014 fossil fuel divestment campaign for those looking to replicate such an effort on their own campus.[6]

In California, faculty are being encouraged to create "service learning opportunities" for their students, such as having social work students volunteer at a local soup kitchen or environmental studies students restore the local watershed. Service Learning is a "teaching and learning strategy that integrates meaningful community service with instruction and reflection to enrich the learning experience, teach civic responsibility, and strengthen communities."[7] In many ways, this integrated learning mirrors Whitehead's ideas about studying life in all its manifestations. While service endeavors have obvious social value, their educational value suffers if students are unable to make connections between their projects and their academic work.[8]

Environmental studies programs are notorious for such disconnected activities. Tree planting is a classic example of a service learning
project with little learning. Sure, it is a worthwhile pursuit, but what
kinds of values and connections does it foster for the student? What
do they truly learn? I am wary of such unattached projects and have
worked to design my own service learning projects so that they are fully
embedded in the curriculum of the course.[9]

I structure my Environmental Thought in Action course, for example, around the annual student elections that occur every spring semester. I require students in the course to participate in the elections by
placing an advisory measure on the ballot as a "service" to the campus;
the "service" is providing a tangible issue, like campus divestment, in
an election that is often devoid of any real issues. As a class, students
research potential campus issues, select a specific issue to work on, draft
acceptable initiative language, collect signatures to place the advisory on
the ballot, and ultimately campaign for the measure's passage. Through
the process they learn a lot about sustainability, social change, and
themselves. It works because, in the words of Whitehead, the students
"feel that they are studying something and not merely executing intellectual minuets."[10]

The course is the capstone course for our environmental studies
minor. Our minor is a smorgasbord of electives with few universal
requirements. So students come into the capstone with little coursework in common. This service learning exercise is the best way I have
discovered to allow students to integrate the diverse courses they have
taken, while also giving them practical skills and confidence in their
ability to change campus culture to a worldview that is in harmony
with the planet.

How to affect a cultural shift is THE question we must now ask
ourselves. To change the campus culture, I believe we need to change
what people are talking about and how they are talking about it. But
how do we get sustainability issues into daily conversation? Those of us
in academia know how hard it is to generate campus wide-discussions.
We can organize forums and events but they are often too small and
too focused to make a difference when we are talking about problems

that need the influence of multiple academic perspectives. One way to broaden the discussion is to take advantage of existing campus-wide platforms. School pride is one popular vehicle. Name plays like "Brown is Green" helped the students at Brown University spread the message of environmental awareness while also implying it is a core value of their campus. Mascot associations like Fresno State's Energy Bulldogs (Bulldogs are the school mascot) are another way to use a widely recognized platform to promote energy conservation in an acceptably aggressive way.

I have found student elections to be an excellent vehicle for introducing conversations about sustainability into campus life. Everyone is already talking about the election. On our small (16,000) campus there is a classic two degrees of separation; everyone seems to have a friend of a friend who is running for one of the sixteen elected positions. Because of this, students are more willing to listen to policy discussions. They are more likely to sign a petition or accept a flyer during election season than they would be a month earlier or later. It is a brief window, but the window is also wide open.

I also point out to my students that the election is the time when they will have their most political power, before the votes are cast. I use our curriculum to teach my students the skills to get their message out. As they do so, they also gain a following. Every candidate is soon angling to get the class's support. Often a candidate will take up the issue, like divestment, and make the advisory measure part of their own campaign. The general rise in awareness and growing alliances combine to create a sense that change is possible if only enough people know to vote for the initiative, lending a sense of urgency to the message. I encourage my students to aim, in the mode of the conference organizers, not just to win an election, but rather to "build a popular movement."[11]

I think the service learning framework functions well in this context because, as Whitehead points out, "theoretical ideas should always find important applications within the pupil's curriculum." Students read outside of class the entire semester and reflect upon the course material in a written journal they share with their peers each week. They write about the issues that concern them based on campus reports. They reflect on the language they should use on the initiative after reading about effective messaging. They discuss the meeting with their peers in elected office while reflecting on how to win friends and influence others. They wrestle with applying abstract theoretical ideals to actual physical problems in the context of social relationships with real people. The experience deepens and improves upon all areas of study.[12]

Most importantly, students learn to collaborate as a team, practicing their interpersonal skills (often the death of community efforts) first as they debate amongst themselves about which issue to choose; again as they engage the public; and once again as they plan and execute the campaign. One main goal is to still like each other at the end of the campaign. We end each class with the same call and response: [Me] "The most important thing?" [Them] "Stay friends!"

By choosing their own issue, writing the initiative, and campaigning, students find their voice and build confidence in their own opinions and their power to effect change. Writing at every step of the process allows them to reflect on the readings within the context of their issue, thereby deepening their understanding of both. Students are able to combine information from a variety of classes they have taken, and from the readings that I assign, and put them into service for something larger than themselves. In turn, students feel an increased commitment to the university and the surrounding community, and this civic responsibility continues on into their careers.

Researching, proposing, collecting, and campaigning all in a single semester is very hard and the students often come in unprepared. It is tempting for faculty to focus on the issues and the solutions at the purely intellectual level without attempting to actually act on them. To do so would be a mistake, however, because as Whitehead points out, "whatever powers you are strengthening in the pupil, must be exercised here and now; whatever possibilities of mental life your teaching should impart, must be exhibited here and now." Simply put, action should never be postponed. Here and now is the exact time and place to act.[13]

Over the years I have identified five key steps in the election process and structured the course around them. Students begin by selecting the campus issue for the campaign. They review our campus sustainability assessment and our latest STARS report. They discuss the issues with other peers in the student sustainability office. Each student comes to the second meeting of class with a list of ten issues and writes them on the board. We discuss the twenty or so different topics, combining and clarifying the issues. Then everyone gets ten votes and we select our Top Ten issues for further discussion. Over the next two weeks we work our way down to our Top Five, Three, Two, and finally *the One*.

Students debate amongst themselves for these first few weeks, gaining the skills necessary to take the issues to the entire campus. There are three main criteria that they use to evaluate each issue. First, they seek an issue that is easy to explain in a two-minute class talk. Students have found the best way to change the culture of the campus is to start in the classroom by asking professors if they can have two minutes at the beginning of class to let their peers know about an important issue in the upcoming campus election. So the first question to ask is: Can they explain the issue to their peers in two minutes or less? Divestment did not score well on this criterion. Nevertheless, they felt passionate about the issue and found they could explain "uninvesting" by starting with fossil fuel's role in climate change. If everyone had to stop using fossil fuels, then it was risky/bad for the university to be investing in the industry.

The second criterion is whether or not the issue is appropriate for an initiative. Students have a litany of complaints about the university and an equally long list of suggested remedies, but are they "legislative?" In other words, can the barriers to action be remedied by mobilizing political power? For example, every year a common suggestion is to demand more recycling, either through more locations or expanded service. The barriers to more recycling, however, are not political will, but rather issues of funding or fire access or markets for the additional material. An initiative, no matter how cleverly worded, will not change those factors.

Lastly, and most importantly, is the resulting action meaningful enough for all the work involved? Running a campaign can be exhausting, and as the students become increasingly invested in it, a campaign can become all-consuming. The rewards at the end need to be equal to work put in, or students will falter. For example, each year, more native landscaping makes the list, and every year folks realize it is too small of an issue in exchange for so much of their time. The cause, should it be accomplished, has to pay off for all the time and effort invested in its success.

Once the students have selected their issue, they then draft acceptable initiative language. Each comes in to class with their text for the initiative. They have been reading about "words that work" during this time and they bring in their favorite set of phrases. To turn their issue into an initiative, it must have a government "action." They are participating in the Associated Students (AS) student election, so the most obvious request is to have the student government do something. There are a host of possible AS actions to call upon. For example, the student government on our campus also runs the foodservice, so a simple action one year was for AS Foodservice to purchase more local food (33% to be exact). The initiative can also direct elected student leaders in AS Government to "strongly encourage" the university to act, as they did with the divestment campaign.

I teach students to use the course readings and training from previous classes to "frame" the issue in their favor, since they are the ones writing the initiative. Many students knew from other classes that conversations around local food often descended from the discussions of community into debates over mileage. Others knew that foodservice was worried about tracking. Their elegant compromise was to define "local" as our county (Butte) and the adjacent counties, which both reintroduced community and made tracking as simple as zip codes. When debating how much of the food should be local, they felt exact numbers were cold and hard, and could scare some peers, but "a third" sounded fair and forgiving. When students wanted to campaign against a suggested parking structure, they avoided a confusing Yes vote by crafting the initiative as supporting the structure and then campaigning for a No vote.

By week four the students are ready to submit language for approval. By this time students have already been discussing the issue with peers and elected student officials, and a few will also have formally presented their ideas to the student government at one of their regularly scheduled meetings. A special meeting is scheduled between the students and the sector of the university affected by the initiative to resolve any concerns over the intent of the initiative. When the issue was local food, students met with senior foodservice staff and discussed the concerns raised above. When the issue was divestment, they met with the staff that oversaw the university endowment and discussed concerns about the timing and scope of divestment. The resolution was to divest from the top 200 fossil fuel companies in four years. During these deliberations the students learn how to give public testimony, how to make their arguments on the fly, and how to agree to concessions they can live with. At the end of the process they walk out with language they can circulate and universally useful skills in public engagement.

Once I get the approved language from the student government, I use it to create the physical petitions for the students to circulate. In addition to printing and signing their names on the petition, students are also required to list the student ID numbers to verify enrollment. The number of signatures required to place an initiative on the ballot is often a percentage of the votes in a previous election. On our campus, students are required to collect 20% of the total votes cast for the office of president to place an advisory measure on the ballot. I require each student to individually collect at least 100 signatures as part of the class assignment. As a class, they try to get twice the number needed, a common tactic when trying to qualify an initiative for the ballot.

The students take the petitions into classes to get signatures, often in conjunction with the two-minute talk about an important campus election issue that I mentioned earlier. Students also organize a weekly table on campus to collect signatures. The signature drive is a test-run for the campaign. The students learn where other students congregate, what arguments sway students, and which ones fall flat. More importantly, they organize themselves, and each begins to find their niche in the group. By the time they turn in signatures at the end of week seven, they are ready to campaign for the measure's passage.

Launching a successful campaign isn't something they teach educators in graduate school. Developing this course required me to read far and wide to educate myself on topics I was never trained in, like how to inform the general public about important issues and convince them to vote for an initiative designed to address them. Fortunately, there are books out there all about the dos and don'ts of effective campaigning. I will mention a few notable books here that have informed my curriculum. [My full reading list is available on my department's website.] The main text for the course is Chris Rose, *How to Win Campaigns: 100 Steps to Success*. Rose was a campaign organizer for Greenpeace, and his book is well written, useful, and available online. Three other books that I have found very helpful are Malcolm Gladwell, *Tipping Point*, Chip Heath and Dan Heath, *What Sticks?* and Jonah Berger, *Contagious: Why Things Catch On*. Each of the latter books references and builds on the previous work, allowing me to see the evolution in thought, and the students have found the ideas particularly helpful when designing their campaigns. They learn from Gladwell, for example, the "law of the few" and early on they begin to look for the "connectors, mavens and salesmen" among their peers to help them spread their message.[14]

I am able to counter criticism of the political nature of the "service" my course provides by staying true to the "learning" that occurs every semester. A shining example of "integrated learning" during the divestment campaign would be the orange squares — the most successful feature of the divestment campaign. Their use developed organically out of the readings and the issue at hand. The national campus divestment movement had already adopted a simple orange square as an "unofficial symbol" by the time we began discussing the issue. Some students knew that public displays of affiliation are powerful signifiers to their peers. So, when the class chose divestment as the initiative issue, those students in the know distributed little oranges patches for everyone to attach to their backpacks. Orange took on further importance after students read the story of the yellow Livestrong bracelets, which Berger argues "stuck" because yellow is a rare color, and this rarity catches our attention from a distance. Students realized the color orange was even more rare than the color yellow once they discovered the only place they could find orange paper was at the local craft store.[15]

Heath and Hearth explain that "unexpectedness" is an important principle in getting people's attention, but "surprise doesn't last." They write that campaigners (and teachers) can hold the public's attention for "a long period of time by systematically 'opening gaps' in their knowledge—and then by filling those gaps." For example, teachers do this by asking rhetorical questions. The students followed their advice quite literally.[16] In a text-saturated world, blank objects stand out. Political "yard signs' dot the campus during student elections. To stand out, students cut old political yard signs into 20-inch squares and painted them bright orange. They slowly began placing the blank/empty orange signs all around campus. They started with ten, then twenty. By the end of the campaign they had placed over forty blank orange squares around campus, and the student activity office (which was in on the gig) was fielding calls daily. Everyone wanted to know, what did the signs mean? The signs had caught people's attention with their absent text and unexplained meaning. Two weeks before voting the signs "disappeared," only to reappear two days later with the words VOTE TO DIVEST in big black letters. The message was clear and "contagious." Students kept the ball (or rather the square) rolling by applying Berger's "game mechanics" to the campaign, offering prizes to students who took pictures of the orange squares and posted them to the campaign's twitter account.

Campaign press events are fun, positive expressions of the issues and a good place for students to build their organizing skills. The local food campaign staged a food fight between local orange and imported banana, tired from all the travel. The parking structure campaign staged a park-in, turning two parking spots into a temporary park complete with chairs and a barbeque. The divestment campaign staged a human oil slick flowing out of the administration building. The latter is posted on YouTube as "Kendall Hall Oil Slick" and is remarkably life-like and easily replicable. The divestment campaign also staged a traditional banner drop off the tallest classroom on campus. The press attended each event and students further shared the stories on social media.

The emergence of Facebook and YouTube has influenced the strategy of our initiative campaigns. For the past five years, each campaign has created its own Facebook page and the last two have created videos.

While the students still participate in candidate forums and visit editorial boards for endorsements, more and more often they are creating
their own media. They also produce traditional campaign materials
like posters, flyers, and t-shirts with cleaver slogans like "Make Love
not Structures."[17]

The campus votes over the course of one day, with the polls open
8 AM to 5 PM. The class used to sit outside the student government
office waiting for someone to "post" the results on the front door. Now
voting is online, so we get to wait at the campus burger joint and stare
anxiously at our phones and laptops. The final tally for the divestment
campaign was 75% in favor. More impressive was the "overvote"—more
students voted on divestment than voted for the office of president. In
other words, divestment, the last item on the ballot, was more popular
than the first item on the ballot.

The students finish the election process by writing. I encourage
them to celebrate the learning as much as the victory. Class activities
after that differ every year. Often the vote is the last stage of the process
and there is nothing more to be done until the newly elected officials
take office in the fall. I schedule activities for the last few weeks of class
but nothing too important in case the students have an opportunity to
carry the current effort forward. Most often, I help the students strate-
gize ways to keep the effort alive until they return from summer break.

The local food campaign created a "local food working group,"
for example, to help AS Foodservice develop a way to track local food
purchases the next semester. AS Foodservice has since increased its purchases of local food and created new programs like the "Local Lunch"
feature in the main dining station, but it has not yet met the one-third
target. When my students expressed frustration at the lack of enforcement and accountability with "advisory measures," I reminded them
that the goal was to change the campus culture. A changed campus
culture is forcing the AS to purchase more local, not the legality of the
initiative.

For the parking structure campaign, students wrote letters to the
trustees who were scheduled to vote on the project at the end of the
semester. Unfortunately, the parking structure was built, but the class

made it widely known that the university built it over student opposition. That seed of cultural knowledge would bear fruit two years later. Following the divestment vote, students worked with staff in university advancement to craft a policy that could be brought to the University Foundation Board of Directors the next semester. They also lobbied the university president and circulated a petition online for faculty support. On December 10, 2014, six months after the election, at the president's urging, the University Foundation voted to divest all holdings from the top 200 fossil fuel companies within four years.

My students have put forward twelve advisory measures over the past decade. All the measures have passed, often with 70–80% support, and most have been implemented to some extent. In addition to becoming the first public university to commit to fully divesting from fossil fuels in four years, Chico State students have campaigned to defeat a parking structure, enact a sustainability class graduation requirement, deny parking permits to anyone living within a mile of campus, and purchase more local food for campus dining. All of these campaigns were born from over ten years of effort to create meaningful courses that operate at the fringe of service learning.

The class is transformative for many of the students. As one student wrote in her election reflection, "I really stepped out of my comfort zone. I can honestly say I never thought I would have been dancing around the middle of campus wearing an orange cardboard box." Others have found the course empowering, a chance to raises their voices for a cause they cared about: "The first week of signature gathering I was very timid but I realized it wasn't scary after all...and soon enough I was in the middle of a major walkway yelling about fossil fuel divestment." The course also gave many students a sense of pride and accomplishment, which one summed up thusly: "There are only three school-related things I have called my parents to brag about: passing physics, passing chemistry and the 80% Yes vote on divestment."[18]

The course also inspires the change-maker in students. While students started the semester focused on a single issue, they learned skills that will help them pursue future activism beyond their university days. One wrote, "I realized that the point is not about winning (though that is wonderful) but about bringing serious issues to light and trying to make a difference." Another wrote, "I never saw myself as an activist and now my feet are itching to get back out there and campaign for more change." The cultural shift even spreads beyond our shores. As one student commented, "Next year I go abroad to Scotland, and I am planning on being just as active on the University of Stirling's campus as I have been on CSU, Chico."

The course builds a popular movement each year that has transformed the campus culture. Things are different now. When the university trustees voted to approve the campus parking structure, one remarked that he had "never received so many letters against *more* parking," and it would cause him to pause when considering another structure. When students campaigned for the campus to divest two years later, the campus paper openly asked if the university would listen to students this time around, in reference to the parking structure vote. The student campaigns have helped make sustainability part of our school culture. When President Paul Zingg addressed the foundation board in December 2014, he urged them to divest from fossil fuels because it represented who we were as a campus; a Yes vote was a reflection of the *values* we uphold. "The bottom line," Zingg said, "is alignment of our enacted values with our professed values."[19]

NOTES

1   Marcus Ford and Stephen Rowe in the introduction to this volume.

2   John Cobb, "The Anti-Intellectualism of the American University" *Soundings,* 98, no. 2 (2015): 218–32. "Philosophy departments today are much like other departments in the university. They understand philosophy should be one academic discipline along others. For this, it requires a subject matter that can be distinguished from others and suitable methodology for dealing with it. What I describe as intellectual activity is seen as speculation, and this is discouraged. The Goal in any academic discipline is the increase of knowledge, and this can be attained only by limiting ourselves to rigorous methods of analysis and testing." Cobb goes on to say, "Two other departments in many universities continued to seek holistic answers to broad questions. Geography expanded from simply learning about the landscape and the location of human habitat

to a deeper reflection on human beings related to their natural contexts and how this affected these contexts. Anthropology sought to understand the world inclusively from the perspective of the people studied. These approaches cut against the trend of university culture, and departments of geography and anthropology began to disappear."

3   William Cronon, PhD, Department of History, University of Wisconsin at Madison. Cronon was on my thesis committee, 1999.

4   Cobb, "The Anti-Intellectualism of the American University," 225–26.

5   Marcus Ford, "On Educational Reform," in *For Our Common Home: Process-Relational Responses to Laudato Si,'* Cobb and Castuera, eds. (Anoka: Process Century Press, 2015), 273. Emphasis added.

6   Marcus Ford and Stephen Rowe, "Introduction," in *From Liberation to Civilization: Seizing an Alternative Education* (Anoka: Process Century Press, 2016).

7   Sarena D. Seifer and Kara Connors, eds. "Community Campus Partnerships for Health," in *Faculty Toolkit for Service-Learning in Higher Education* (Scotts Valley: National Service-Learning Clearinghouse, 2007), 4.

8   Alfred North Whitehead, *The Aims of Education* (New York: The Free Press, 1929).

9   Mark Stemen, "Keeping the Academics in Service Learning Projects, or Teaching Environmental History to Tree Planters," in *The History Teacher* 37, no. 1 (November 2003).

10 Whitehead, *The Aims of Education,* 10.

11 Ford and Rowe, "Introduction."

12 Doug McKenzie-Mohr, *Fostering Sustainable Behavior: An Introduction to Community-based Social Marketing* (Vancouver: New Society Publishers, 1999); Dale Carnegie, *How To Win Friends And Influence People* (New York: Gallery Books, 1981; 1936).

13 Whitehead, *The Aims of Education,* 6.

14 Malcolm Gladwell, "The Law of the Few," in *Tipping Point: How Little Things Can Make a Big Difference* (New York: Little, Brown, and Company, 2000); Chris Rose, *How to Win Campaigns: 100 Steps to Success* (London: Earthscan, 2005); Chip Heath and Dan Heath, *Made to Stick: Why Some Ideas Survive and Others Die* (New York: Random House, 2007); Jonah Berger, *Contagious: Why Things Catch On* (New York: Simon and Schuster, 2013).

15 Berger, *Contagious,* 146.

16   Heath and Heath, *Made to Stick,* 16.

17   https://www.facebook.com/Wildcats-Against-Parking-Structure-195178440514597/?fref=ts

https://www.facebook.com/ChicoStateAdvoCatsForWaterConservation/

https://www.facebook.com/DivestChicoState/

https://www.facebook.com/RealFoodChico/

https://www.youtube.com/watch?v=wZ5AfW_1NiQ

https://www.facebook.com/RealFoodChico/videos/1623490287869886/?theater

18   Reflections on file with the author.

19   Tom Gascoyne, "Investment change, Chico State moves to divest from fossil fuels," *Chico News and Review* (Chico, CA), Dec. 18, 2014.

13. REDESIGNING EDUCATION IN A GRADUATE PROGRAM IN SUSTAINABILITY

Sandra B. Lubarsky

ABSTRACT: *This essay recounts the establishment of the Master in Sustainable Communities degree program at Northern Arizona University in the early 1990s. Mid-sized public universities have not been, on the whole, a hot-bed of curricular innovation. And yet, under the right circumstances, it is possible to create something that is radically new. The success of this particular program suggests that other public universities might want to institute a similar sort of program study.*

IN 1996, WITH THE HELP OF A SMALL GROUP of faculty from many quarters of the campus, I led the founding of one of the first masters degree programs in sustainability in the country, what is now the Master of Arts in Sustainable Communities program at Northern Arizona University. Our success hinged on several factors to be outlined below, but, above all, the program's vitality was the result of the remarkable desire of both faculty and students for new ways of structuring higher education—and the willingness to step beyond traditional boundaries to create it.

THE M.A. SUSTAINABLE COMMUNITIES PROGRAM

Northern Arizona University in Flagstaff, Arizona, is a mid-sized state university in the high-altitude, semi-desert of the Colorado Plateau. In the 1990s, it had strong, faculty-led grassroots support for making sustainability a part of its ethos and identity. Nonetheless, the birth of this innovative masters program was mostly the result of good luck. It began incognito, as a Master of Liberal Studies degree, a program that had been approved several years earlier by the governing board of the Arizona state universities as a degree for mid-career students who wished to return to school as a matter of personal fulfillment. But budget short-falls had thwarted the start of the program. When, a few years later, a far-sighted vice provost determined to fund the program and handed it off to me in my capacity as Assistant Dean of the Graduate College, it became possible to create a graduate program free of disciplinary bounds and responsive to the contemporary world.[1]

Two of us who were involved from the start, myself and Marcus Ford, co-editor of this volume, had been significantly influenced by John Cobb's thinking about the environment, economics, and social justice. Ford was in the midst of writing his own book on what a postmodern university might look like.[2] We immediately sought and were given permission to rethink the original structure of the program. At our first curriculum development meeting, we put the following questions out to the faculty for consideration: "At the close of the twentieth century, what ought we to be teaching in the university? What should be the scope of a graduate education? What are the most pressing issues facing this generation and, as well as we can predict, those that will follow closely behind? And, in light of these issues, what is our responsibility as members of the academy, as citizens, and as part of the human species, to our students?"

While the majority of graduate programs in liberal studies were not, at that time, thematically structured, the committee agreed that without a focus, interdisciplinary education risks becoming an educational buffet—a sumptuous but disordered spread of courses. We took seriously the double entendre in David Orr's now-classic essay, "What is Education For?" and gave consideration to the aims of education as well as the values fostered by it.[3] We decided on the theme "Visions of Good and Sustainable Communities" to shape our issue-based, interdisciplinary graduate program. Ford made the case for conjoining the terms, arguing that it is naïve to assume that the word "sustainable" presupposes an ethics of social justice or participatory democracy or that it necessarily promotes the flowering of individual talents and the strengthening of community capacities. The amazing engineering feat of the Llahasa Express, China's cross-country train from Qinghai to Katmandu, illustrated his point. Hailed as a model of environmental sensitivity to the fragile environment it traverses, the train's effects on the cultural integrity of the Tibetan people have been of great concern to those who defend an independent Tibet. If sustainability includes cultural sustainability as well as environmental sustainability, we knew that we must attend to questions of justice as well as efficiency.

We were consciously influenced by the earlier work of those who had recognized the urgency and strategic importance of teaching sustainability within formal educational institutions. When I read Wes Jackson's recollections about establishing the Environmental Studies program at Sacramento State University in the early 1970s, I was struck by how much our process resembled his—and was probably influenced by his. "None of us would be a Rachel Carson, a heroine of ours," writes Jackson,

> but we were not about to allow environmentalism to be defined in a narrow "clean-up-the-mess" sort of way, because we, in fact, did see that war, racism, poverty, the growing gap between rich and poor, destruction of our environment, and consumerism were one subject. . . . [W]e made sure that the curriculum was not restricted to wilderness issues and conservation or simply pollution or the exploding population. We talked about worldviews, and we did not pretend to embrace that hopelessly naïve view that it was possible to be objective. We had a sense of oughtness. . . ."[4]

In consenting to the double adjectives, "good and sustainable," we provided a double helping of fodder for those who would be set against the program. Not only would we hear the repeated accusation that inter-disciplinary work lacks the rigor of discipline-based training, we would also hear the program incriminated for being simultaneously trendy—an academic fashion that would soon pass—and retrograde, a throwback to the era when values were imposed. But our answer to the question "What is education for?" included the intention to educate scholar-activists, to make "liberal education" a force for good in the world.

Our mission was to provide interdisciplinary graduate education on the *very complex* issues of sustainability, focusing on the "commons" of our community life. The eclipse of community life is one of the most insidious consequences of modernity. In studying the collapse of com-munities—both human and non-human—and the reconstruction of them, we understood sustainability as extending beyond the technical to the structural and beyond the physical to the psychological, socio-logical, and metaphysical. We aimed to educate students for commu-nity leadership, preparing them to contribute to the well-being of their communities.

Our initial target audience was non-traditional students who in many cases were already active in bettering their communities. They fit the description of "Cultural Creatives," a term coined by sociologists Paul Ray and Sherry Ruth Anderson to name the forty million people whose lives are oriented around such things as concern for the environ-ment, gender equality, new spiritualities, invigoration of community life, and embrace of cultural pluralism.[5] (Twenty years later, it is tradi-tional students with undergraduate degrees in Environmental Studies, Environmental Sciences, and various sustainability-focused degrees who constitute the majority of participants in the program.)

Six years after we began, we were recognized at the national level as a model for other graduate programs. By 2008, the program had achieved legitimacy both because sustainability was very much a topic of public discussion and because the program had proved itself to be acceptably rigorous, practical (our students were getting jobs or going on for terminal degrees), and viable (attracting more than enough high quality graduate students). The program name was changed to the M.A. in Sustainable Communities to better reflect its mission and focus.

SOME REFLECTIONS ON SUSTAINABILITY

The word "sustainability" has become something of a "familiar unknown"—a word now integrated into our vocabularies, but still conceptually murky. I have been at more than one faculty meeting, at more than one university, where a department chair or a marketing director or an admissions counselor inevitably admits, "I'm just not sure what you mean by sustainability. How are you defining it?" And more often than not, the response comes in the form of the 1987 statement, issued as part of the Brundtland Commission: "Sustainable development is development that meets the needs of the present without compromising the ability of future generations to meet their own needs." To my repeated surprise, heads nod and there is no request for further explication.

Yet those of us who are immersed in the complex effort to reorient our lives and our teaching around sustainability know that the inquiry into sustainability goes well beyond the confines of seeking parity between current and future generations. We also know that to ask about "sustainability" as if it were some kind of Cartesian substance, a thing that can stand on its own without reference to anything else, is to risk the error of misplaced concreteness. Sustainability is better understood as a directional—a *way* of thinking, acting, and being, an *orientation in* the world and *to* the world. It gains its vigor in companionship with other nouns. Absent that, we lose what the word itself implies: a commitment to wholeness, complexity, pattern, design, and relations.

Though the full description of sustainability given in the Bruntland report includes concerns with such social conditions as poverty and inequity, the fact that economics is given a status of its own, named apart from such social needs, is a telling sign of the power of economism in shaping conceptions of sustainability. Indeed, the second most-cited definition of sustainability comes in the form of the "three E's of sustainability: economy, ecology, and equity." Economics is awarded a distinct province as if it were somehow separate from other social dimensions.

It is not just the inordinate influence of economics on our modern way of thinking that poses concerns for the study of sustainability. It is also, especially within our universities, our deeply rooted commitment to structuring intellectual inquiry and knowledge around the disciplines. Because this is the dominant paradigm in higher education, even a highly interdisciplinary inquiry like "sustainability" quickly defaults to discipline-defined units, often science or technology departments. Our national funding programs reinforce this focus on the science and technology dimensions of sustainability. Rather than understanding sustainability as a site of common concern for the sciences, social sciences, and humanities, it is seen as a topic to be examined by discrete disciplines. I once urged a dean to consider funding courses in sustainable food systems within our program on sustainable communities. His dismay belied his attachment to disciplinary modes of thought. Why would a social science college offer courses in agriculture? "We're not an ag school!" he exclaimed. In his mind, agriculture was a topic for agricultural schools and culture was topic for anthropology departments; if the burgeoning interest in sustainable food systems couldn't be addressed within those units, then it wasn't an appropriate topic for higher education.

But the idea and practice of sustainability can and ought to outflank the dominion of the disciplines. And, in fact, we saw our graduate students in the sustainable community program do this, taking classes, for example, in forest restoration and then going into fire-ravaged communities of the White Mountains and helping people to heal through creative arts narratives; studying the ecological oral histories of ranchers and native land stewards in order to record their wisdom and assess land changes over the decades of a lifetime; tracking down the data of species extinction on the Colorado Plateau and then designing a memorial in the memory of extinct species.[6] Rather than a discipline, students learn an "issue"; their depth came not in a discipline or even in the relation between two disciplines, but in their focus on the issue-solution — a compound inquiry that transcends artificial boundaries and the separation of study from practice.

Because creating and supporting sustainable communities depends on the capacity to understand and generate connections, learning to think relationally is an essential part of teaching for sustainability. It is not enough to work between disciplines, seeking to understand the connections that arise between them. If we only do that, we continue the mistaken belief that the whole is nothing more than the parts. An issue-based curriculum gives centrality to the "whole" and ensures that the relationship between disciplines is not simply additive.

Even then, an issue-based approach is not immune from the perils of reductionism. Unless the issue is understood as part of a larger pattern of relations, an issue-based curriculum can nonetheless fail on account of settling for a too-small understanding. Wendell Berry's notion of "solving for pattern" expresses a central notion of both process philosophy and ecological thinking. "It is the nature of any organic pattern to be contained within a larger one," writes Berry, echoing the ecological idea of nested systems. In order to arrive at a "good solution," the whole pattern of relations must be considered:

> A good agricultural solution, for example, would not pollute or erode a watershed. What is good for the water is good for the ground, what is good for the ground is good for the plants, what is good for the plants is good for animals, what is good for animals is good for people, what is good for people is good for the air, what is good for the air is good for the water. And vice versa.[7]

A good solution sacrifices neither part nor whole. It "improves the balances, symmetries, or harmonies within a pattern" and it "preserves the integrity of the pattern that contains it." While Berry's principal focus has been agricultural practices, his guidelines for "solving for pattern" are equally relevant to the redesign of educational practices and cultural issues in general.

GREEN KNOWLEDGE AND EDUCATING SCHOLAR-ACTIVISTS

Because discipline-based education favors method as a means for managing knowledge, the question about method arose again and again as a concern about programmatic rigor, student competence, and the legitimacy of the entire endeavor of interdisciplinary education. It was an ongoing conversation among affiliates and students and is indeed a conversation underway wherever interdisciplinary education and research is undertaken. But the desire to define a methods course for interdisciplinary work runs counter to the recognition that knowledge cannot be neatly boxed up and stacked like cartons in a warehouse. What kind of methods course would be appropriate for an interdisciplinary program that deals with both social and environmental sustainability? At first we simply advised students into one or another methods course offered through various departments on campus once they had chosen a thesis topic. Most took a qualitative research class, but some enrolled in courses in oral history, ethnography, creative writing, or quantitative methods. Eventually we realized that there was in fact a method to our programmatic intention to educate scholar-activists. That method involved situated, participatory learning, sometimes called action research. In his work on social movements and environmentalism, Andrew Jamison uses the term "change-oriented research" to describe the method appropriate to the production of "green knowledge."[8] This is research that is directed by purpose and value, but grounded in empirical realities and critical awareness.

In 2009, we introduced a new element into the required portion of our graduate curriculum, called "Action-Research Teams." Each team had responsibility for a community-based research project to be developed in collaboration with community organizations. Working on such local issues as water, weatherization, youth empowerment, immigration, and sustainable food practices, students immersed themselves in the details and circumstances of their project. They learned to develop collaborative networks and to work with community members, not as subjects for study but as partners in research and engagement.

Two colleagues, Dr. Romand Coles and Dr. Kimberly Curtis, developed this framework for teaching the art of community-building by way of the methods of change-oriented research. They drew heavily on the principles of citizen organizing proposed by Harry Boyte in his model of "Public Achievement"—"a theory-based practice of citizen organizing to do public work for the common good."[9] Boyte often cites the phrase from a southern civil rights movement song, now made famous by President Obama, "We are the ones we've been waiting for," as a clarion call for the responsible application of theory to praxis. They also incorporated the methods of relational meetings and public narrative developed by the Industrial Areas Foundation (IAF) and its Interfaith Network.[10] In this pedagogy of praxis, theoretical work and practical action are interwoven. For example, students in the action research team on "Water Advocacy" studied forecasts of a regional mega-drought and the critical challenges raised by insufficient water on the Colorado Plateau. They learned about local ecological, political, and social conditions related to water use and also contributed, on campus and off, to developing and implementing water-saving strategies. In partnership with several groups to "Take Back the Tap," they helped to install water bottle refill stations in several sites on campus (an act that can reduce the use of plastic bottles by tens of thousands), organized workshops on rainwater harvesting and permaculture landscaping, and contributed to the creation of local water-use policies.[11] In the process of cooperating in context, integrating theory and practice, and engaging in real-world issues, students generated "green knowledge."

In achieving our program goal to educate people who have both a depth of understanding and the ability to engage in community work, we came to realize that scholar-activists need a lot of skills. Our students were eager to do something, now, to improve the world. But it took time for us to learn how to integrate content and application and how to make it sufficiently rigorous to merit graduate credit. The literature on craftsmanship was helpful in this regard, reminding us of the intellectual complexity that often accompanies skilled practice. In its ideal form, craftsmanship is a coordinated relationship of head and hand, an embodied comprehension given material expression. To teach skills for social change, we developed a Summer Institute for Sustainable Communities in which students could learn such things as grant writing, conflict mediation, documentary videography, community assessment, fundraising, bee-keeping, and permaculture. We found that these capacities could be successfully taught in an intensive format, often in one-unit portions. In this way, we are able to provide additional competencies necessary for community-building, competencies that also made our graduates more attractive to potential employers.

In our Summer Institute, we also included short courses that were deeply interdisciplinary and otherwise not available in the university. Our program relied heavily on courses offered within the disciplines throughout the university — a cost-effective way to offer an interdisciplinary graduate program — but this meant that, aside from the program core, students mostly took discipline-based courses. Though they took courses from a wide range of disciplines, they nonetheless studied material presented in a discipline-bound way. In our summer courses, we were able to offer special topics classes that were not linked to a single discipline. Often nationally renowned guest faculty taught these courses, giving students the opportunity to study with leading thinkers in sustainability. John Cobb taught a course on "Spirituality, Economics, and the Environment"; Wes Jackson gave a course on "Agriculture and Culture"; the ethnobotanist Gary Nabhan taught courses on "Mapping the Indigenous Southwest" and "Community Food and Economic Development"; William R. Jordan, the ecologist who coined the term "ecological restoration," gave a class on "The Practice of Reinhabitation"; Yi Fu Tuan, the well-known geographer, lectured on "The Good Life"; and C. A. Bowers, a leading voice in education, offered a course on "Educating for a Sustainable Future." NAU faculty members were encouraged to develop deeply interdisciplinary classes of their own. One colleague from the Business College offered a class on "Community-based Economics"; an anthropologist taught classes on "Sustainability in the Southwest"; with my colleague William Burke in the English department, I developed a class on "Ecology, Art, and Sustainability." These cross-cutting courses were an important supplement to the discipline-based courses available during the regular academic year.

Over time it became clear that the entire program, in structure as well as content, needed to exemplify the values we wished to teach. Shifting the dominant paradigm entails systemic curricular changes, including how papers are written, how theses are shaped, what counts as appropriate research, what voice we give ourselves in our writing and speaking, and how we make ourselves present in the community. We believed, for example, that effective agents of change must be able to write in ways that are cogent and emotionally satisfying to their readers. But if we taught students to do this yet still insisted that their course papers and theses be written in a traditional, academic voice, not only would our message be mixed but our own commitment to changing the dominant paradigm would rightly be suspect. So we worked with students to develop their skills in creative non-fiction writing—a style that has its own significant rigors—and we permitted them to shape their papers and theses along these lines. We realized that if we spoke of the community as our site of responsibility and yet ignored contemporary community issues, we would have failed our heuristic convictions. In Flagstaff, the debate continues to rage over the use of reclaimed water for artificial snow-making on the San Francisco Peaks, sacred ground to thirteen native tribes. Though fraught with passion and potentially explosive, not to have taught a class on this issue, especially while it was under consideration by the Supreme Court, would have been to hide in the safe haven of the academy even as we called our students to grapple with issues of a similar intensity. To nurture responsible participation, to teach about the relocalization of culture, we had ourselves to create a curriculum responsive to our home base.

From the beginning, we embraced the idea that "the personal is the political," that sustainability and community cannot be taught as something "out there" to be interrogated by those with specialized training. In our first core course, "Self, Other, and Community," we explored questions about happiness, goodness, evil, and power, helping students to find their own answers to these perennial human concerns. The frame of "liberal studies" served us well in making a close examination of values a central feature of our curriculum. Had we not made a space in which students could reflect together on these basic questions, given the overall program ethos embedded in the theme of "good and sustainable communities," we could have descended into a presumptive ideology. Though almost all of our students came into the program aligned with politically progressive values, we needed to be sure that they had the chance to develop their positions with deliberation and that they could articulate them to their classmates, knowing that these conversations are at the heart of rebuilding culture.

But though we knew early on that in providing a curriculum that was not value-neutral we would have to be intentional in the teaching of values clarification, we did not also realize the importance of a good philosophical map in guiding our students. We thought, incorrectly, that students would naturally absorb the metaphysics that underlay so much of the literature in sustainability. Eventually it became clear that the metaphysics of modernity is so powerful that even people who want to escape its grip cannot do so without formal strategies for deconstruction and reconstruction. After a number of years of introducing process metaphysics in modest, unsystematic doses, we began to intentionally teach process thought in our second core class. Some students balked at the requirement to study philosophy because it was so foreign to them, but many more were grateful to have a philosophical way to express and understand their ideas. The lesson we learned is that teaching sustainability must include teaching a philosophical alternative to modernity in a purposeful, systematic way.

INTO THE FUTURE

As an experiment in crafting sustainable education, we relied on the boldness and enthusiasm of faculty and students alike. Again and again, our affiliate faculty indicated their desire to be more deeply engaged in the program. What kept them from doing so were departmental demands and constraints on faculty to participate in extra-departmental activities. Though faculty members are often encouraged to give time to university projects that enrich their intellectual life, departmental commitments are given precedence over non-departmental ones. Thus sustained participation in an anomalous program that is not housed in its own unit was difficult. Until universities dismantle the departmental, discipline-defined structure—or at such a time that departments become deeply interdisciplinary—free-standing interdisciplinary programs will remain subordinate to the competing needs of departments. As more and more students seek out programs like this, universities will do well to devise ways to regularize faculty participation in interdisciplinary programs.

In the twenty years since the Master of Sustainable Communities program was established, programs in sustainability have multiplied. What is meant by sustainability, what a study of it ought to include, and how programs ought to be organized, is now part of a vibrant discussion at many universities. But these programs are still relatively young and vulnerable. Though the Sustainable Communities program at Northern Arizona University has one of the longest track records thus far among graduate programs devoted to sustainability, like any educational project that is unconventional and innovative, it requires constant attention to and reflection on new issues, an enduring vigilance (especially in times of declining budgets), and the ongoing zestful commitment of faculty and students to shaping a new kind of education. The future of programs like this is not clear. We can hope that they will become increasingly common and that as they succeed, we will see a much-needed shift in our understanding of the structures and purposes of higher education.

NOTES

1   Dr. Henry Hooper, then Vice Provost for Research and Graduate Studies and one of the most able administrators with whom I have worked, handed me the fortunate task of implementing this new graduate degree. He served as a role model to me for how to accomplish creative change within a large, conventional institution.

2   Marcus P. Ford, *Beyond the Modern University: Toward a Constructive Postmodern University* (Santa Barbara: Praeger, 2002).

3   David Orr, "What is Education For?" in *Earth in Mind* (Washington, D.C.: Island Press, 1994), 7–15; also online: <http://www.context.org/ ICLIB/IC27/Orr.htm>.

4   Wes Jackson, *Consulting the Genius of the Place* (Berkeley: Counterpoint, 2010), 62.

5   Paul H. Ray and Sherry Ruth Anderson, *The Cultural Creatives: How 50 Million People Are Changing the World* (New York: Harmony Books, 2000).

6   Patty Kohany, "A Quilted Landscape: The White Mountain Collaborative Quilt Projects, Community Restoration and Visual Narrative" (NAU, M.A. Sustainable Communities, 2004); see Peter Frederici, *What Has*

Passed and What Remains: Oral Histories of Northern Arizona's Changing Landscapes (Tucson: University of Arizona Press, 2010). Friederici's book drew on two graduate seminars on "Ecological Oral History" offered in the Sustainable Communities program; Michele A. James, "Envisioning a Memorial for Extinct Species" (NAU, M.A. Sustainable Communities, 2003).

7   Wendell Berry, "Solving for Pattern," in *The Gift of Good Land: Further Essays Cultural & Agricultural* (New York: North Point Press, 1981).

8   Andrew Jamison, "In Search of Green Knowledge: A Cognitive Approach to Sustainable Development," in *Pragmatic Sustainability,* Steven Moore, ed. (London: Routledge, 2010). See also Jamison, *The Making of Green Knowledge: Environmental Politics and Cultural Transformation* (Cambridge: Cambridge University Press, 2001).

9   See "Humphrey School of Public Affairs," *University of Minnesota,* April 25, 2011, <http://www.hhh.umn.edu/people/hboyte/>.

10   See "Who We Are," *Industrial Areas Foundation,* <http://www.industrialareasfoundation.org/>.

11   For current examples of the work of Action Research Teams in the Sustainable Communities Program see "Green NAU," *Northern Arizona University,* <http://green.nau.edu/cbart.html>.

14. ENCOUNTERING THE OTHER:

A CASE FOR APPLIED LIBERAL EDUCATION

Robert Neustadt

ABSTRACT: *This essay makes a case for what we might call applied liberal arts instruction, an experiential approach to teaching that takes students out of the classroom in order to teach them to care about and engage with the world in which they live. Caring is crucial to successful learning experiences and is central to the concept of postmodern Whiteheadian education — a process that aims to teach the whole student, to lead students to care about the environment, to care about people, and to realize that human beings are part of nature. Since 2010, the author has brought seven different classes of students on five-day field trips to the Arizona/Mexico border in courses that focus on the topic of undocumented immigration. The bulk of this essay describes and discusses students' experiences on these trips — learning experiences that have been life changing. The author's goal, through applied liberal arts education, is to teach students to care about moral and ethical principles, to learn compassion, and to assume a sense of personal agency.*

HOW CAN WE GET STUDENTS to care about their education? As a professor, I have found that the most effective way to get students to care and engage with a course is, paradoxically, to get them out of the classroom. Environmental Education. Experiential Education. Field Trips. Action Research Teams. Community Service. Theatrical performances in the community. Study Abroad. Engaged Education. These are some of the approaches, projects, exercises, and pedagogical strategies that can get students to care. Getting students to care is crucial, since caring about one's education is the key to motivation, hence learning. Caring is also the first step towards making the world a better place—an idea which is central to the concept of postmodern Whiteheadian education—a process that aims to teach the whole student, to lead students to care about the environment, to care about people, and to realize that human beings, as Stephen Rowe points out in the introduction to this volume, are part of nature. If we conceive of ourselves as elements of nature, not independent handlers that exist above or outside of our environment, then a commitment to become stewards of the Earth and to care for the planet rises naturally. As Howard Woodhouse writes in his chapter, Whitehead evoked "a buzzing world amid a democracy of fellow creatures," a world we share with interrelated "populations" and "communities." Our goal, then, in envisioning alternative models of education, is to teach students to care about moral and ethical principles and to assume a sense of personal agency.

This essay describes a pedagogical case study of what we might call *applied liberal arts instruction*, an experiential approach to teaching that takes students out of the classroom in order to teach them about the world in which they live. Since 2010, I have brought seven different classes of students, a total of over 100 students, on five-day field trips to the Arizona/Mexico border, in courses that focus on the topic of undocumented immigration. The bulk of this essay describes and discusses students' experiences on these trips—learning experiences that for them and for me have been life changing. Ultimately, my hope is that students will take what they have learned on the trip and in the class, and will engage in, and with, the "real world" in whatever manner proves meaningful to them.

It is important to underscore that I work in Arizona, where the issue of undocumented immigration remains a very controversial topic. Tenure has given me the protection that allows me to persist in teaching courses that could very easily "ruffle feathers" of parents, administrators, or politicians. Without tenure, I would not have had the confidence to take on such politically sensitive endeavors. And yet it was precisely through teaching politically controversial material that I have discovered my appreciation for applied experiential education, which has been the most pedagogically significant development of my career. I maintain that a comprehensive college education should embrace political controversy. It should encourage students to explore and critically interrogate their opinions and newfound knowledge within the context of their humanity. This, I think, is how we can strive to educate *the whole student*.

The question of mixing the "messy" world of politics with a liberal arts education is in many ways linked to interdisciplinarity. Marcus Ford argues that "the organization of knowledge into isolated disciplines" is implicated in the failure of contemporary universities to educate the "whole student to repair the world."[1] Instructors are encouraged to stay within the confines of their discipline. We are told that as educators we need to be objective and politically neutral. By this logic, I should teach only Spanish language and Latin American literature. Language instruction should be merely grammar or skills-based, and literature, analogously, should only involve the comprehension of story lines and plots. The fallacious idea that teaching language or literature can be apolitical stems from a false dichotomy, a deceptive division attempting to isolate liberal arts content from political controversy. Both language and literature, when studied in context, are inherently political. To ignore the political underpinnings of language and literature corresponds to a politically biased decision hidden within the discourses of modern disciplinarity and neoliberal specialization.

Whereas I certainly understand, and agree, that faculty should not use their platform to manipulate their students, the idea that we are not supposed to engage students politically, to provoke them to think critically, to expose hidden inequities and abuses that are rife in contemporary political systems, correlates to relinquishing our goal to serve as educators of the whole student. Of course, our students have every right to disagree with us. If we inspire them to think critically, students' analyses will interrogate not only the "world" but also their professors' worldviews. I encourage students to examine the facts and to form, and voice, their own opinions. I remain in contact with former students of different, more conservative political ideologies who enjoy sharing and exploring their ideas with me. But this type of critical inquiry will only arise if and when we, as educators, take the risk to cross borders—disciplinary boundaries, political boundaries, and humanistic boundaries—and engage, rather than avoid, the problems of the world with our students. Let us look specifically at the issue of undocumented immigration to underscore the need of interdisciplinarity in this specific case.

Today, in the popular press, there exists an enormous "wall" of disinformation about the causes, conditions, and consequences of undocumented immigration in the United States. Politicians, from both sides of the political spectrum, manipulate the public by exploiting tropes of fear, instability, and economic and social disorder.[2] Before taking my students to the border, then, it is necessary to sort out the facts so that we all draw our (varying) conclusions from the same foundation of verifiable information. It is also incumbent to prepare the ground conceptually, through readings, films, and discussions. Many students have never thought about what a border actually is, how international borders get re-drawn over the course of history, or how a plethora of discursive and conceptual borders affect all of us in our everyday lives. If we want a comprehensive understanding, it is necessary to study the border from across a spectrum of different disciplines. If we limit our study to economic factors without taking into account cultural, environmental, sociological, and political consequences, then we are contemplating only an isolated fragment of a very complex puzzle.

It is crucial to read about the 695 miles of walls and vehicle barriers that have been constructed along the nearly 2,000 mile U.S./Mexico border to assess the economic cost of "securing the border." Who are the people who cross the border, why do they enter the country illegally, and how have our strategies of border security affected the patterns of illegal immigration? To answer these questions we need to explore transglobal economic factors and take into account the practices and consequences of undocumented labor in the United States. In order to understand the root causes of mass migration, we also need to understand the connected economic policies of globalization, free trade, and the resulting violence decimating Mexico and Central America.

Questions of social justice, including what actually happens to people who are detained without documents, intersect with the evolution of immigration law — the criminalization of undocumented people — and neoliberal economic structures such as the rise of the private "for-profit" prison industry and the Border Industrial Complex.[3] A cost benefit analysis obliges us to take into account the border wall's efficacy as infrastructure vis-a-vis its environmental impact. Never have I had a student come into class already aware that the border wall will likely cause multiple species to become extinct.[4] Only a handful of students have begun class with anything more than a vague awareness of the extent of migrant deaths in the borderlands. Virtually no student has had prior knowledge that the increase in border deaths — over 7,000 human remains have been discovered since 1994 — is directly attributable to changes in U.S. border enforcement strategies.[5] In addition to studying Border Patrol policy papers, journalistic descriptions, scholarly assessments, and documentary films, we deepen our understanding by analyzing how the border wall and the issue of immigration have been represented aesthetically, in art, feature film, music, and literature, including poetry, performance art, theater, and narrative.

All of the above are excellent and necessary approaches to learning about the border and immigration. And yet all of them, even in combination, yield a partial and inadequate perspective. It is one thing to read about the border wall; it is another to touch the wall and to see Mexico, only inches away, through the slats. I take my students to the wall, and we even go so far as to *play* the wall as a musical instrument. Our experiences playing the wall are facilitated by sound sculptor Glenn Weyant, who attempts, by musicalizing the wall, to transform a barrier built to separate people into a collective and unifying musical experience.[6] To play the border wall, and to hear it vibrate, produces an ineffable feeling, especially in the context of other aspects of our trip (which I describe in the remainder of this essay).

With respect to teaching style, I lead very interactive classes. Whenever possible, we sit in a circle and I encourage students to dialogue amongst themselves, in small groups, in large groups, and with the entire class. Even so, on my first border field trip, when we jumped in the vans after two months in the classroom, I heard one of my students ask another student his name. I was flabbergasted to realize that this far into the semester these students still did not know each other's names. It is as if there are "border walls" that divide and separate us. I am referring here not only to the political borders that divide one nation's citizens from "foreign Others," but to psychological border walls that divide students from their peers and professors from students.

Obviously, social boundaries — different races, ethnicities, and sexual preferences — divide us, but here I am discussing an even more generalized division. In our contemporary state of continual *busy-ness*, students come to class with a smart phone in their hands and social media on their minds. Social media helps us to connect with people around the globe, yet paradoxically, such "connected" students often may not notice the person sitting next to them. When taking students on field trips I see, over and over, how students become friends. On one trip, a student took my guitar from the back of the van and began to play and sing *La bamba*. While driving down the highway, a van full of my students sang *La bamba* together at the top of their voices. Then, when we stopped at a rest stop they got out and started to stretch and practice yoga in a group. On another trip, one student taught the others how to play a game, "My Cow," which she grew up playing with her family on road trips. It is beautiful to see my students laugh, play, and become close to one another in ways that I have never seen occur in a traditional classroom.

On these field trips we camp in the desert. In most classes I usually have some students who have never camped before. They work together, problem solving, to figure out how to set up their tents before dark. Sometimes they sleep huddled together, in "dog piles," to stay warm. I often think, while watching them bond, that even if they learned nothing more from the class, the group dynamics combined with the impact from the outdoor experience would be enough to make the trip a success. Getting students out of the classroom is a way to help students transcend the interpersonal walls that divide us.

Of course, this is not just an arbitrary outdoor experience—we camp at the basecamp of a humanitarian organization called No More Deaths/No más muertes, a volunteer group that places water in the desert and provides medical aid to migrants in an effort to keep people from suffering and dying in the desert. On several trips we have met and befriended migrants who were receiving medical assistance at the base-camp. They have shared their stories with us and given us a much more personal understanding of what crossing the border without documents entails. On one trip, a Guatemalan man named Lalo told us about how he had become separated from his group when a Border Patrol helicopter scattered his group. He lost his backpack, all of his supplies, and spent two nights alone shaking from the cold. Lalo told us that he passed several days without food or water and thought he would die. One can read about the average temperatures in the desert in November, but to feel these temperatures adds another level of understanding. My students and I shiver while wearing jackets and hats. We cozy up to the fire and sleep in sleeping bags inside tents. For my students to hear Lalo's story, and to realize how viscerally the cold affects *us,* brings an awareness of how truly difficult and dangerous the journey is for migrants who cross the border without proper gear. Regardless of a student's political perspective, my experience is that this awareness brings compassion.

Though it might sound trivial, even the experience of singing songs around the campfire proves educational on these trips. Sharing music by a fire under the stars is a social activity during which I feel close to those around me. Singing around the fire with my students gives me the opportunity to share some of who I am, via the music of my generation, and vice versa. This goes much deeper, nevertheless, than a simple social gathering. On one trip, a Honduran migrant, Óscar, told us his harrowing experiences during his repeated attempts to cross the border. He first crossed Mexico on top of a freight train known as "*la bestia*" (The Beast). We had watched a documentary film about this train, but to hear someone tell us that he personally had travelled on the Beast, and that he saw people fall off the train and die, brought our memories of the film alive.[7] Óscar also saw another woman fall off the train and lose her legs. On his first attempt to cross into the United States, a woman collapsed in the desert. He abandoned his quest to reach a city in the U.S. and carried her back across the border to Mexico. Then, on his second attempt to cross the border, a man in the group he was travelling with died in the desert. Óscar's group took the time to bury the body under desert rocks. To read about and discuss such topics in a classroom is a learning experience, but it mainly corresponds to filling in background material. To listen to these testimonials in the desert, on the other hand, conveys a more profound, human impression.

I can remember that night vividly, all of us sitting around the campfire, sharing music. I pass my guitar to Óscar and he plays and sings us a song in Spanish. Huddled around the fire singing, for a brief few moments, we are not "migrants," "professor," and "students"; we are friends—fellow humans in a buzzing democracy, trying to make sense of the differences conveyed by our citizenship, our nationalities, and the privileges conferred to us by the various places we were born. To sing Woody Guthrie's "This Land is Your Land," in Spanish and English, with these new friends in the middle of desert, brings a lump to my throat.

The experience helps students move beyond the walls that separate them and even goes so far as to build bridges between them. On one of my trips, one of my students, I'll call her Sabrina, told us that she had been particularly interested in the class because she was planning to become a Border Patrol agent. A politically conservative student from a Latino family, she had not really thought about the human costs involved in "securing the border." Before the class, by her own account, she did not understand the complexity of the issue and had no idea how much migrants suffer while attempting to cross the border. She also had not heard about the abuse migrants often receive from immigration authorities, or about Operation Streamline, a federal program that sends thousands of undocumented people into for-profit prisons for lengthy periods of incarceration prior to deportation. Earlier in the trip we had attended an Operation Streamline session in the federal courthouse in Tucson where we observed 70 shackled and chained migrants plead guilty in a group hearing that took just over two hours.

At the No More Deaths basecamp, Sabrina spent a day caring for a group of migrants who had become ill and injured during their journey. Over the course of that day they told jokes and talked about their families, their tastes in music, their religious beliefs, their political allegiances, and their lives in Honduras, Guatemala, Mexico, and Flagstaff. They also explained the reasons that had informed their decisions to migrate.

Later, when we were debriefing our experiences, Sabrina spoke about the arbitrary nature of our privilege, that we could get in vans and drive back home to take showers and sleep in our beds, while the migrants, now her friends, would leave the camp hoping to avoid arrest, imprisonment, deportation, even death. She said that she had never thought about what her parents must have gone through to cross the border, a journey that resulted in her being born a citizen of the United States. She said that she kept imagining her parents out in that desert. As she tried to express her feelings, she started to cry. Another student named Reyna, a left-wing political activist who had not been particularly friendly with Sabrina before the trip, moved over to rub her back. As I watched these two students hug I realized that the ideological differences that separated them — the "walls" that only a few days prior had kept them from being friends — had crumbled.

On another trip, at the campfire, a student who I'll call Rebecca surprised us with her candor. Rebecca was a quiet student who never participated much in class. I couldn't tell if she was simply unmotivated or bored, but she didn't seem to enjoy class. When we took an orientation workshop with No More Deaths volunteers, she embarrassed many of us by falling asleep right in front of our speakers. Later, at the No More Deaths basecamp, she took us off guard at the campfire when she told us that she used to "hate" migrants. "I used to hate migrants," she said, "because they cross our borders and break our laws." Then, she paused and added, "but I don't think people should be dying out here." The rest of the class and faculty who were helping me lead the trip were as surprised as I was. We looked around at each other's faces as if to ask if she really said what we heard her say. I felt shocked, and at the same time was happy to see that she had become comfortable enough to share her feelings and opinions. Later, at the end of that trip, when we got back to Flagstaff (a mountain town at 7,000 feet elevation), it was very cold. I was dropping off students at their dorms and happened to catch Rebecca's eye. "It's cold," I muttered. "At least you have a jacket," Rebecca responded. I looked at her, a bit confused, and asked what happened to her jacket. "I gave it to a migrant" she replied. Rebecca had learned compassion. I don't think any amount of classroom readings and activities could have affected her so profoundly.

During these field trips we also walk across the international border into Nogales (Sonora), Mexico. After passing through a turnstyle you realize that you're in Mexico when you see a sign reading, "Bienvenidos a México." Students are always surprised to realize that they've entered Mexico without so much as having to show their passports. While in Nogales, Mexico, we serve meals to recently deported people at the Kino Border Initiative "*Comedor*" (Soup Kitchen). Here, students hear stories, face-to-face, from men, women, and children who describe their experiences crossing the border, in the desert and/or in Border Patrol custody. We have also visited with Border Patrol agents and visited their facilities. In Nogales, students have the opportunity to try to square what they've heard from Border Patrol authorities with what they hear from people who have been deported.

After the soup kitchen, we visit with residents at a Women's Shelter in Nogales, also run by the Kino Border Initiative. It is said that 60–80% of migrant women are raped at some point while they are crossing the border.[8] The rate is so high that many women take birth control pills prophylactically. Whereas anti-immigrant activists, politicians, and Border Patrol agents may assert that all "illegal aliens" are "criminals," talking with mothers who are attempting to give their children a better life opens up the possibility of different, more nuanced perspectives. We listen to the women explain their need to cross the border. One woman tells us that she was seeking medical treatment for a child who cannot walk. These are emotional encounters. One of these women has U.S. citizen children waiting for her in the United States. Another, an indigenous woman from Oaxaca, has children in southern Mexico, and they are depending on her to send money for food. Another tells us that she has children on both sides of the border, and she simply wants to have them together under one roof. A woman at the shelter,

Rosie, describes her three harrowing attempts to enter the United States to care for her U.S. citizen child (who is handicapped). On her most recent try she had hidden in the trunk of a car, which flipped over while the driver attempted to flee from the Border Patrol. After the accident, Border Patrol pursued the driver while this woman lay injured, locked in the trunk. Rosie thought she would die. We listened to all of this, all the while aware that we walked freely across the border into Mexico without even having to show documents.

In the shelter we hear stories that contradict information that we have heard earlier. The Border Patrol agents described the *coyotes,* the guides, as evil people who only care about money. One woman in the shelter reinforced this view when she told us that her guide tried to rape her in the desert. She escaped and then spent two terrifying nights alone in the desert. Another woman told us that when she was detained, four male Border Patrol agents yelled at her in a cell for three hours, pressuring her to identify the *coyote* from their group (so that they could charge him with human smuggling). In her case, she said that the guide was a nice man; he had already crossed her sister and she knew that in the future he would help her get into the United States. After intimidating this woman verbally, the Border Patrol left her sitting on a bench alone from 8 PM to 6 AM with no food or water. We later asked Border Patrol agents about her story, and they replied that it would clearly be in violation of policy and that she should have complained. Obviously, these are specific examples. Everyone's experience is different, and other deported people have told us that the Border Patrol treated them professionally. I am not trying to demonize the Border Patrol. That said, there exists ample documented evidence, in addition to the anecdotal evidence that we have encountered when speaking with deported people, that points to a preponderance of abuse experienced at the hands of both the Border Patrol and *coyotes.* Consistently, the migrants, those at the bottom of the "chain," those who are most vulnerable, are the people who suffer the mistreatment of unscrupulous individuals from both sides of the issue.

While in Nogales we also visited the site where a 16-year-old boy, José Antonio Elena Rodríguez, was shot and killed by Border Patrol on October 10, 2011, on the Mexican side of the wall. Only recently has the agent who shot him been charged, and the videos of the killing have still not been released (in spite of numerous FOIA requests).[9] Border Patrol maintains that José Antonio was throwing rocks and, furthermore, that they have the right to use lethal force against rock throwers. Witnesses on the Mexican side of the border deny that he was throwing rocks. It is enlightening, however, to visit the site because one becomes immediately aware of the fact that it would have been impossible for José Antonio to hit a Border Patrol agent with a rock from that place. The boy was shot eight times in the back and twice in the head. It is one thing to read about this case. It is another experience entirely to visit the place where he was shot and to try to make sense of this event. Prior to the class, and the trip, most of my students had no idea how many credible abuse allegations have been made against U.S. Border Patrol agents, officers who are almost always given immunity.[10]

I also take students out into the Arizona desert to hike on trails used by migrants when entering into the United States. Having read about the experience of crossing the border gives an idea, but actually walking on the trails provides a tangible experience. Even so, the experience is partial. We cannot know what it is like to flee for our lives, for example, as do refugees who are fleeing violence in Mexico and Central America. Likewise, we cannot know how it feels to be compromised physically by years of malnutrition, to walk/run for days without food and water, to feel afraid to die. To hike, stumble, get scraped by cacti, and from time to time feel lost on these trails, nevertheless, gives students an inkling of what this journey can be like for undocumented border crossers. To visit places in the desert where people have died adds an even more poignant layer to this experience. When we visit the site where a 14-year-old girl from El Salvador, Josseline, died, many of my students cry. They have all read about her story beforehand in Margaret Regan's book, *The Death of Josseline: Immigration Stories from the Arizona/Mexico Borderlands*, but still there is something about being in this place that makes one feel personally connected to Josseline. I have seen some of my students pray at Josseline's altar. I have seen others leave offerings: flowers, stones, a ring; others hug. On one trip, a student announced, with tears in his eyes, that if Josseline were alive, she would be their same age. He went on to say that since we now know about what is occurring, it is our responsibility to try to keep this type of tragedy from continuing.

Here, in the Sonoran desert, my students have become acutely aware of a humanitarian crisis that is taking place in their own state, a tragedy seldom mentioned in discussions of undocumented immigration. In the classroom, before the trip, the students had debated whether or not it was appropriate for humanitarian groups like No More Deaths to cache water in the desert. In class there was some disagreement—they struggled with the idea of whether such aid would serve as an incentive to other would-be migrants. Now, in the desert, with the knowledge that some 200 human remains are found in the Arizona desert every year, with an awareness that it is legal to leave water, and with a map in their minds of how lucky a migrant would have to be to encounter the cached water, all of my students have reached consensus. Just as important, from my perspective, here in the desert my students have learned compassion. No one, they say, deserves to die of thirst in the desert.

Before concluding, I would like to describe one more example of how getting students out of the classroom can lead to a more nuanced understanding of issues that, for many people, remain hidden behind walls of ignorance and political discourse. On a recent trip we visited the Tohono O'odham reservation, an indigenous nation that spans both sides of the U.S./Mexico border. In spite of the fact that the Tohono O'odham reservation is the second largest Indian reservation in the U.S., and even though the names of Arizona and Tucson derive originally from O'odham words, very few people, even in Arizona, have heard of the tribe, and even fewer know where they live. One can, and should, read about poverty on Indian reservations, but to see it first-hand brings new levels of empathy and understanding. In an area essentially devoid of employment opportunities, one can understand the temptation for O'odham to engage in smuggling. Our visit to the O'odham Nation helped us to deconstruct the concept of a binary border neatly separated into the "1st" and "3rd" worlds and allowed us to see a more complex border that is inscribed within the logic of land ownership and control. The Nation is surrounded by Border Patrol check-points. You cannot leave the Nation without being asked to prove your citizenship. Yet, how can a U.S. Border Patrol agent from Ohio, for example, demand that an O'odham person, whose people have lived in this area for thousands of years, show proof of citizenship on the O'odham nation?

We stood at the San Miguel gate, an area where the O'odham Nation is divided by vehicle barriers demarcating the U.S./Mexico border. Looking south, one becomes aware of the arbitrary nature of political borders. From a nationalistic perspective, we were standing on the international border dividing two countries, the United States of Mexico and the United States of America. From a Native American perspective, on the other hand, we were standing in the middle of an area that has been inhabited by an indigenous people for millennia. An indigenous tribe that, as a consequence of U.S. border policy, can no longer conduct its traditional, cultural, and spiritual gatherings because the international boundary that bisects their nation prohibits them from moving freely within their own homeland.

Sadly, the O'odham nation is the most deadly corridor for border crossers. And many of the migrants who die on the nation are indigenous people from southern Mexico and Central America, people who have lost their livelihood due to the free trade treaties (NAFTA and CAFTA), signed by the governments of the U.S., Mexico, Canada, and most recently, Central American countries. Our O'odham guides, Mike Wilson and David Garcia, help us to understand the political paradoxes. The O'odham Tribal Government, we learn, refuses to allow humanitarian groups to operate on the reservation. "The Tribal Government does not want to bite the hand that feeds it," says Wilson. The tribe receives funding from the federal government, so they give the U.S. Border Patrol free run on the reservation and have allowed the Department of Homeland Security to construct a border barrier, even when this occupation corresponds to the restriction of O'odham people's rights. As a consequence, Wilson, Garcia, and other O'odham individuals provide humanitarian aid to migrants on the reservation, simultaneously defying both the U.S. government and their own tribal government. The question of indigeneity, then, throws a monkey wrench into the simplistic binary concept of border politics. It is not simply an *us versus them*, north/south geographical division. There are O'odham living on both sides of the international border, and in the U.S., there are O'odham on both sides of the issue. Certainly these international, economic, and cultural divisions, resulting in the deaths of thousands of indigenous people on an Indian reservation, run counter to the indigenous concept of living in, with, and as part of the land (as Woodhouse describes in his essay in this volume).

On my border field trips students come to know one another and form rich, meaningful, and lasting relationships. The class "chemistry" becomes transformed by the trip. My own relationship with my students is also significantly enhanced by the time spent together outside in the "real" world. Engaging with "Others," talking with recently deported people on the Mexican side of the border, singing with undocumented migrants at the No More Deaths basecamp, meeting with Border Patrol, observing Operation Streamline hearings in the federal courthouse, contemplating the complexities of the Tohono O'odham Nation, and playing the border wall as a musical instrument — all of these experiences make the inequities of undocumented immigration tangible, understandable, and palpable. On these trips, what was once course "content" becomes experience, material of deep and profound intellectual and ethical comprehension. One student wrote on his course evaluation that the course "made me realize I have a soul." By getting students out of the classroom and into the world, by exposing them to the complexities of an issue that lies largely hidden behind a wall of political discourse and media "blah blah," students become both informed and compassionate. I am hopeful that their compassion will inspire them to transcend the hyperspecialized limitations of modern education — what Whitehead called "minds in a groove" — that they will continue to learn, and that they will find ways to make this world a better place.

NOTES

1   Unpublished manuscript, paper presented at the "Seizing an Alternative for an Ecological Civilization" conference, Pomona College, Claremont, CA, June 4–7, 2015.

2   The popular image in the contemporary United States, for example, is that Democrats, favoring comprehensive immigration reform, are

"pro-immigrant," whereas Republicans, calling in contrast for enhanced "border security," are "anti-immigrant." The fact that the Obama administration has deported over 2 million people, more than any other administration in history from either party, is one significant example of the fact that the situation is more complex than a two-party binary opposition implies.

3   By "Border Industrial Complex" I am referring to the phenomenon of massive spending on security hardware (Predator B drones, helicopters, sensors, walls, vehicle barriers, a 22,000 "man" Border Patrol agency, etc.) concentrated on the border. We currently spend $18 billion per year on border security. For more information, see Todd Miller's book, *Border Patrol Nation: Dispatches from the Front Lines of Homeland Security* (San Francisco: City Lights Open Media, 2014).

4   According to Dan Millis, director of the Sierra Club's Borderlands Campaign, there are 33 threatened and endangered species living in the vicinity of the border wall that are being put at serious risk. For more on the impact of the wall on wildlife, see Krista Schlyer, *Continental Divide: Wildlife, People and the Border Wall* (College station, TX: A&M UP, 2012).

5   This figure provided by Kat Rodríguez (via personal communication), formerly with *Derechos Humanos,* currently with the Colibrí Center for Human Rights in Tucson. The actual number of people who have died in the borderlands is not known, though some estimate that the number of deaths could be anywhere from 2 to 10 times the number of recovered human remains. The wall and border security strategies are directly implicated in these deaths because such strategies funnel border crossers through remote, hostile terrain. For a historical and demographic analysis of the phenomenon of border crosser deaths in Arizona as a result of the "funnel effect," see "Structural Violence and Migrant Deaths in Southern Arizona: Data from the Pima County Office of the Medical Examiner, 1990–2013" by Daniel Martínez, Robin Reineke, Raquel Rubio-Goldsmith and Bruce O. Parks in *Journal on Migration and Human Security* 2, no. 4 (2014): 257–86.

6   For more on Weyant's work, including audio files, see his web page, <http://www.sonicanta.com>. To hear one of Weyant's compositions with a poem about the border wall by Margaret Randall, listen to "Offended Turf"/"Droneland Security" on *Border Songs: A Collection of Music and Spoken Word,* eds. Robert Neustadt and Chuck Cheesman, Tucson: No More Deaths, 2012, Track 7, Disc 1.

7   Thousands of the most impoverished Central American migrants ride on top of freight trains to travel through Mexico. They call the train *"la bestia"* (the beast), presumably because of the danger involved from

falling off, or getting thrown off, of the train and getting sucked under the wheels. For a film that follows the experiences of migrant children on the trains see Rebecca Cammisa's powerful documentary film, *Which Way Home* (Los Angeles, CA: Mr. Mudd Production, 2009).

8   See Eleanor Goldberg, "80% of Central American Women, Girls are Raped Crossing into the U.S." *Huffington Post* (September 12, 2014) <http://www.huffingtonpost.com/2014/09/12/central-america-migrants-rape_n_5806972.html>.

9   On the case of José Antonio Elena Rodríguez and the still un-released video, see Perla Trevizo, "Border Agent's Murder Trial Postponed," in the *Arizona Daily Star* (January 5, 2016) <http://tucson.com/news/border-agent-s-murder-trial-postponed/article_561ac027-ef47-5d29-8d01-9c073669afff.html>.

10   See, Charles Davis's article, "U.S. Customs and Border Protection has Killed nearly 50 People in 10 Years. Most were Unarmed." *The New Republic* (January 4, 2015) <https://newrepublic.com/article/120687/border-patrol-officers-get-impunity-anonymity-immigrant-killings>.

CONTRIBUTORS

JIAHONG CHEN received completed her Ph.D. in Social Sciences and Comparative Education from UCLA. Her research runs across the philosophy of education, dialogue among civilisations, and cross cultural inquiry of humanist education. Previously she served as Vice Director of the Centre for Dialogue among Civilizations at the Institute for Advanced Humanistic Studies, Peking University, as well as Secretary General of the World Ethics Institute at Peking University. She was a fellow at the East and West Centre, Asia Pacific Higher Education Research Partnership and now a research director of Dialogue of Civilisation Research Institute and a visiting research fellow at Peking University.

JOHN B. COBB, JR. is an American philosopher, theologian, and environmentalist and is often cited as one of the most important North American theologians of the twentieth century. He is the preeminent scholar in the school of thought associated with the philosophy of Alfred North Whitehead. The author of more than fifty books, Cobb is also a member of the American Academy of Arts and Sciences. Cobb is known for his transdisciplinary approach to knowledge, integrating insights from many different areas of study and bringing different specialized disciplines into fruitful communication. As a result, Cobb has been influential in a wide range of disciplines, including theology, ecology, economics, biology and social ethics.

FRANCE H. CONROY's varied experiences include Danforth scholar, ship fitter, radical journalist, and organizer of seminars on Confucian humanism. As a Danforth scholar at Yale and Union Graduate School, he completed a PhD project at the intersection of philosophy, sociology, and political movements under Continental philosopher George Schrader. As an East-West Center (Hawai'i) fellow under Confucian scholar Tu Weiming, he organized seminars on Asian texts for Paul Desjardins' Adirondack Work-Study center. In between, he taught 35 years at Burlington County College in Pemberton, New Jersey. He is co-author of *West Across the Pacific* with his father, historian Hilary Conroy.

ABIGAIL E. DEHART, a graduate of Grand Valley State University, is a J.D. Candidate at the University of Michigan Law School. She holds an MPhil from the University of Cambridge in Political Thought and Intellectual History. Her work has mainly focused on interrogating the relationship between education and citizenship in eighteenth-century political thought. In the future, she hopes to work on issues of law and public policy pertaining to educational access.

MARK DIBBEN is a professor in the Tasmanian School of Business & Economics, Hobart. He is on the Advisory Board of Process Studies, co-editor of *Philosophy of Management* and Academic Director of the International Process Network. He has worked in Applied Process Thought — the thoroughgoing, serious minded, hard-core common-sense application of process metaphysics to topics in the sciences, social sciences, and arts — his entire academic career, and uses Whitehead's "speculative inquiry" as a basis for his philosophical questioning (cf. scientific answering) approach to student learning.

MARCUS FORD taught Environmental Humanities at Northern Arizona for twenty years and is the author of *Beyond the Modern University: Toward a Constructive Postmodern University* and *William James's Philosophy: A New Perspective*. He currently is involved in starting a very-small college is Flagstaff Arizona and is working with others to promote the establishment of other, very-small, mission-driven, educational institutions around the U.S. and abroad.

LAURA GARDNER, Ph.D., began her career teaching art to young children and currently prepares university students to be artist-teachers in schools and arts organizations. She is a letterpress printer and book artist. Dr. Gardner has received numerous grants and awards in the areas of pedagogy, service learning, arts education, book arts, and letterpress printing, most recently a National Endowment for the Humanities Summer Seminar for College Teachers Grant to lead a transdisciplinary investigation into the commonplace book.

JOSEPH T. HOGAN is pursuing his MA in English and American literature at New York University, where he is a Charles Wickham Moore fellow. A recent graduate of Grand Valley State University, Joseph was program manager of the Common Ground Initiative at the Hauenstein Center, and currently hosts a podcast called "Common Ground," in which he interviews scholars, critics, and writers about the shifting political and cultural landscapes of twenty-first-century America.

SANDRA LUBARSKY founded the M.A. Sustainable Communities program at Northern Arizona University and chaired the Sustainable Development Department at Appalachian State University. She writes on process thought, interreligious dialogue, aesthetics, and sustainability.

ELIZABETH MINNICH, a professor of moral philosophy and Senior Scholar at the Association of American Colleges & Universities, has chaired Committee on Public Philosophy of the American Philosophical Association and the N.C. Humanities Council. Since earning her Ph.D., when she served as Hannah Arendt's teaching assistant, she has practiced her fieldwork philosophizing through a wide variety of projects that bring people together to think, talk, and act, from serving on boards (e.g. Medicine & Morals; the Center for Humans and Nature) to writing op eds. Her first book, *Transforming Knowledge* (Temple, 1990), won the Frederic W. Ness Award for "best book in liberal learning" of its year. She has papers in 16 anthologies and 3 textbooks as well as journals and magazines. Dr. Minnich has held the Hartley Burr Alexander Chair for Public Philosophy, among other academic appointments. Her most recent book, *The Evil of Banality: On the Life and Death Importance of Thinking*, will be released by Rowman & Littlefield in mid-December, 2016.

Robert Neustadt is Professor of Spanish and Director of Latin American Studies at Northern Arizona University in Flagstaff. He has published two books focusing on performance and experimental art, *CADA día: La creación de un arte social* (Santiago: Editorial Cuarto Propio), now in a second edition, and *(Con)Fusing Signs and Postmodern Positions: Spanish American Performance, Experimental Writing and the Critique of Political Confusion* (New York: Garland Publishing, 1999). Since 2010 he has been taking classes on field trips to the U.S./Mexico border where students experience, firsthand, the human, environmental, and political dimensions of immigration. In 2012, he co-produced and contributed a song to the album Border Songs, a double CD of music and spoken word about the U.S./Mexico border. The album raised nearly $100,000 for a humanitarian organization, No More Deaths/No más muertes, a volunteer group that places water in the Sonoran desert in an effort to keep migrants from dying in the Arizona borderlands.

Peimin Ni is Professor of Philosophy at Grand Valley State University. He has served as President of the Association of Chinese Philosophers in America, President of the Society of Asian and Comparative Philosophy, Editor-in-Chief of the ACPA book series on Chinese and Comparative Philosophy, visiting Professor at the University of Hawaii and the University of Hong Kong. His publications include over 70 articles and seven books, including *On Confucius, On Reid, Confucius—The Man and the Way of Gongfu, Wandering—Brush and Pen in Philosophical Reflection*, and *Understanding the Analects of Confucius: A New Translation of the Lunyu with Annotations*.

Vandana Pednekar-Magal is Professor of Journalism and currently Director of the School of Communications at Grand Valley State University. She has authored refereed journal articles on topics of media and society and global communication, and has produced two documentaries—*Divided by Language: India's Newspapers;* and *From Somewhere Else: Transnational Communities and Global Media.*

SHERYL PETTY, Ed.D., has worked in educational systems change and organizational development for 20 years, practices Tibetan Buddhism, and is a priest in an African-based indigenous tradition. She is a consultant through Movement Tapestries, as well as Management Assistance Group (Washington, D.C.), and Movement Strategy Center (Oakland, CA). She is also a Fellow with the Mind & Life Institute, and Adjunct Faculty with Teachers College, Columbia University. She has been an executive director and consultant to school districts, universities, nonprofits and foundations. Her expertise includes equity-driven change process design, facilitation, cross-sector field-building, strategy development, alliance and network development, equity assessments, qualitative research, visioning, and life coaching to promote our collective vibrancy and healing.

STEPHEN ROWE is Professor of Philosophy, Liberal Studies, and Religious Studies at Grand Valley State University. He is also actively engaged in intercultural dialogue and consultation on liberal education though several universities and institutions in China and the U.S. An award winning teacher, his books include *Rediscovering the West: An Inquiry into Nothingness and Relatedness* (SUNY Press, 1994, in Chinese, Shanghai Translation Publishing House, 1996), and, most recently, *Overcoming America / America Overcoming: Can We Survive Modernity?* (Lexington Books, 2012, and forthcoming in Chinese).

BRENDA SORKIN teaches Somatics, Movement Education. She is a certified Feldenkrais® Practitioner and Senior Trainer for Movement Intelligence. Movement Dialogues, LLC

MARK STEMEN is Professor of Geography and Planning at California State University, Chico, where he teaches courses in sustainability and civic engagement. In 2008, Stemen was named "Sustainability Champion" at the California Higher Education Sustainability Conference. He is also President of the Butte Environmental Council, as well as Chair of the City of Chico's Sustainability Task Force. During his eight years as

Field Director of the Butte Creek Ecological Reserve, he created a set of restoration practices that put into practice William Jordon's ideas about restoration and ritual. Mark has a PhD in Environmental History from the University of Iowa.

HOWARD WOODHOUSE is Professor in the Department of Educational Foundations and Co-Director of the University of Saskatchewan Process Philosophy Research Unit. He is author of more than 70 book chapters and articles in refereed journals on such topics as the philosophies of education of Bertrand Russell and Alfred North Whitehead; academic freedom and university autonomy; cultural and economic dependency in Africa; the importance of critical thought in education; and most recently storytelling in university education. His book, *Selling Out: Academic Freedom and the Corporate Market,* published by McGill-Queen's University Press in 2009, was short-listed for a scholarly writing prize by the Saskatchewan Book Awards. In 2010 he was given the University of Saskatchewan Faculty Association's Academic Freedom Award.

www.ingramcontent.com/pod-product-compliance
Lightning Source LLC
Chambersburg PA
CBHW031119020426
42333CB00012B/142